Carving Cheetahs

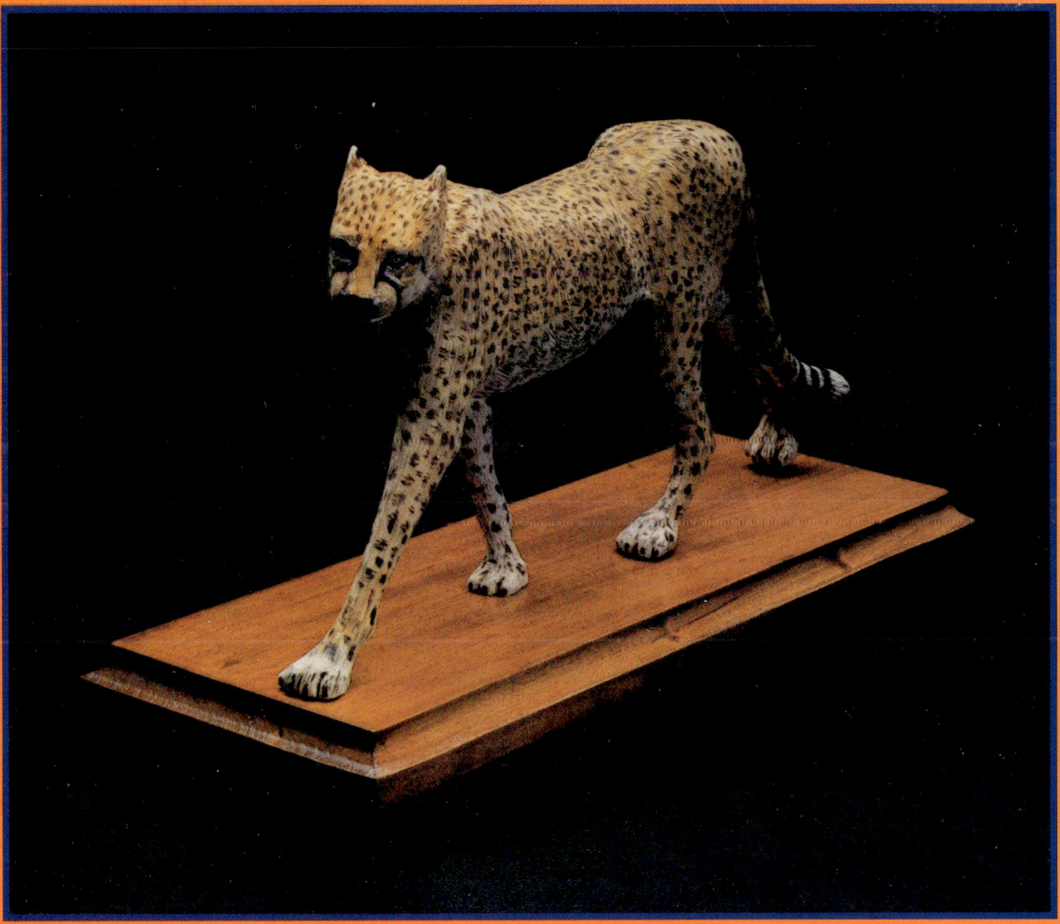

Dale Power

Text written with
and photography
by Jeffrey B. Snyder

Schiffer Publishing Ltd
77 Lower Valley Road, Atglen, PA 19310

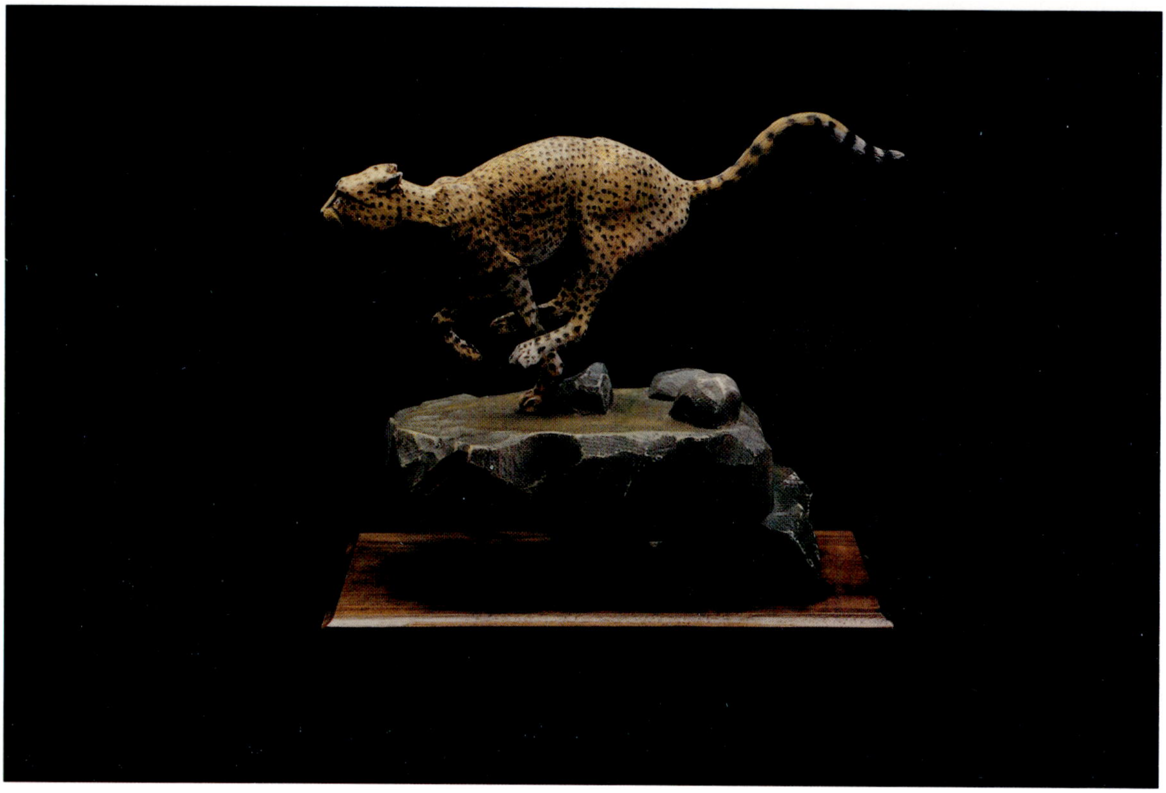

Contents

Library of Congress Catalog Number: 94-66199

Printed in China
ISBN: 0-88740-696-3

Published by Schiffer Publishing Ltd.
77 Lower Valley Road
Atglen, PA 19310
Please write for a free catalog.
This book may be purchased from the publisher.
Please include $2.95 postage.
Try your bookstore first.

Introduction

Cheetahs are the fastest animals on land, using long legs and slender bodies to reach speeds of up to seventy miles per hour for short distances. These felines belong to the class of big cats including lions, tigers, jaguars, leopards, snow leopards and clouded leopards. Cheetahs differ from these other big cats, however, in three important ways.

Cheetahs are not powerful, they can't roar and they are the most gentle of the big cat family. Because they aren't fighters by nature, other predators take advantage of cheetahs. Predators steal their food, eat cheetah cubs and even attack the adults. In the wild cheetahs survive only four to five years. In captivity they may reach fifteen years of age.

The five things that help the cheetahs stay alive are long legs, a springy backbone, a slender build, long claws and a long tail. The average cheetah is seven feet long including the tail. It weighs about one hundred and twenty-five pounds.

Roughly one million years ago, the ancestors of cheetahs roamed all over Europe, Asia, North America and Africa. However, today cheetahs may only be found in Africa and, in very small numbers, in Asia.

This cheetah is carved out of Basswood (also known as American Linden) to achieve the high quality and durability desired of the final product. Basswood is classified as a hardwood but I find it great for either hand or machine carving.

To familiarize yourself with the shape and movement of the cheetah before carving, find as many photographs of cheetahs as possible. Sporting magazines and children's books on animals make good references. The more you know about cheetahs, the easier carving them will be.

While we're speaking of carving, I use a bench knife, a set of assorted hand gouges, an Automat Power Chisel, a Detail Master Wood Burning System, a Foredom flexible shaft machine, and an Optima-2 high speed grinder. Both the Foredom and the Optima-2 are fitted with assorted carbide burrs for this project. The paints are acrylic washes.

Whenever you use sharp tools a Kevlar woodcarvers glove is a wise choice to protect your hand from the blade. **However, it is important to remember NEVER to use the glove with rotary power tools. The potential for getting the blade wrapped in the glove and causing serious personal injury is simply too great.**

Whenever you use power tools, it is always wise to protect your lungs with a dust mask or a dust collection system.

Good luck carving your Cheetah.

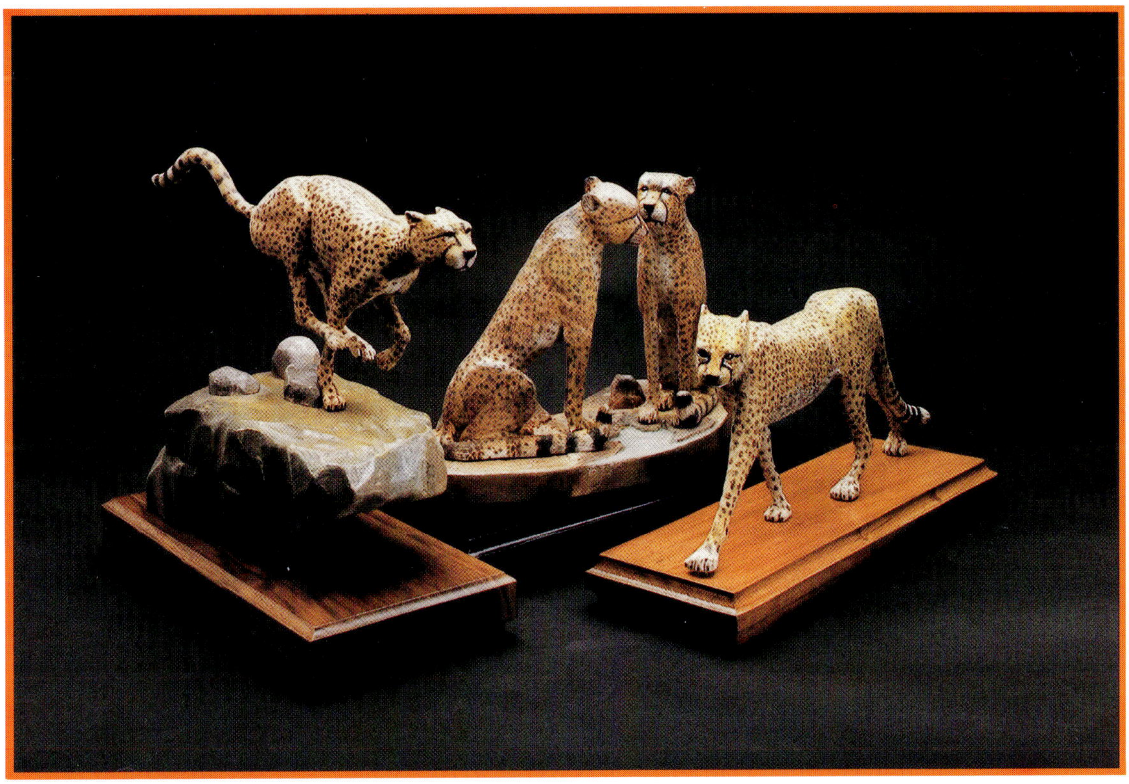

Patterns

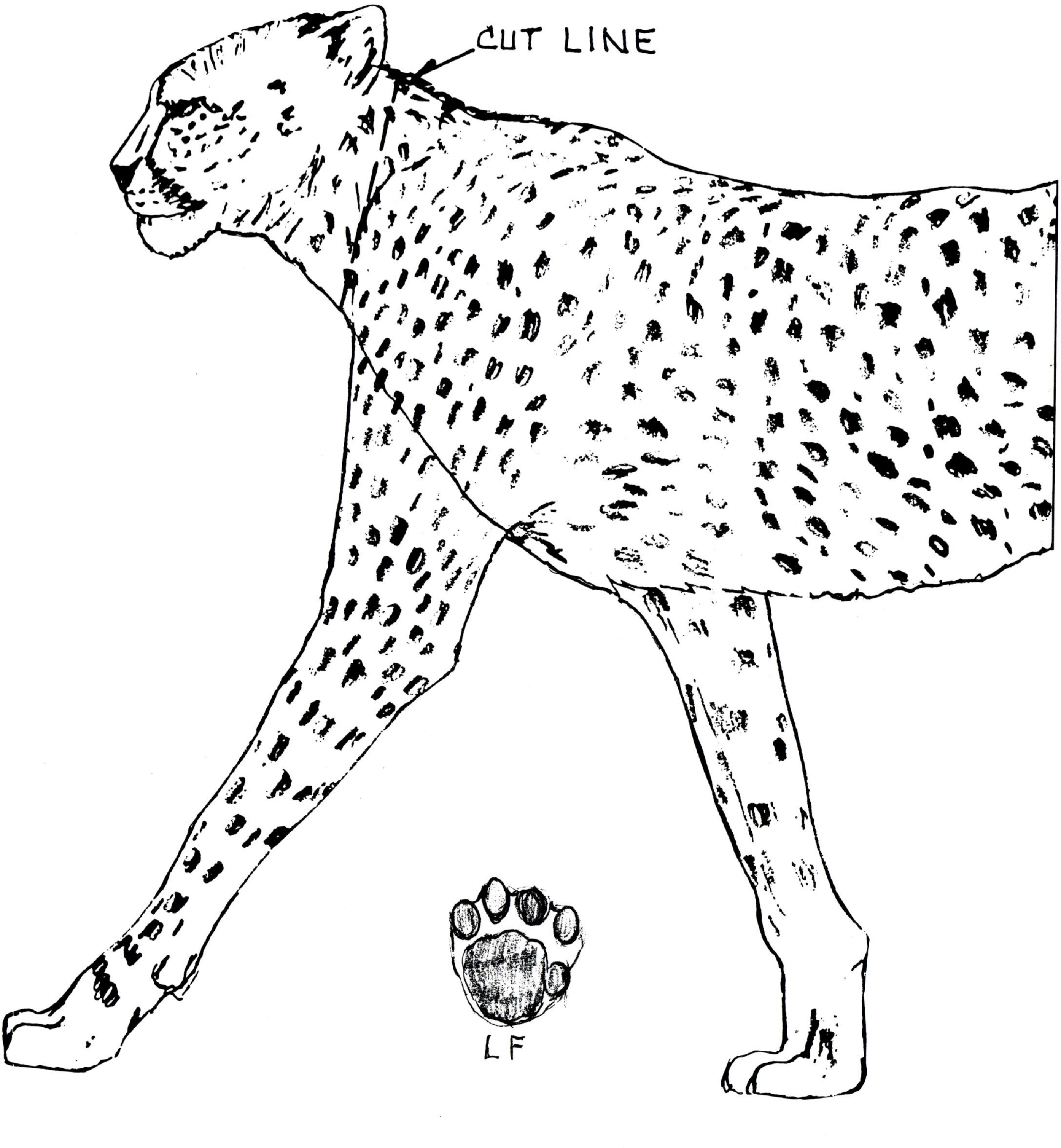

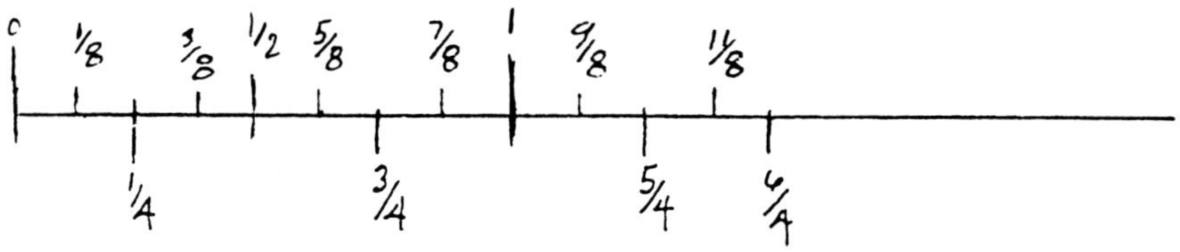
0
1/8
3/8
1/2
5/8
7/8
1
9/8
11/8
1/4
3/4
5/4
6/4

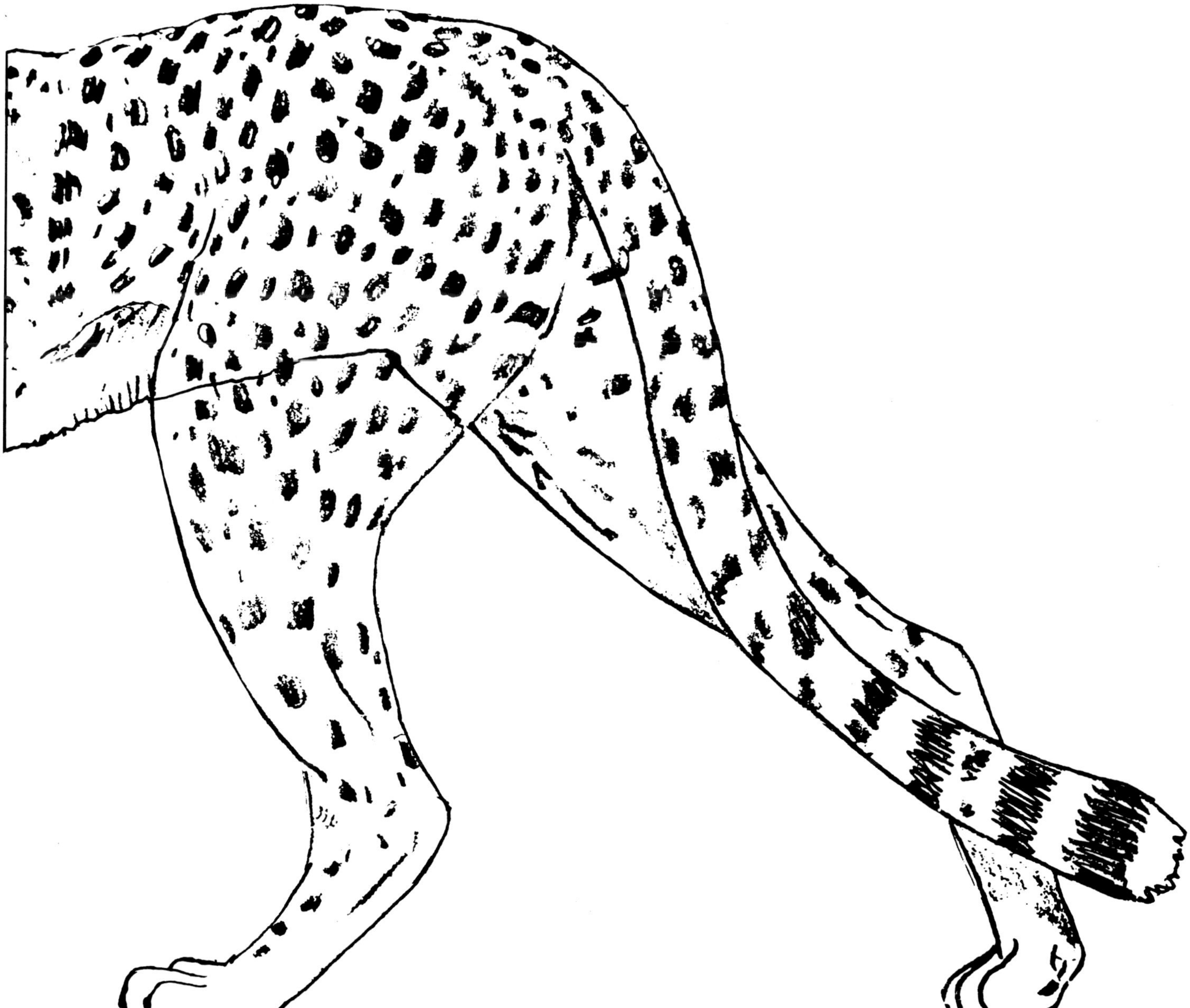

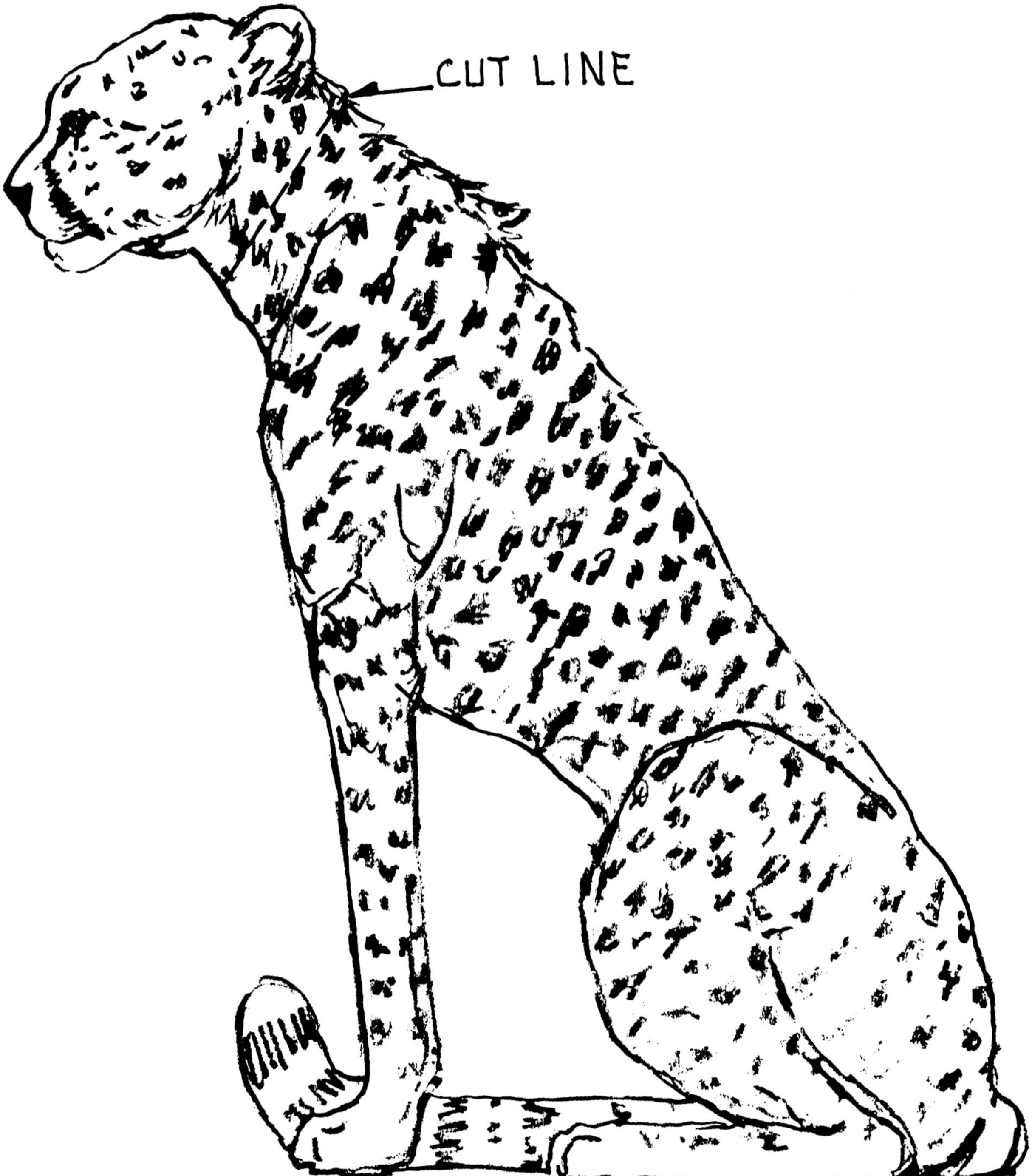
CUT LINE

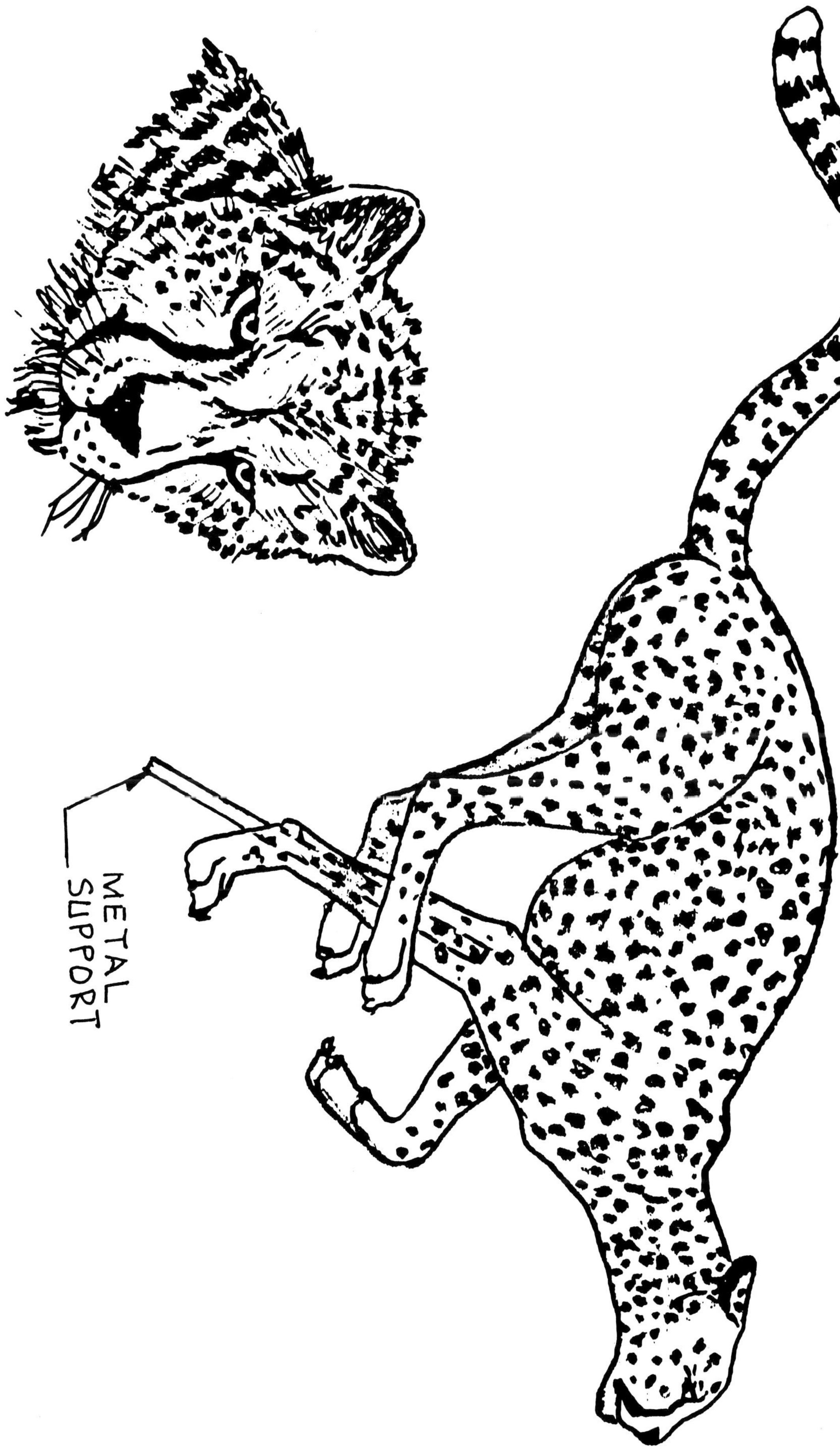
METAL SUPPORT

Carving the Cheetah

To follow Dale step-by-step through this book, proceed from the upper left, down the left column, then to the upper right and down the right column. It's just like reading a newspaper.

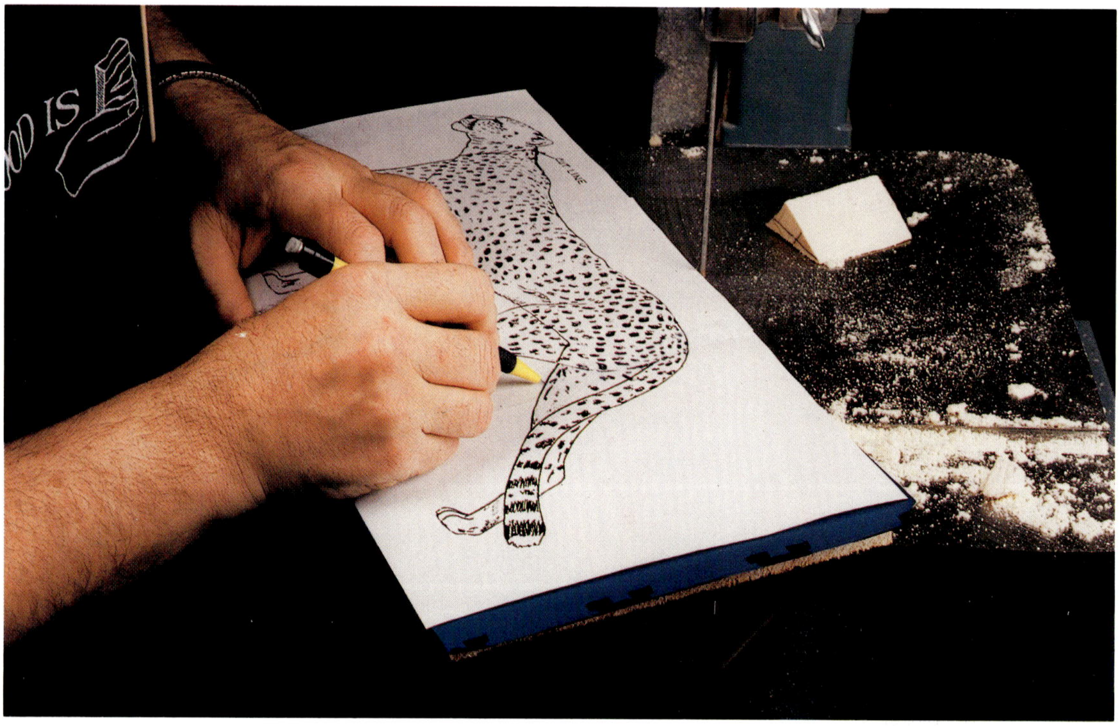

Transfer the cheetah pattern to A 1" x 8" basswood board. Carbon paper may be used to aid in the transfer.

Here is the traced pattern. Trace it on two pieces of basswood.

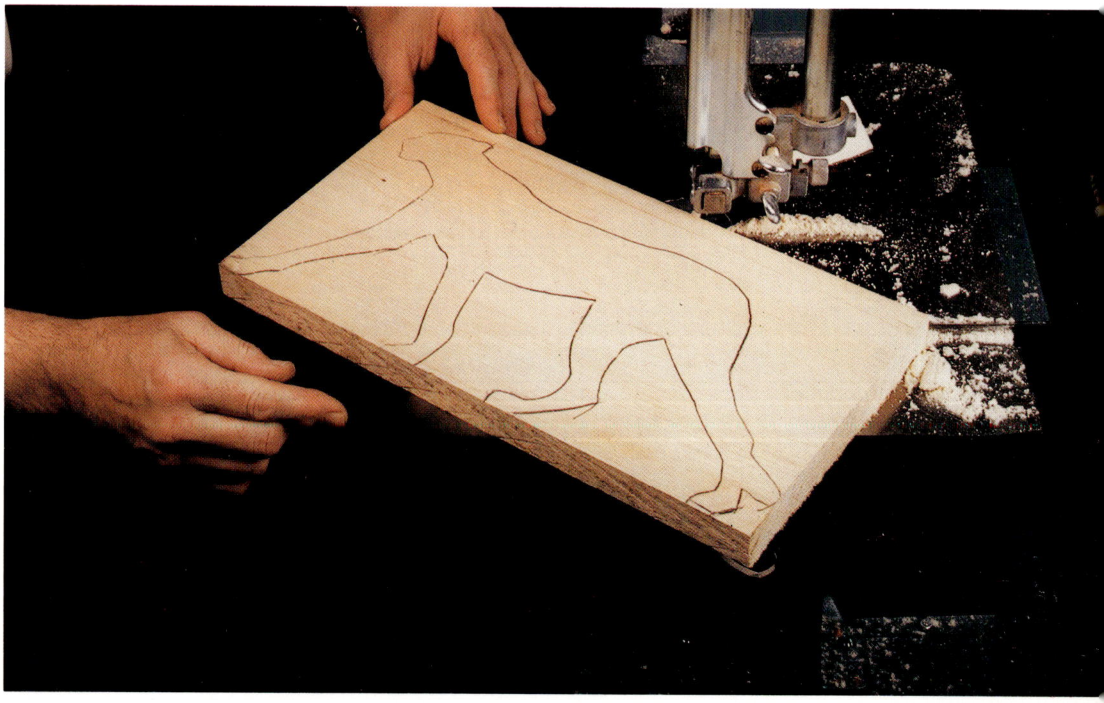

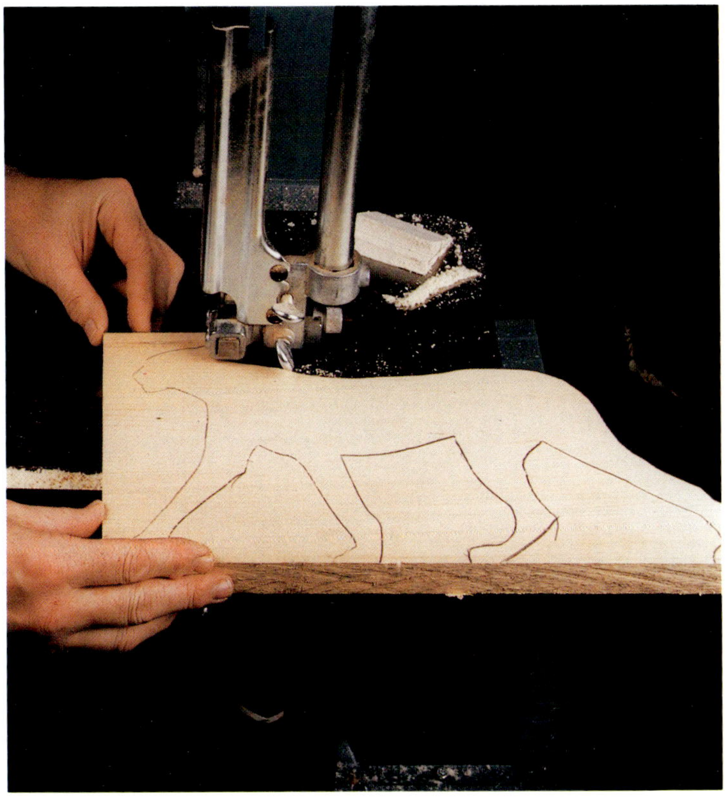

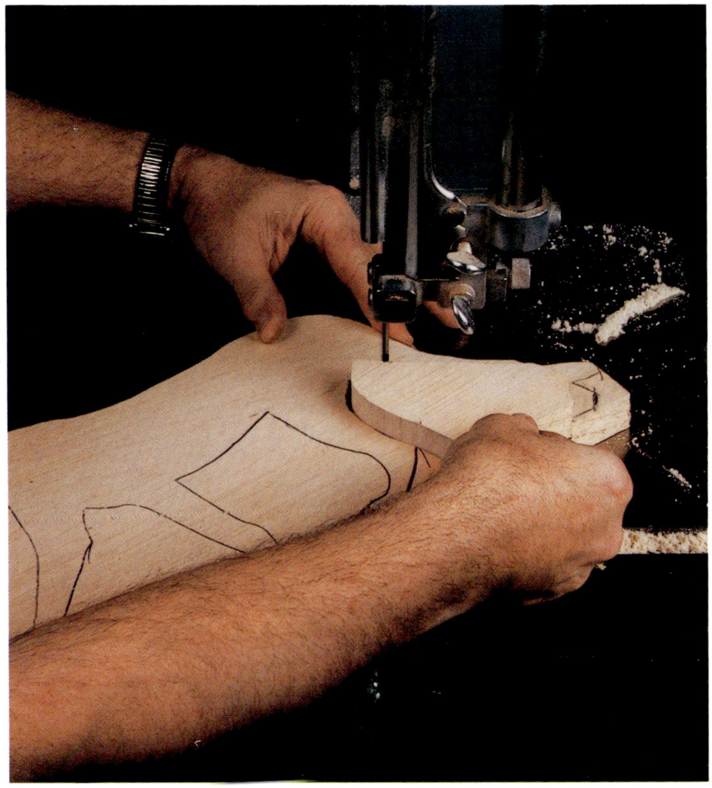

Cut along the outside of the pattern line, removing the excess wood.

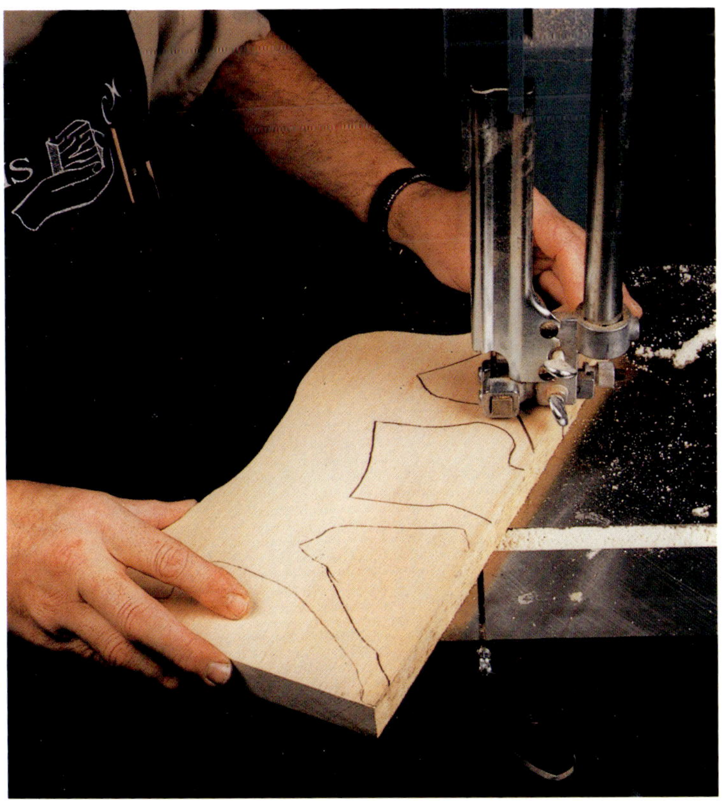

To cut out the back legs, first cut the back of the leading rear leg. Then cut along the front of the trailing rear leg, meeting where the legs join the body, allowing you to free the piece and easily remove your blade.

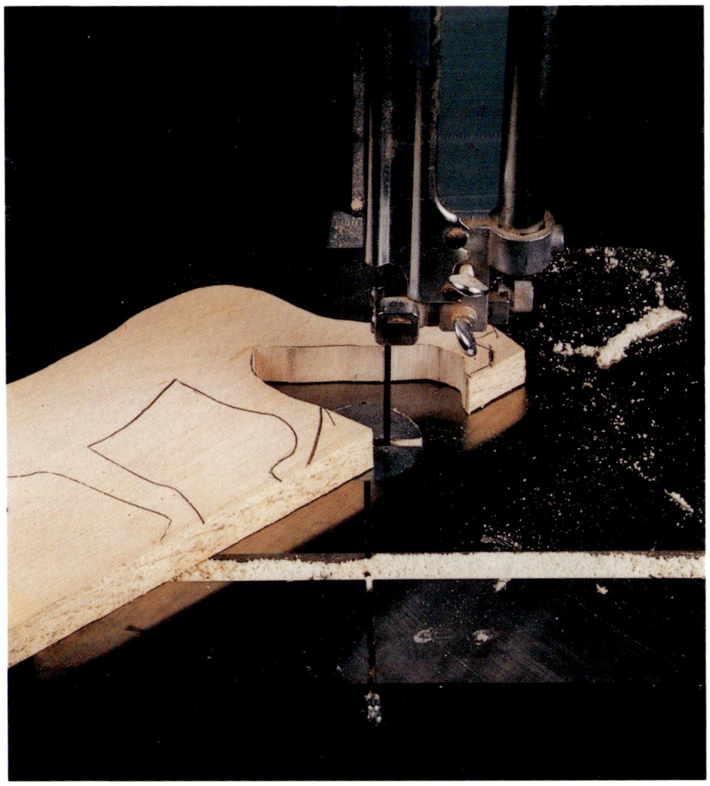

Remove the excess and free the blade.

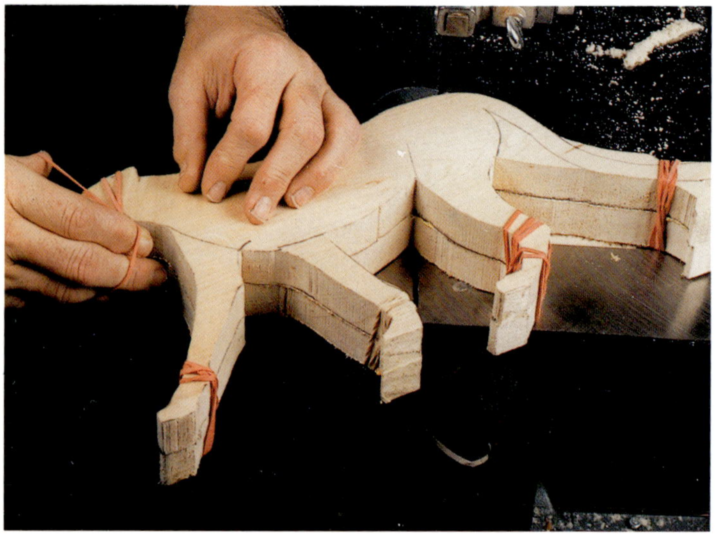

When both blanks are cut, apply yellow carpenters glue liberally to the insides of each. Clamp them together. If clamps are not available, large rubber bands may be used. Set the clamped or banded blank aside for twelve hours or longer to allow the glue to dry properly.

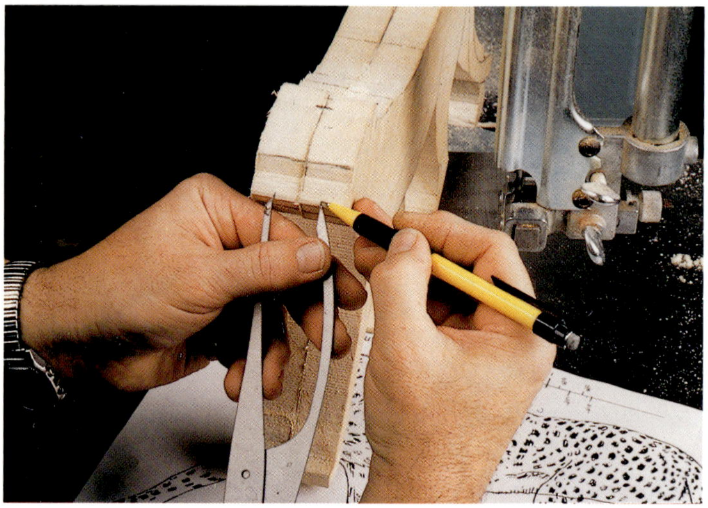

Draw in the centerline around the cheetah blank. We are ready to measure the dorsal view using the head as our standard measurement, marking the measured locations with pencilled dots and connecting the dots as we go. The length of the head will be the standard unit of measurement. The measurement across the end of the muzzle is 1/2 of the total length of the head.

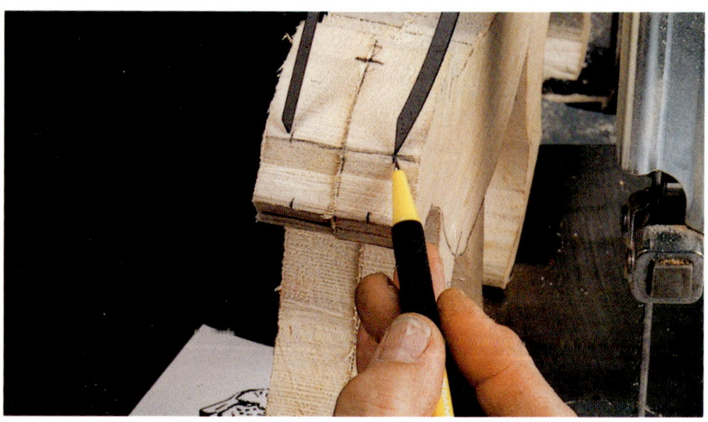

The measurement across the brow is 5/8 of the total length of the head.

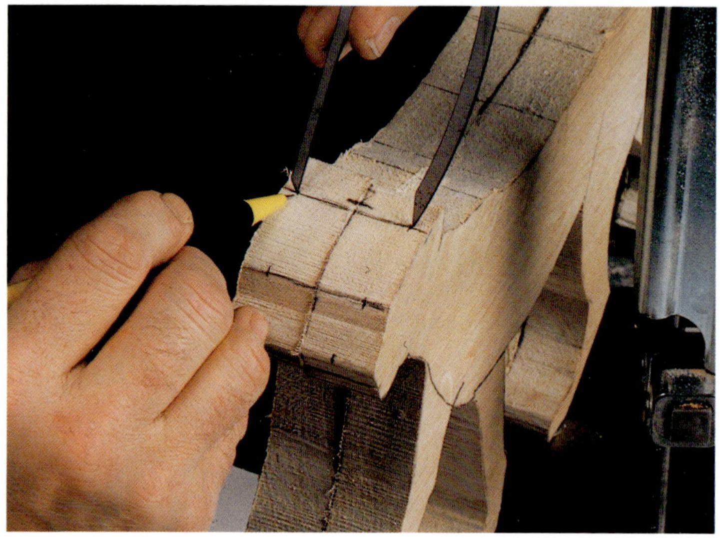

The measurement at the front of the ears is 3/4 of the total length of the head.

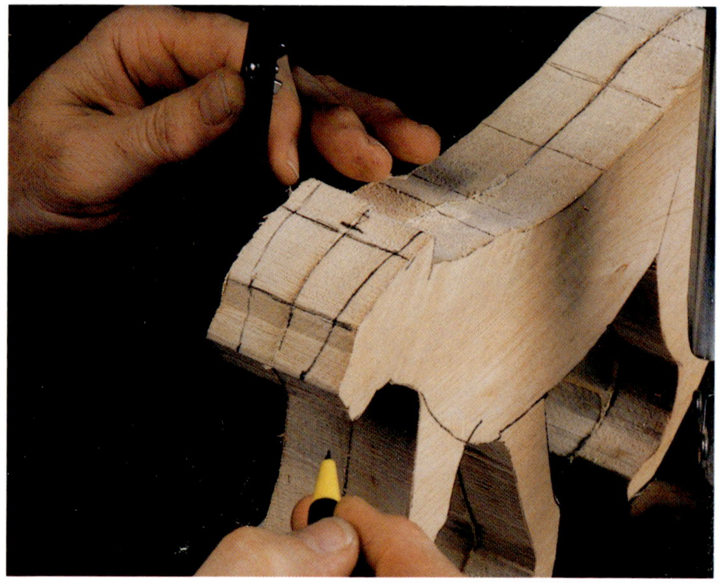

The same measurement extends to the tips of the ears.

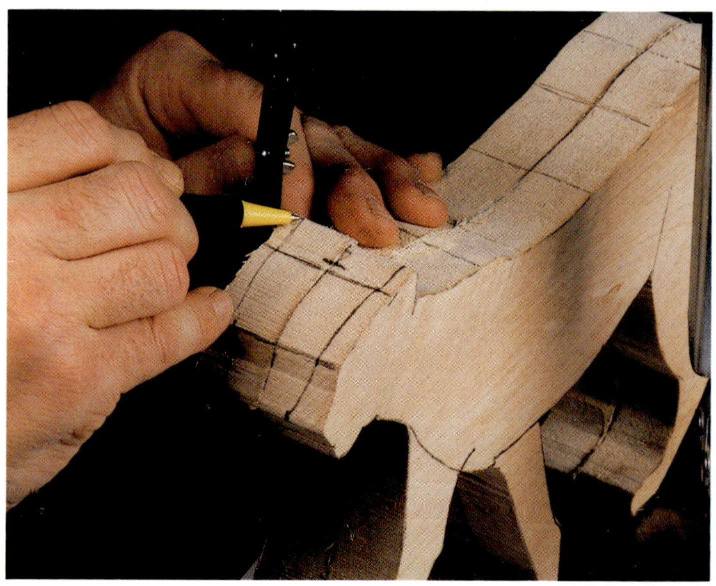

Connect the measured points on the cheetah's head.

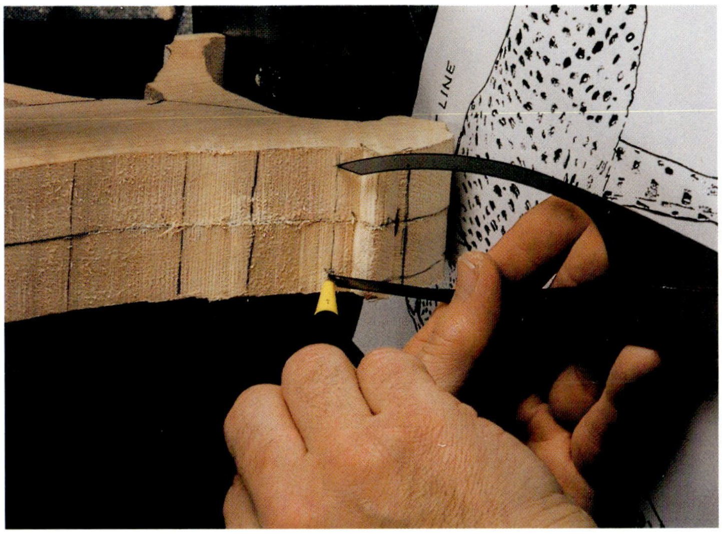

The neck also measures 3/4 of the total length of the head.

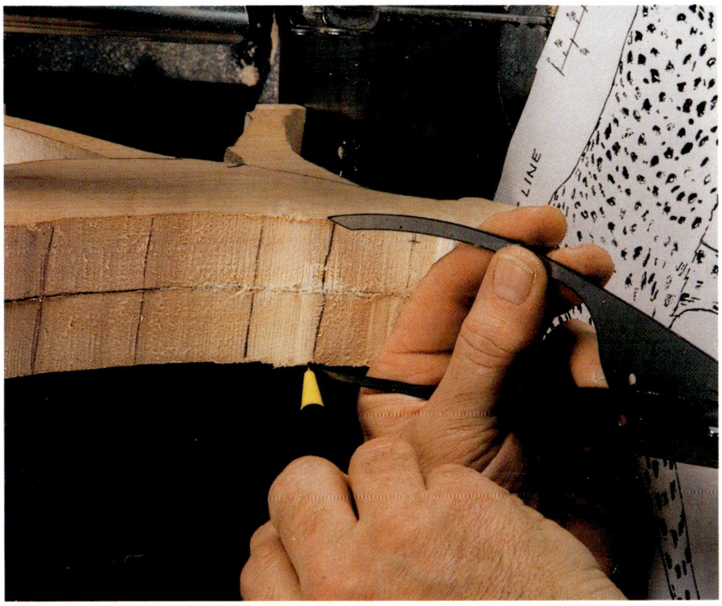

The front of the shoulders is exactly one full head length wide.

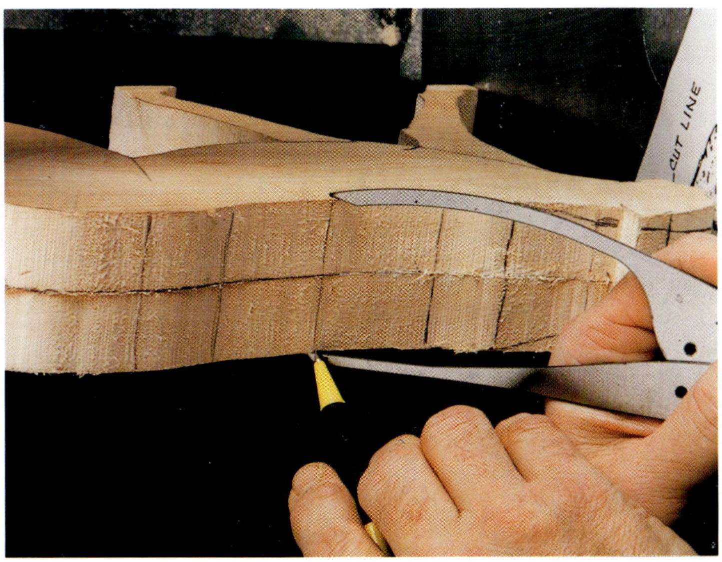

The same full head measurement extends to the widest (middle) point of the stomach.

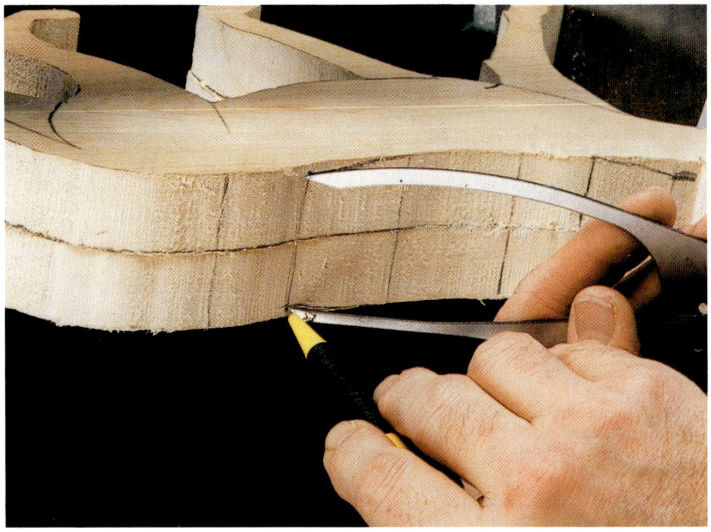

The next measurement at the point just in front of the rear hips is 7/8 of the total length of the head.

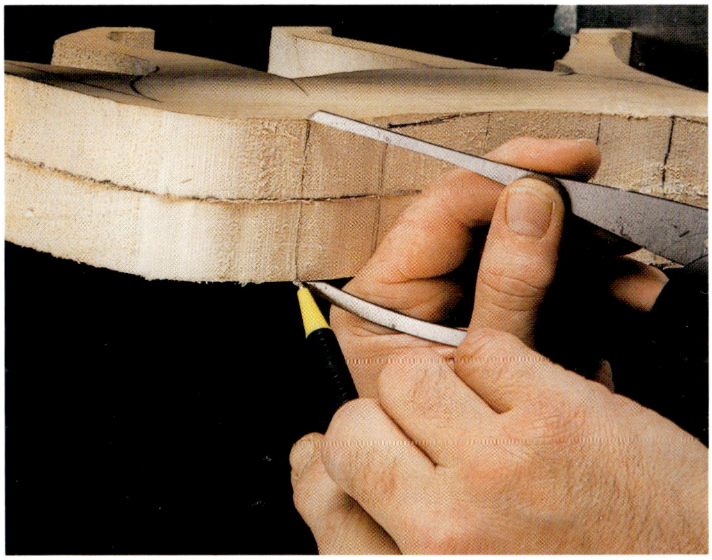

The measurement through the broadest point of the hips is one full head length.

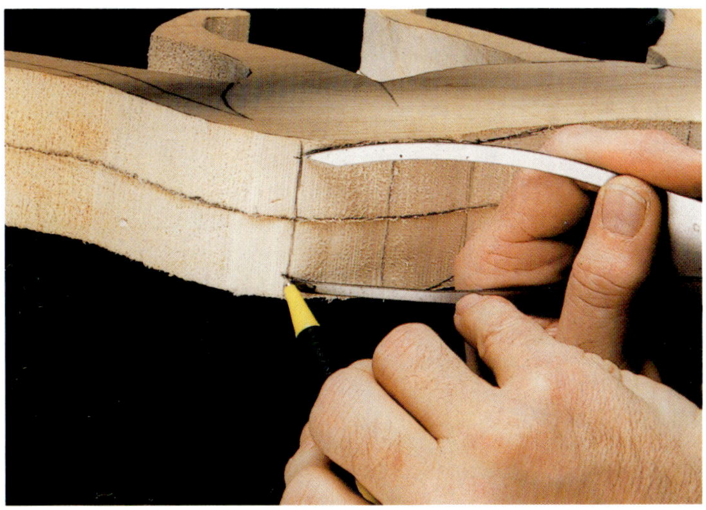

At the root of the tail, the measurement is 3/4 of the total length of the head. This is a good time to draw in the dorsal view of the cheetah's body. Using a pencil, connect the dots, creating the dorsal view.

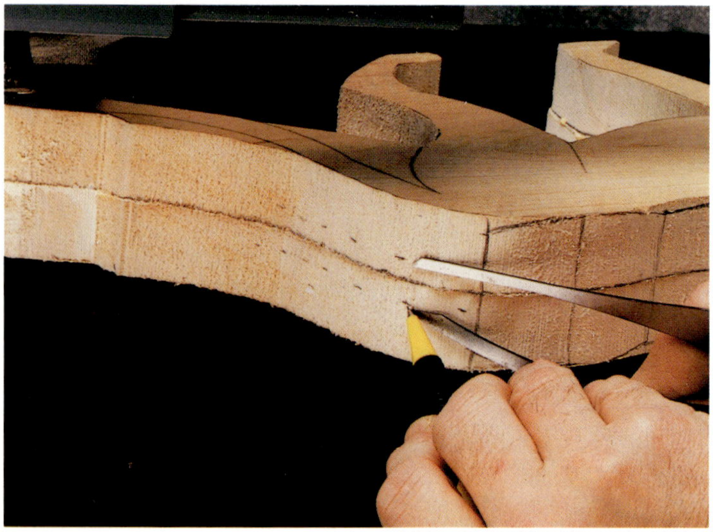

Starting at the root of the tail we will mark in the tail on either side of the center line, keeping it a constant 1/4 of the total length of the head.

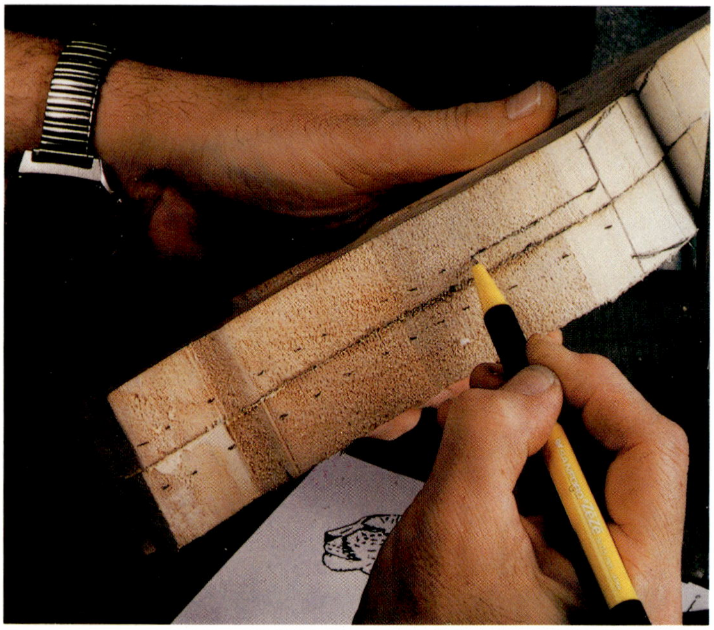

Connect the dots down through the tail.

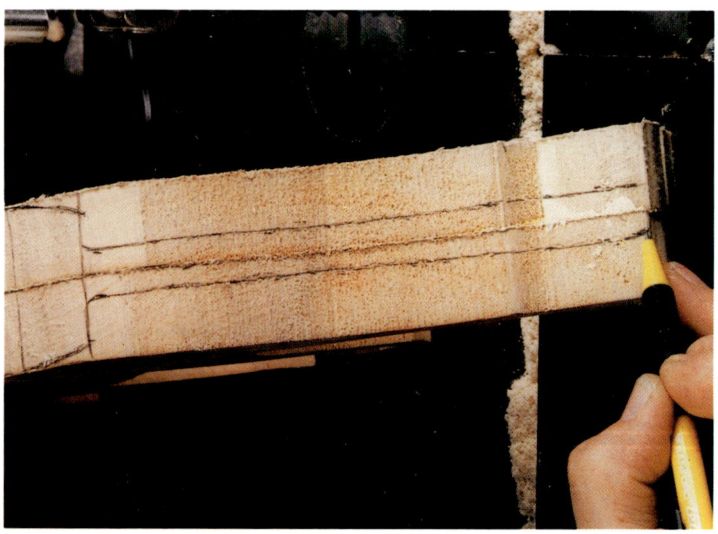

The finished tail should look like this.

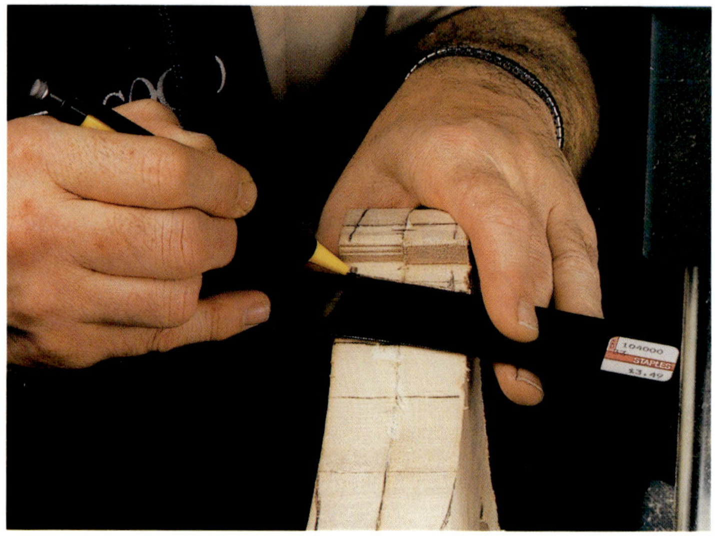

It is time to turn the cheetah's head. To accomplish this first draw a line from just ahead of the front shoulder to just behind the ear at a 15 degree angle or less.

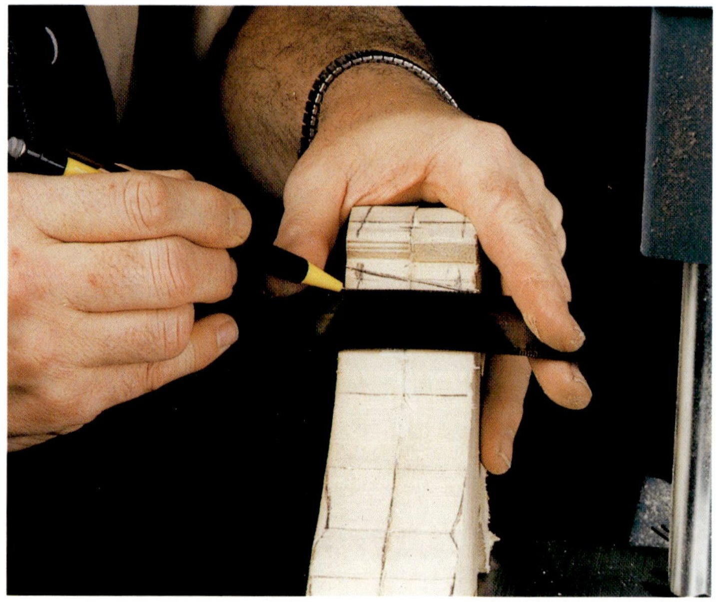

Draw a straight line across the neck, making the guide line for the square portion of the cut.

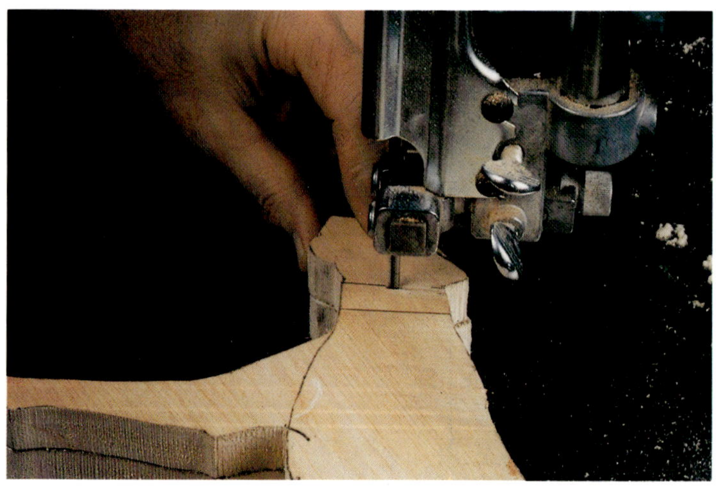

Before you cut, tilt your band saw table to a 15 degree angle. Now it is easy to make the angled cut.

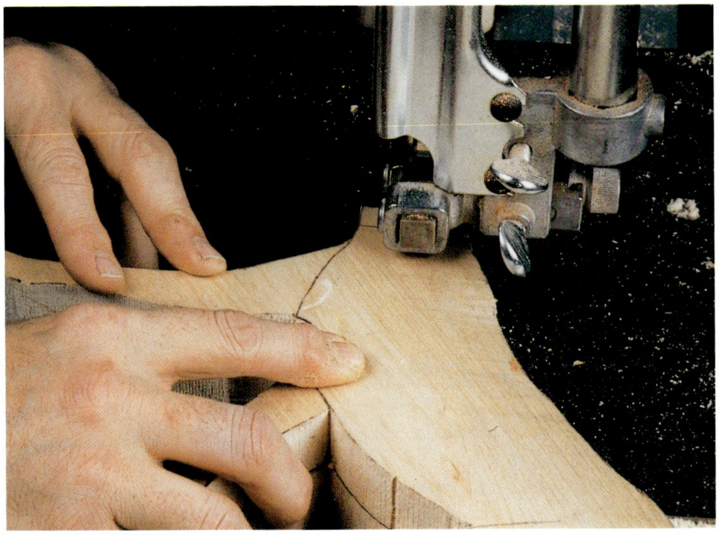

Reset the table to 0 and make your second bandsaw cut, the square neck cut.

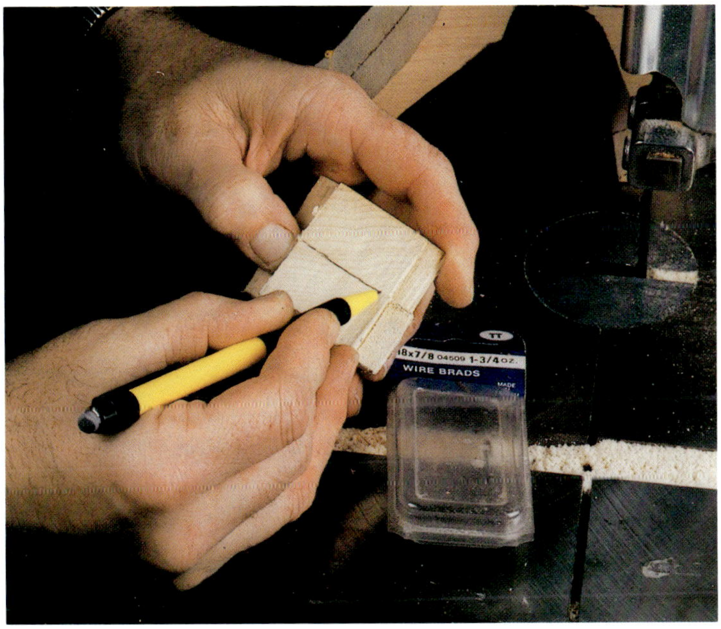

Draw the center line on the newly cut inner surface of the neck to act as a guide for reattaching the angled head.

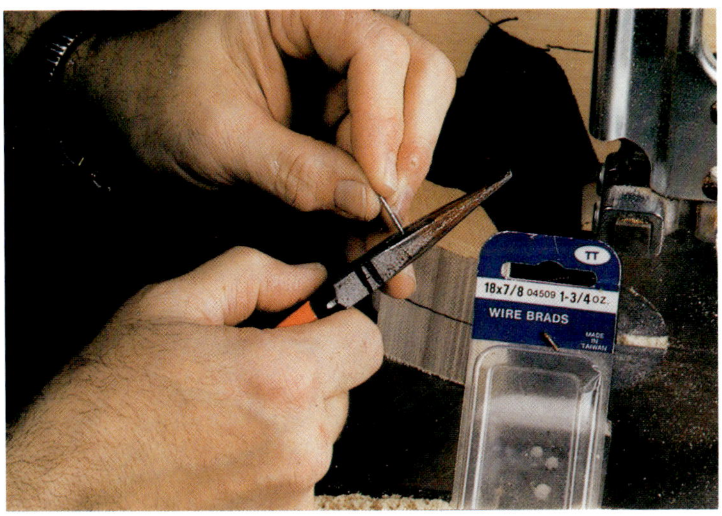

Cut the heads off two brads.

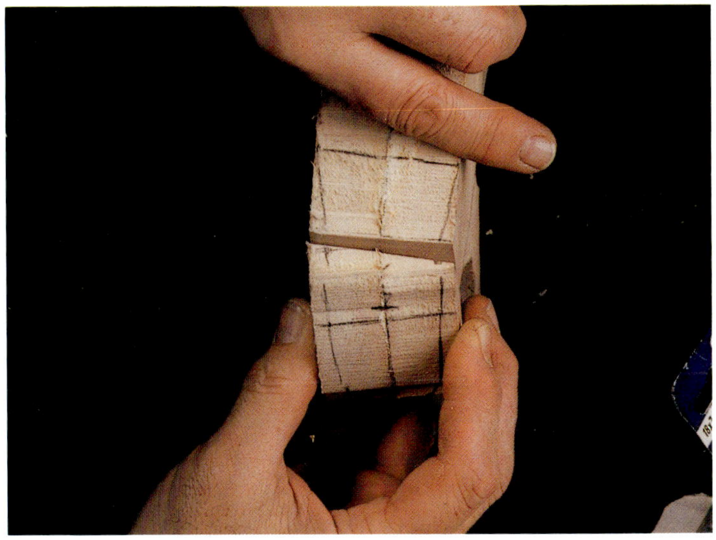

Insert the brads in the detached head along the guide line on the inner surface of the neck. This will allow you to mark the location of the holes in the body that will correspond with the holes in the neck. Positioning the two exposed points of the brads along the body's center line, force the head and body together.

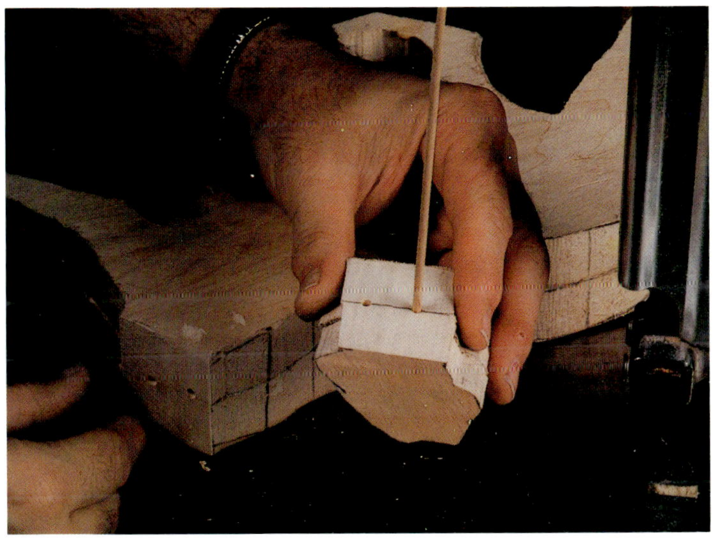

Remove the brads and use a 1/8 inch drill bit to drill holes at the indicated locations into the head and body. Insert a 1/8 inch dowel into each hole in the head section and trim to an appropriate length.

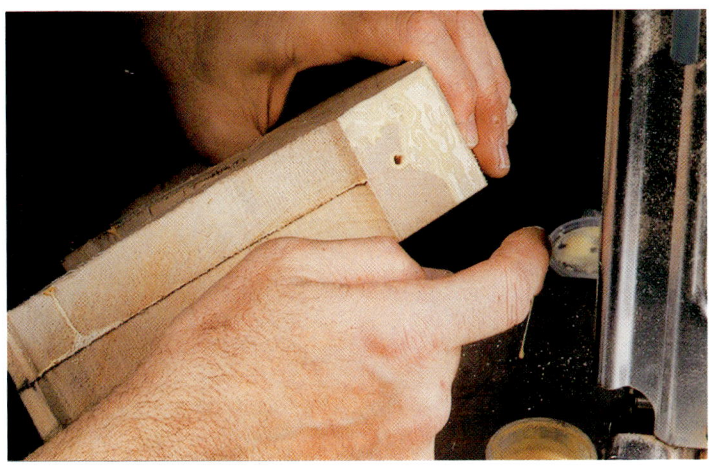

Spread a uniform layer of carpenter's glue on the exposed inner neck surfaces.

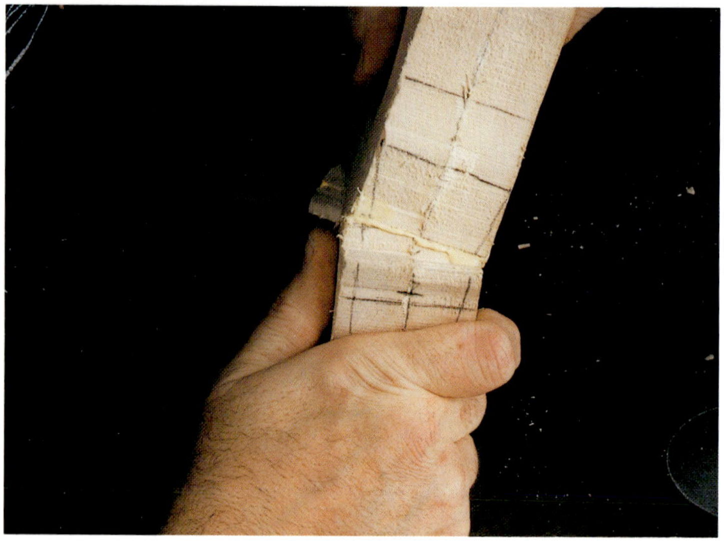

Press the head firmly into position, allowing the doweling to line up the head and body.

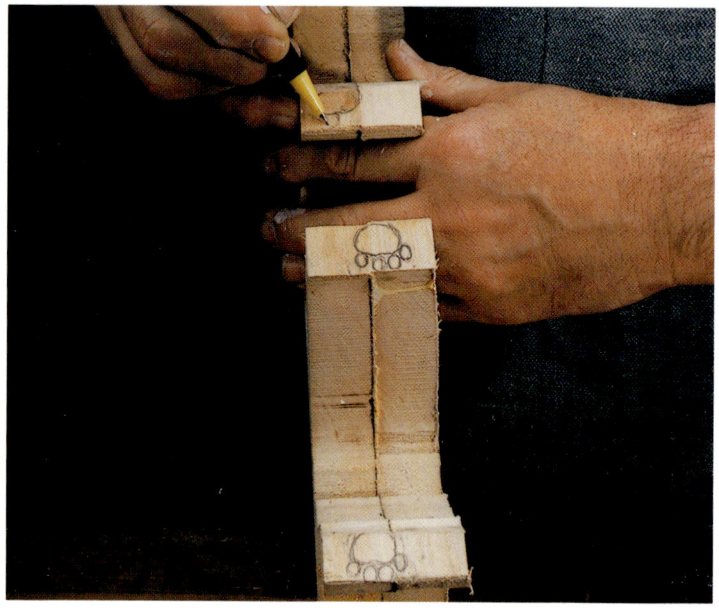

It is time to locate the paws. First draw the location of the paws on all four legs. Each foot slightly overlaps the centerline.

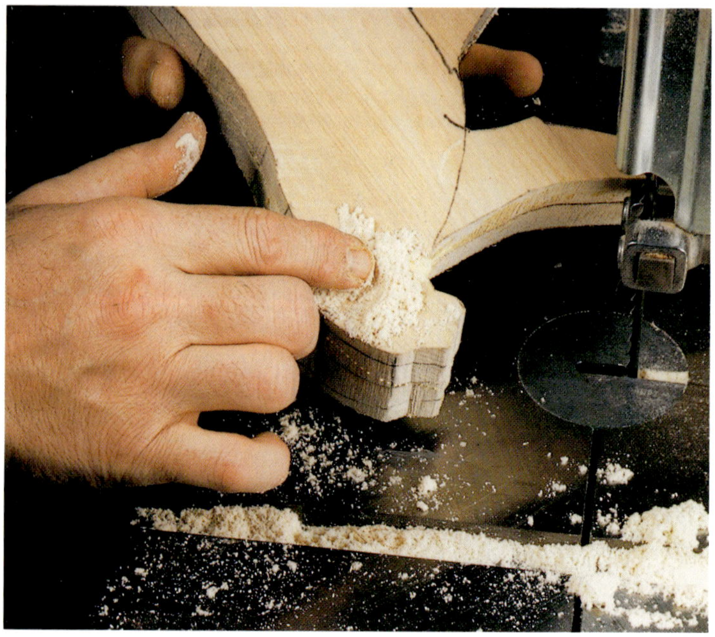

Any obvious gaps that appear may be filled with a mixture of sawdust and carpenter's glue.

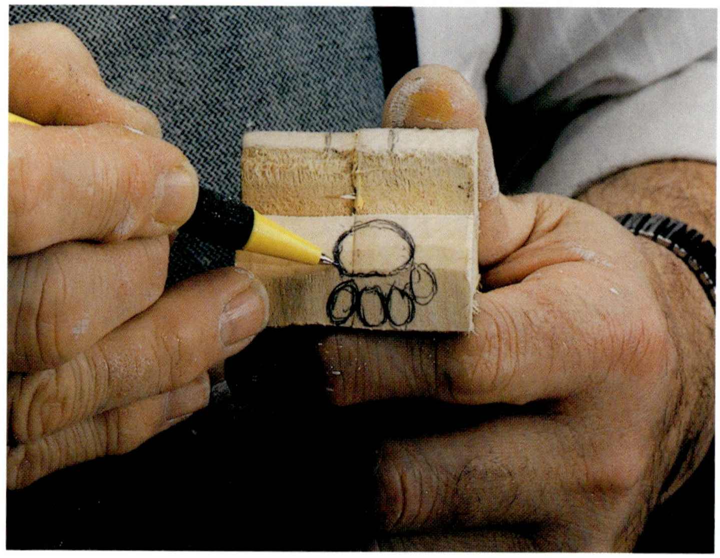

The trailing hind foot is different. The cat is in mid-stride and the ball of this foot can be seen from the back. The appearance is of the cat being up on his toes on this foot.

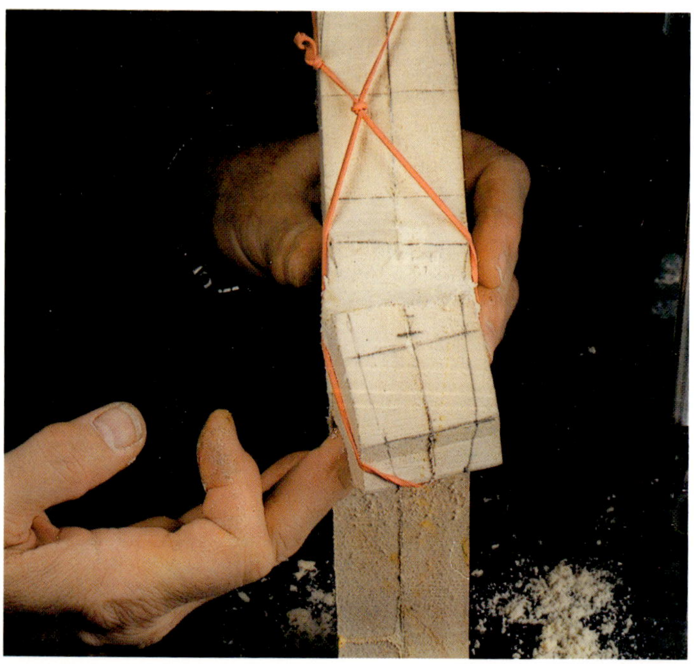

Place a rubber band around the head to hold it in place. Set the cheetah aside for twelve hours or more to allow the glue to set.

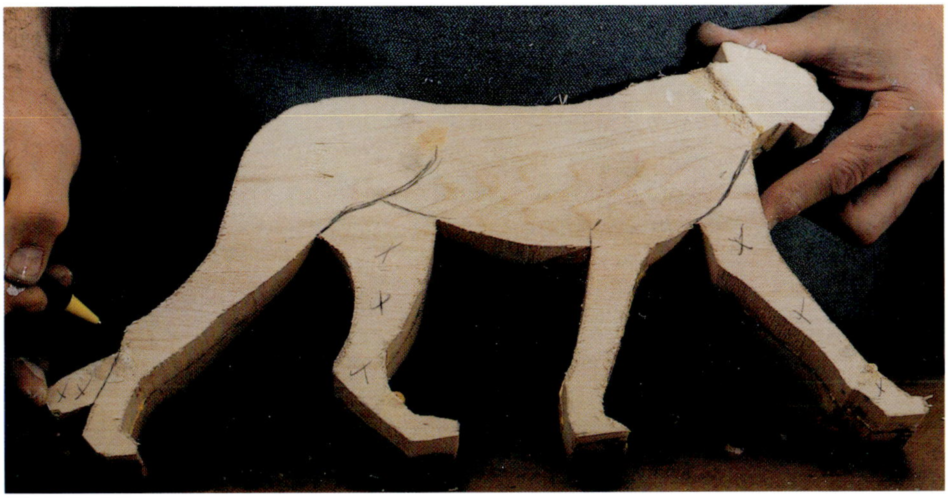

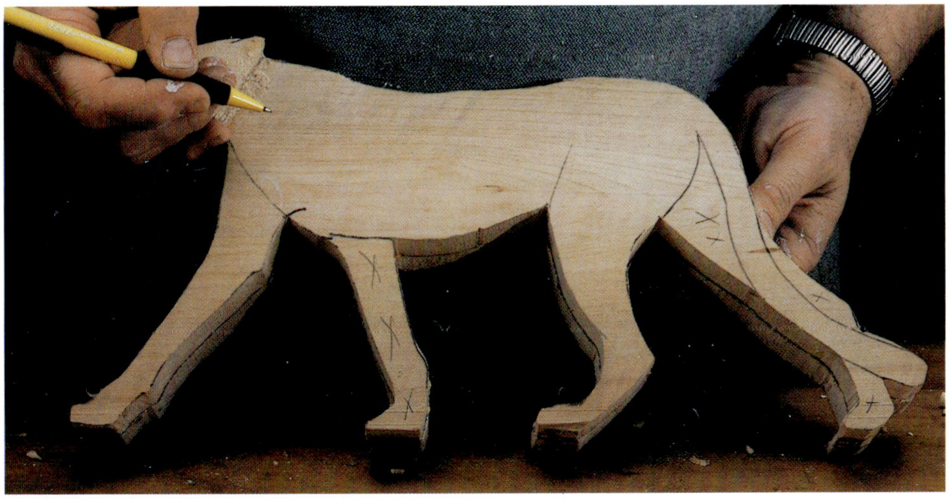

It is time to remove wood that is not needed. Unnecessary wood is indicated by the X's.

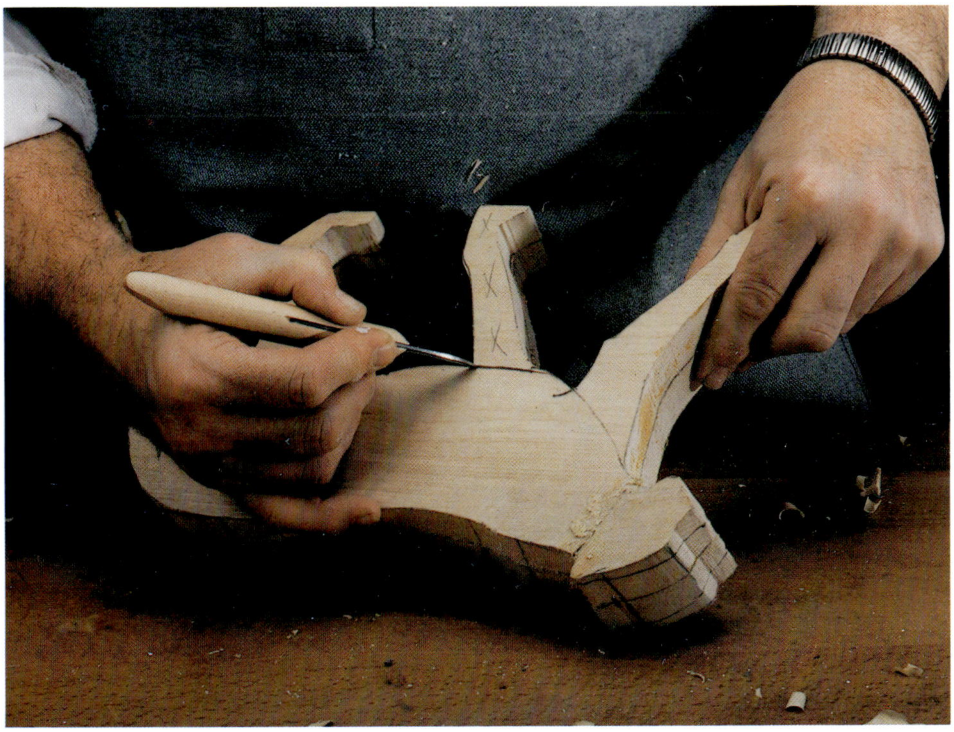

Scribe a stop cut line along the body for the trailing front leg with a bench knife.

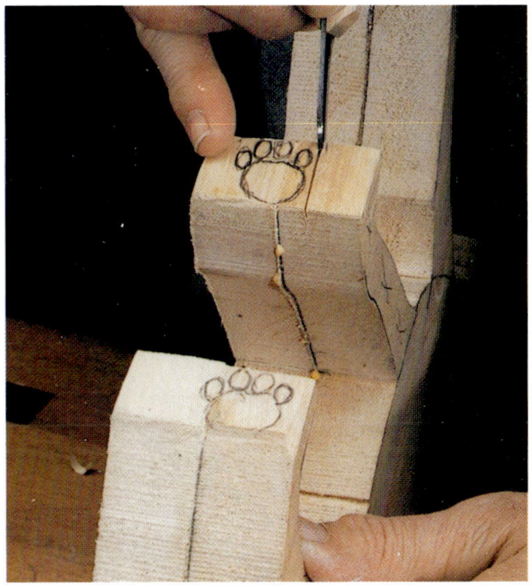

Scribe a stop cut line along the side of the trailing front foot as well. When the excess wood is removed, this cut will help prevent you from breaking the foot.

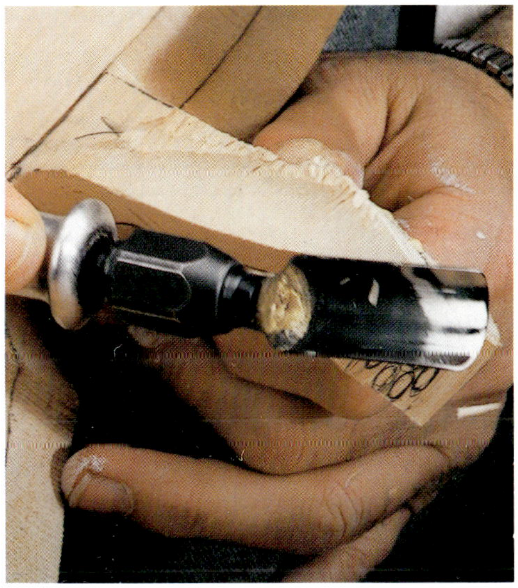

Use an Auto Mach power chisel with its largest gouge to reduce the leg.

The easiest way to maintain a sharp enough blade to do the job is to use a strop.

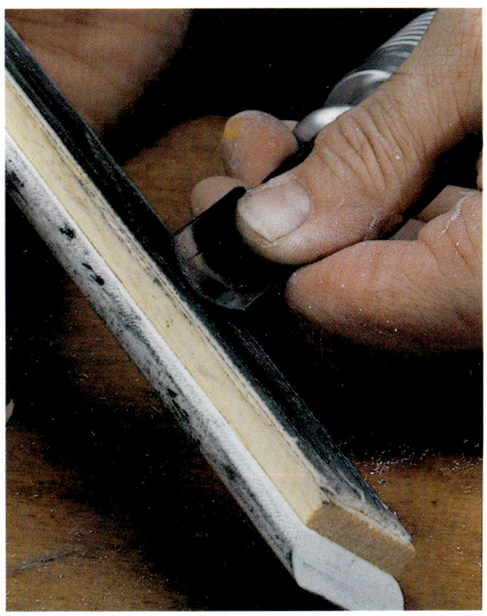

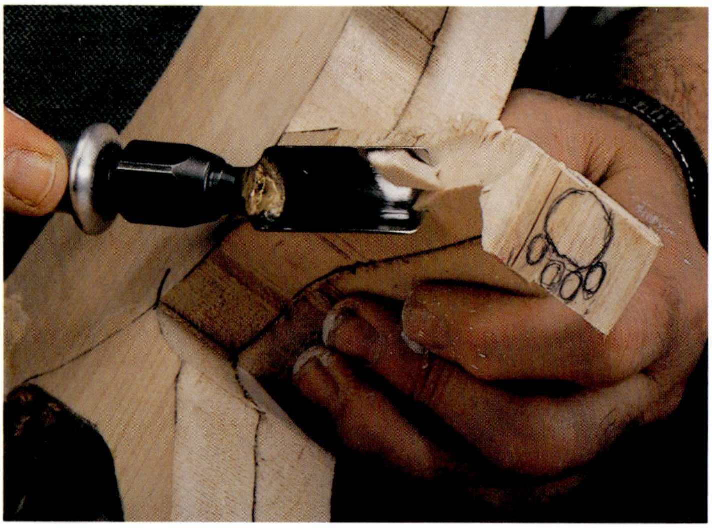

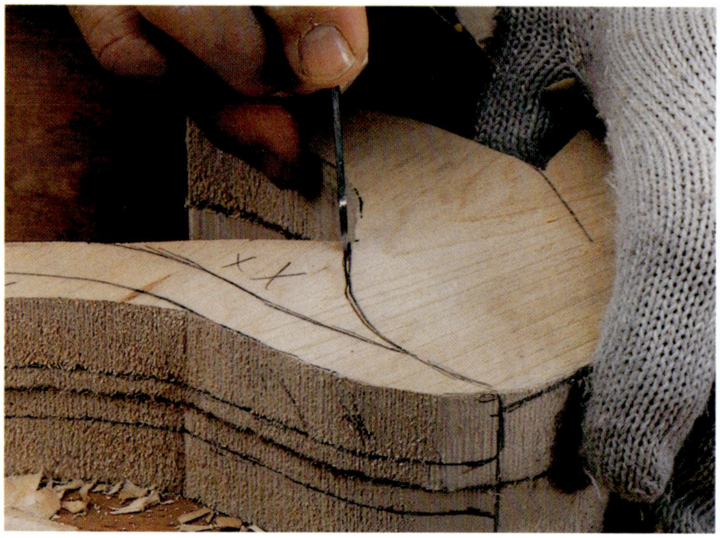

Moving to the rear legs, scribe stop cut lines on the left rear flank and underneath the tail before removing the wood behind the left rear flank to the base of the tail.

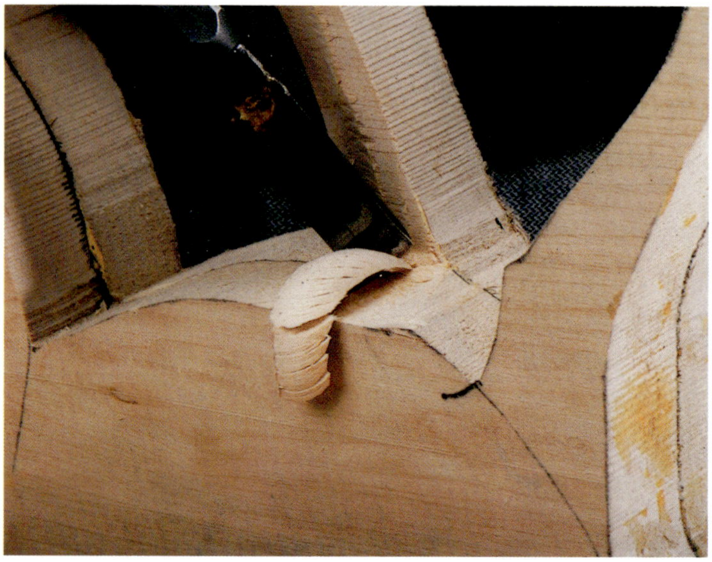

Remove the excess wood from the trailing front leg.

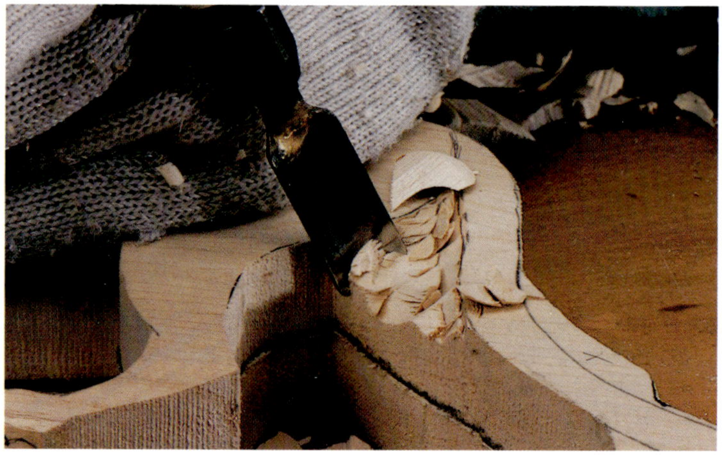

This wood should be removed to the center line.

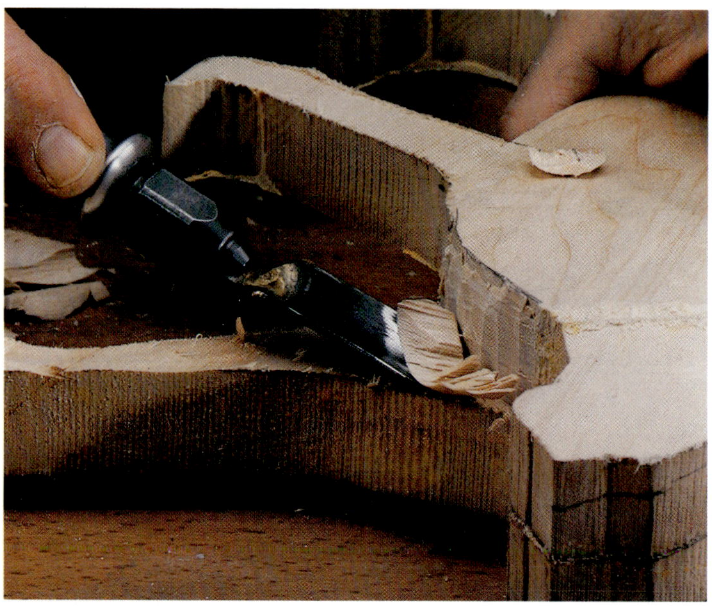

Repeat the process on the leading front leg and remove the excess wood here as well. The excess wood has been removed from the front leg.

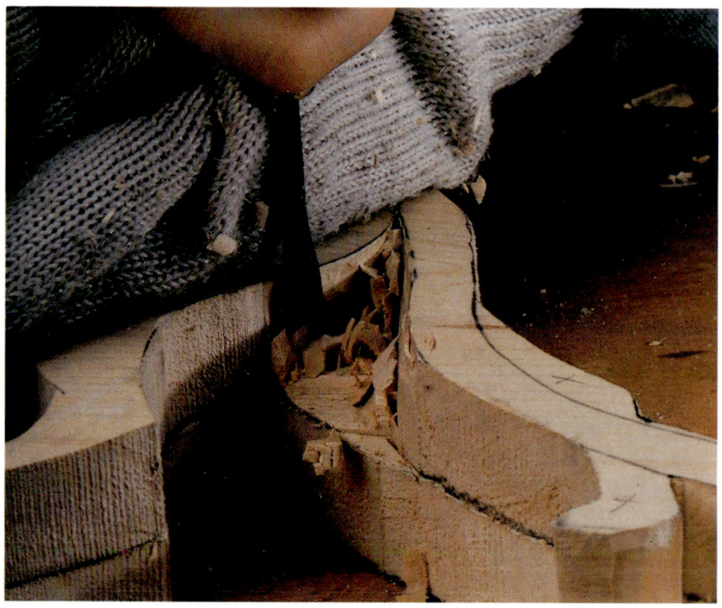

Once this area has been roughly cleared with the power chisel, we can finish cleaning up close to the root of the tail with a square-nosed gouge.

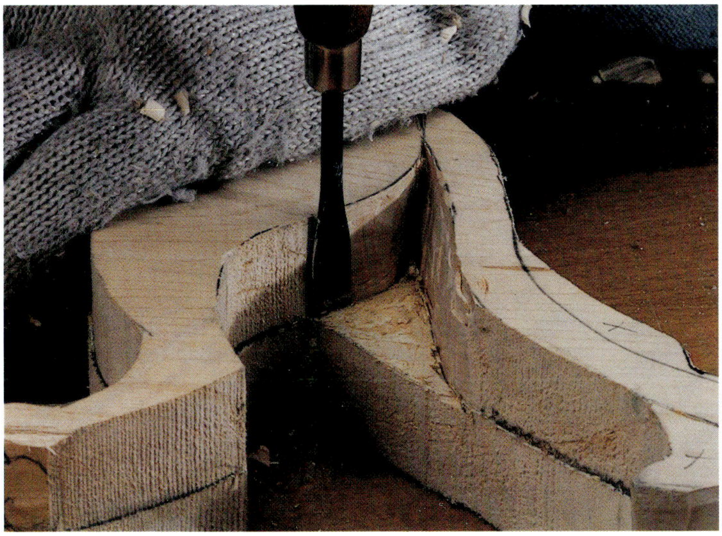

Here is the finished left flank area, clear of wood to the center line.

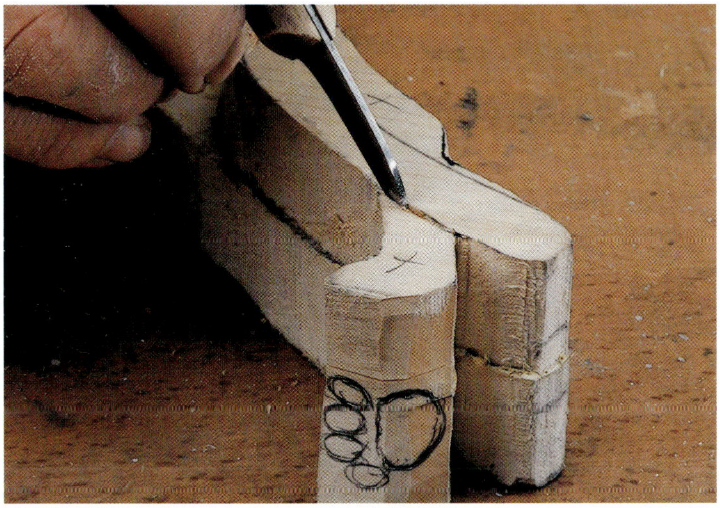

Making a stop cut with the bench knife along the line of the tail will prevent breakage of the tail when excess wood is removed from the trailing (right) rear foot beside the tail.

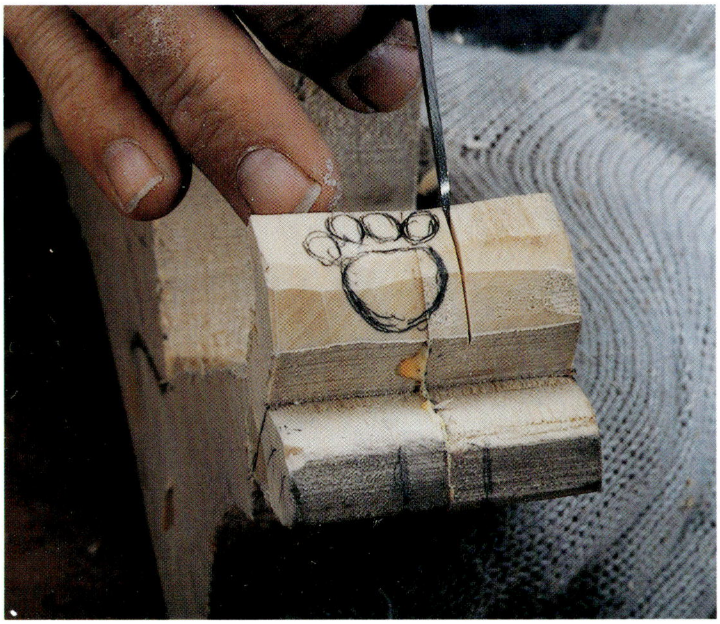

A second stop cut line is made along the side of the foot.

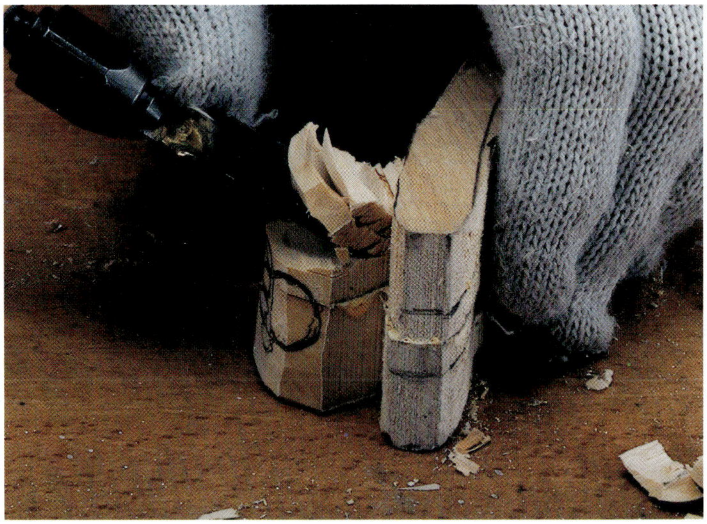

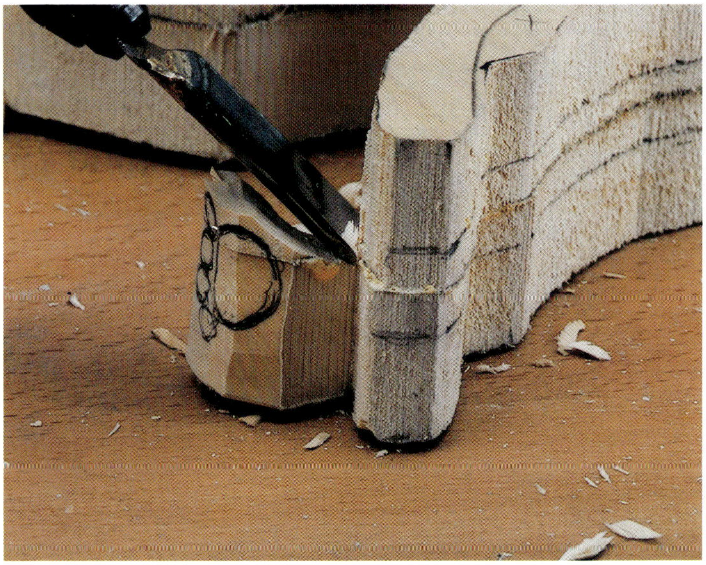

Remove the excess wood with the power chisel. Note the slanted angle of the side of the trailing leg. A Kevlar woodcarvers glove is recommended to prevent injuries to your hand while working with any sharp tools. However, do not use this glove when you are using a rotary tool; the glove could catch and and wrap up in the tool.

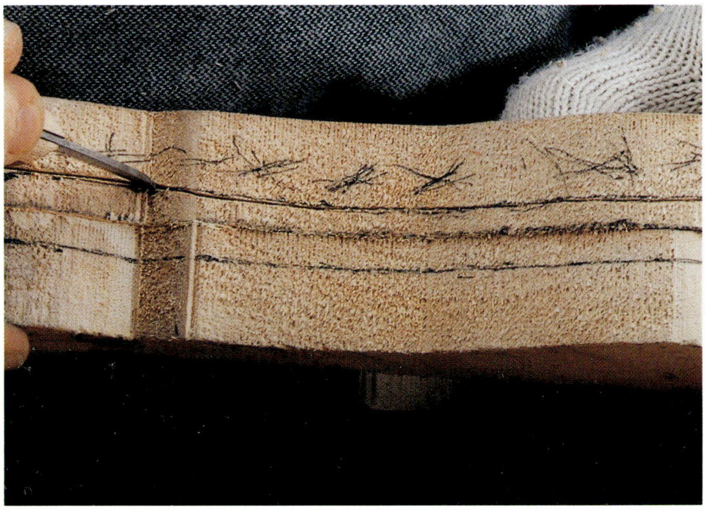

Now we will remove the wood that remains along the left edge of the tail, first by making a stop cut with a bench knife along the length of the tail.

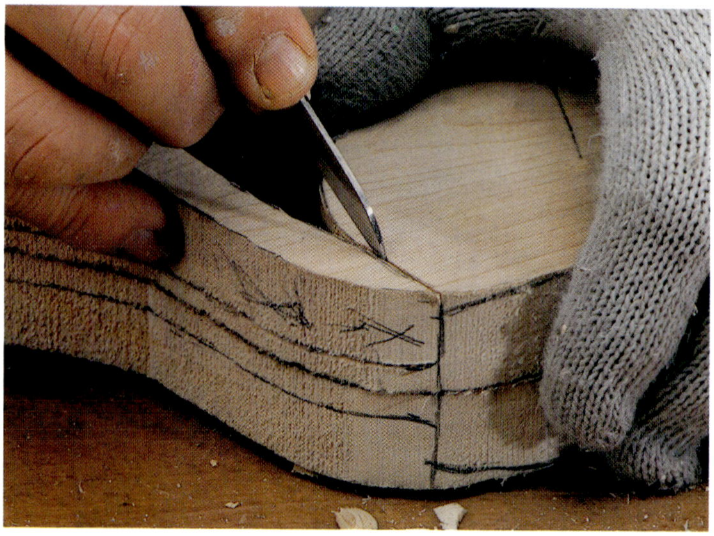

Make a second stop cut along the left flank.

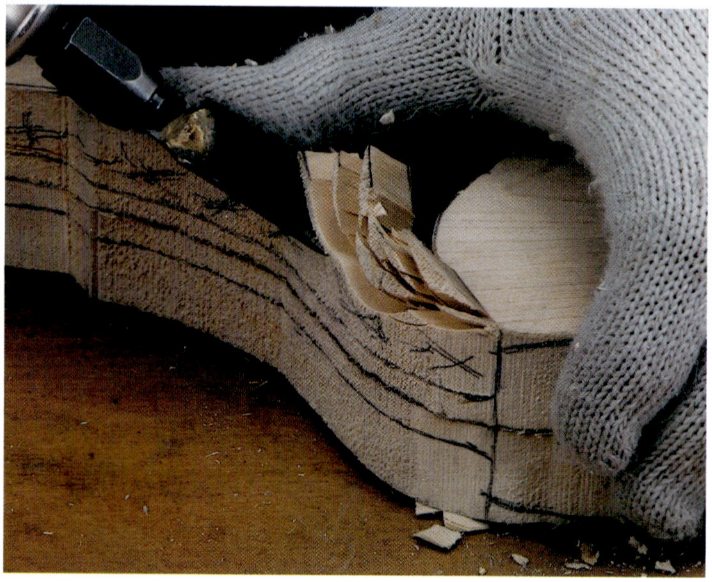

Begin removing the excess wood with the power chisel.

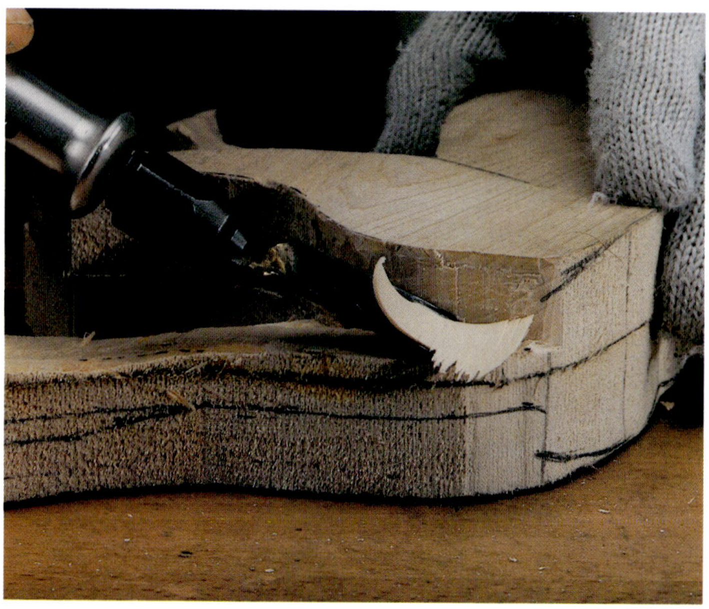

The excess wood has been removed from the left side of the tail.

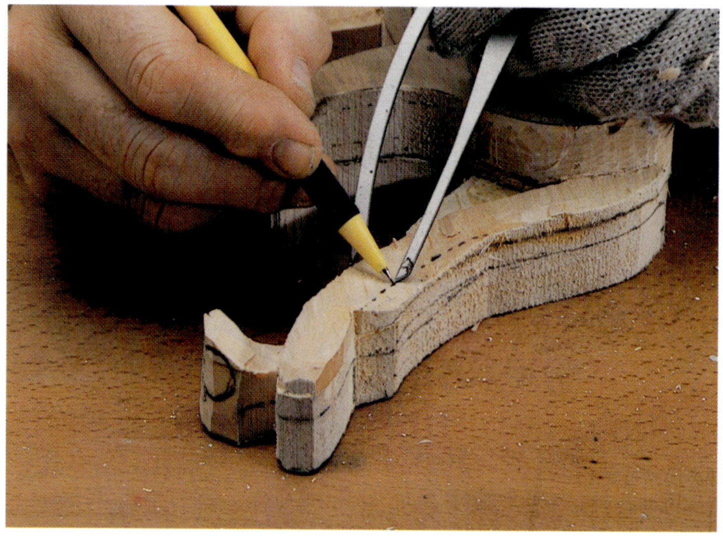

Redraw the tail to indicate the new area to be removed along the trailing back leg.

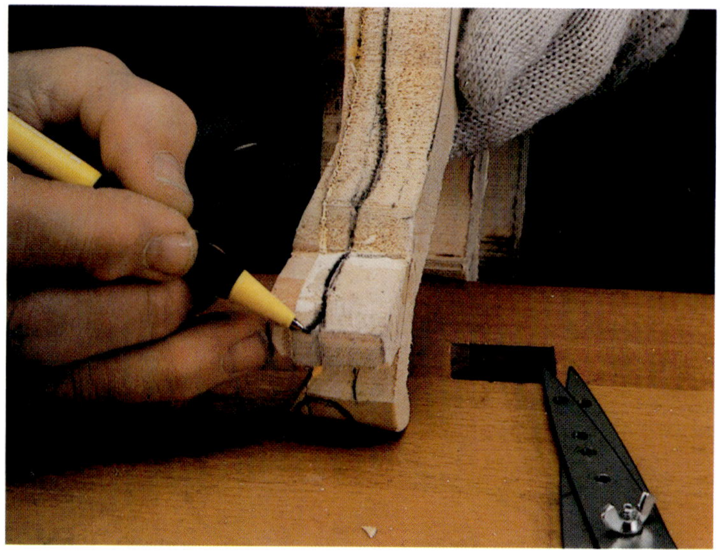

To add more life-like movement, redraw the tail line, adding a slight S curve

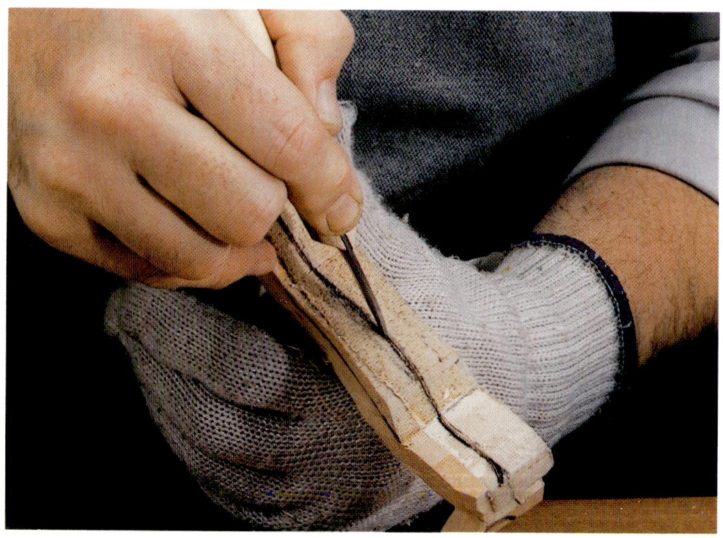

Remember to scribe stop cut lines with a bench knife before you start to remove any excess wood so that you won't accidentally remove either part of the leg or the tail as they are exposed.

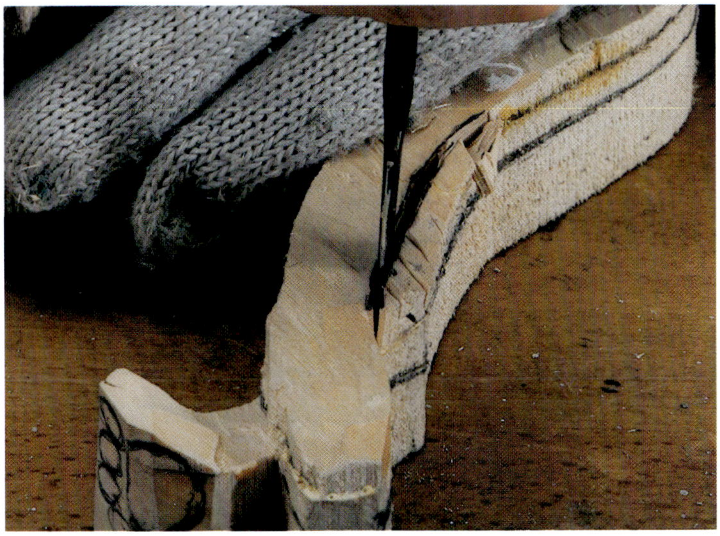

Remove the excess wood from the top of the tail using a small square-nosed chisel, exposing part of the trailing rear leg as well.

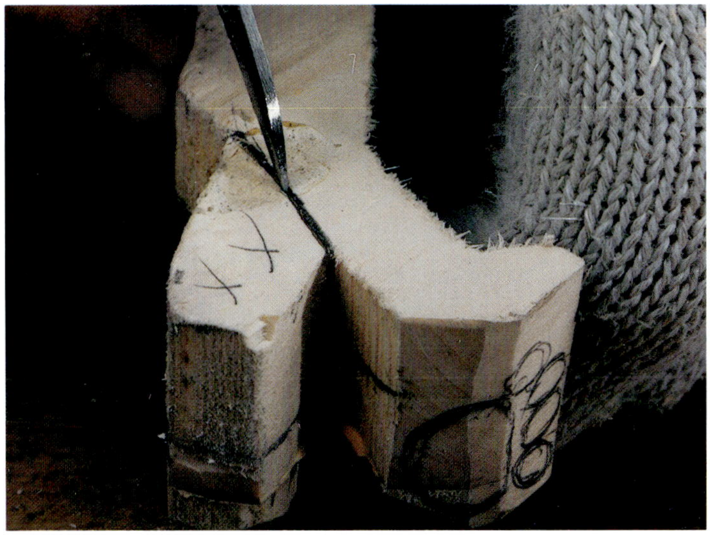

The second stop cut line will be down along the side of the same leg.

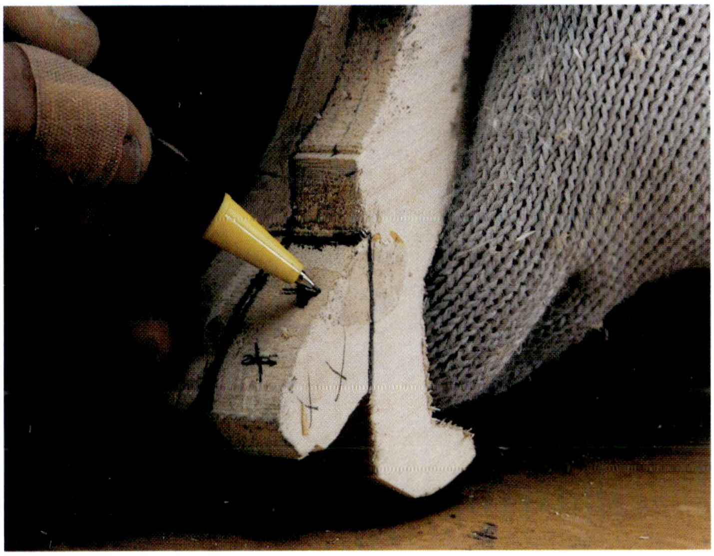

Next prepare to free the end of the tail. The excess wood to be removed is indicated with X's.

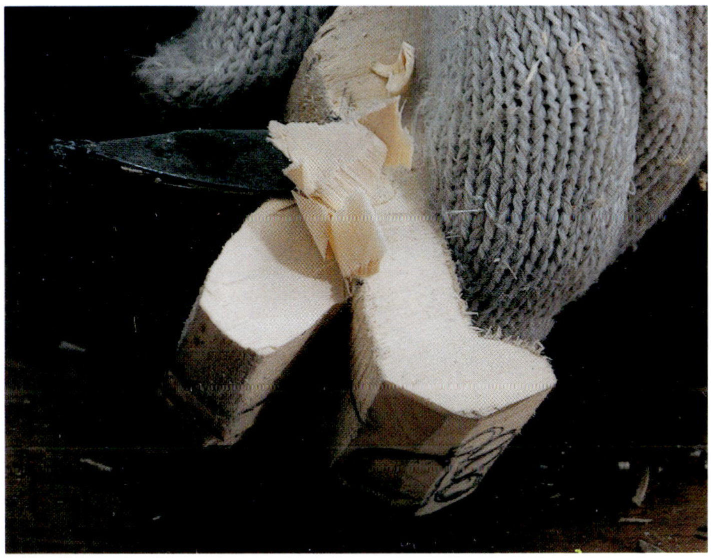

Remove the excess wood to free the tail with a small square-nosed chisel.

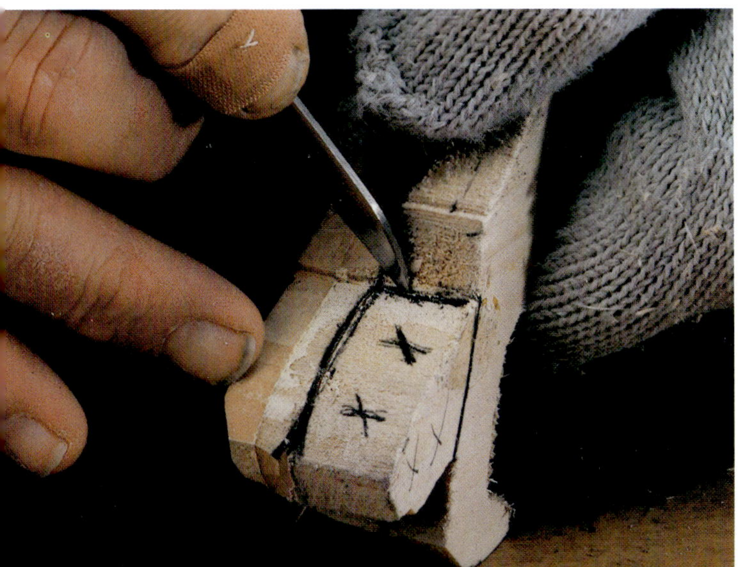

Make the first stop cut line across the back of the trailing leg.

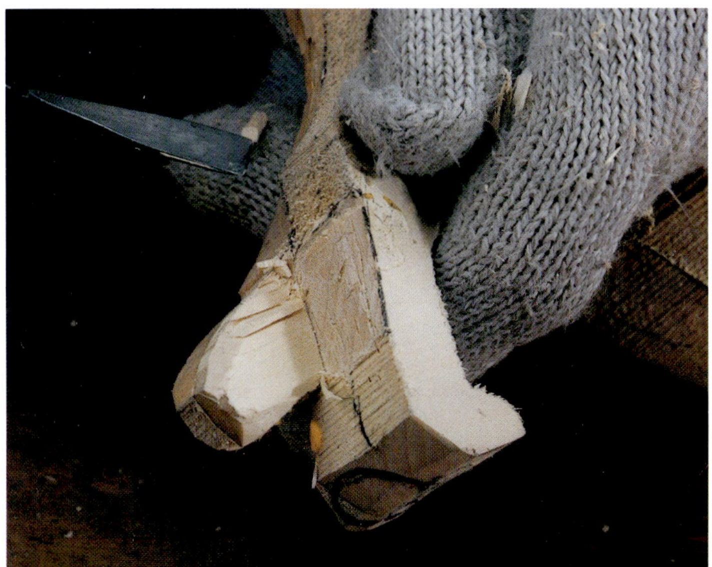

The freed end of the tail.

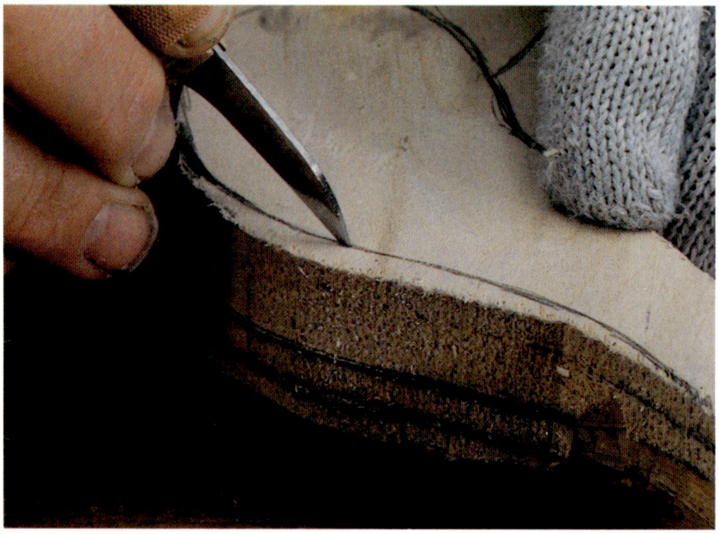

Scribe a stop cut along the back line of the trailing (right) rear leg with a bench knife where the wood is to be removed, freeing the right side of the tail.

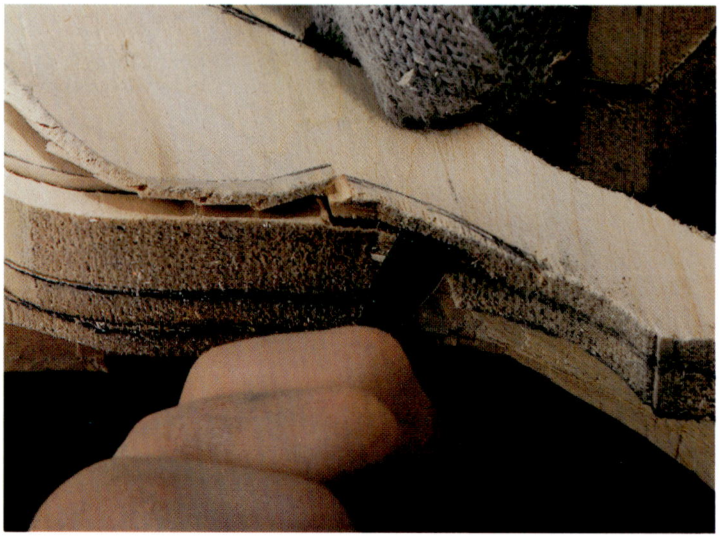

Begin to remove the wood from the right flank to further free the tail.

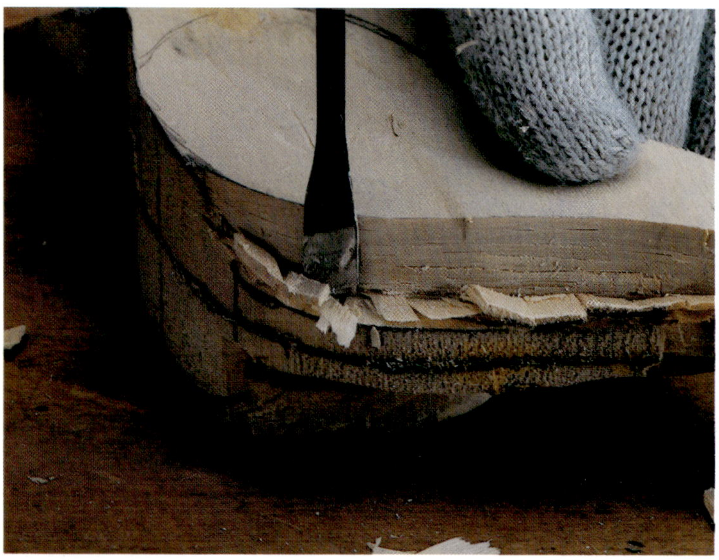

The wood has been removed from the right flank and tail, freeing the tail. This is how it should appear at this time. Let's leave the tail now for rounding later.

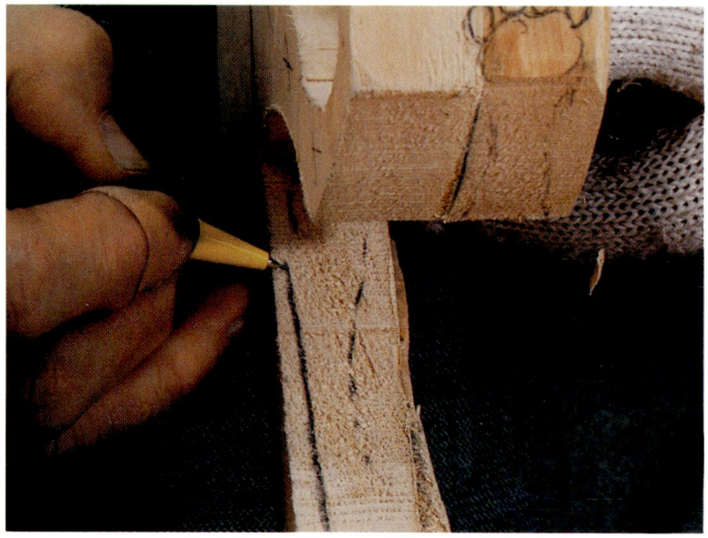

Because the legs are so thin, great care will have to be used to remove the excess wood around them, starting at the feet and working up the legs. We will be using a square-nosed chisel, a V gouge and a bench knife. Before doing this, it is best to stop and make sure these tools are extremely sharp. Once they are sharp, sketch in the outside of the leg prior to removing any wood. We are working on the trailing (left) rear leg here.

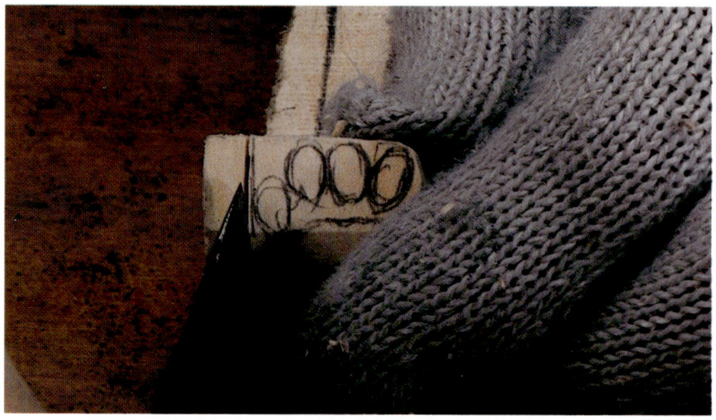

Scribe a stop cut along the side of the foot prior before removing any wood. This will help prevent breaking off the toes and feet.

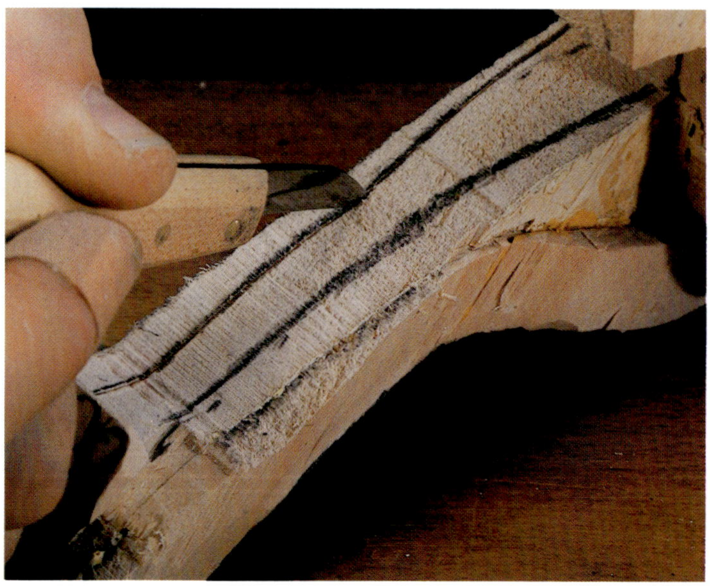

Scribe a stop cut along the side of the leg as well.

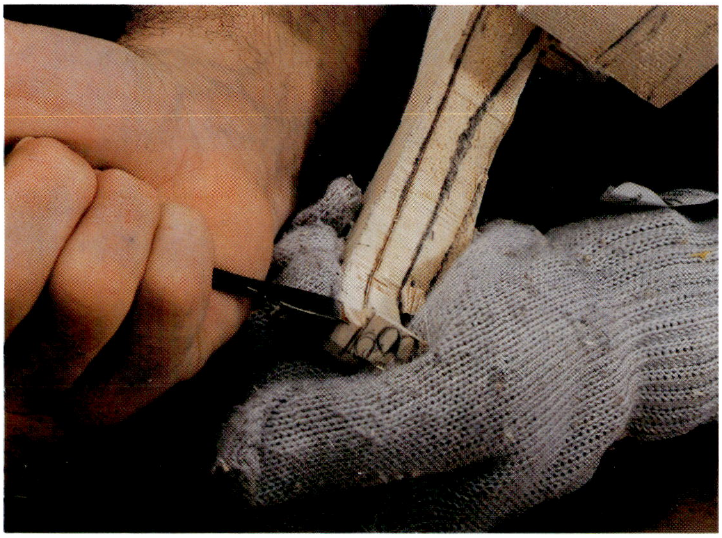

While making your cuts with the square-nosed gouge, be sure to support the foot and leg with your other hand. This is a critical time when breakage could occur.

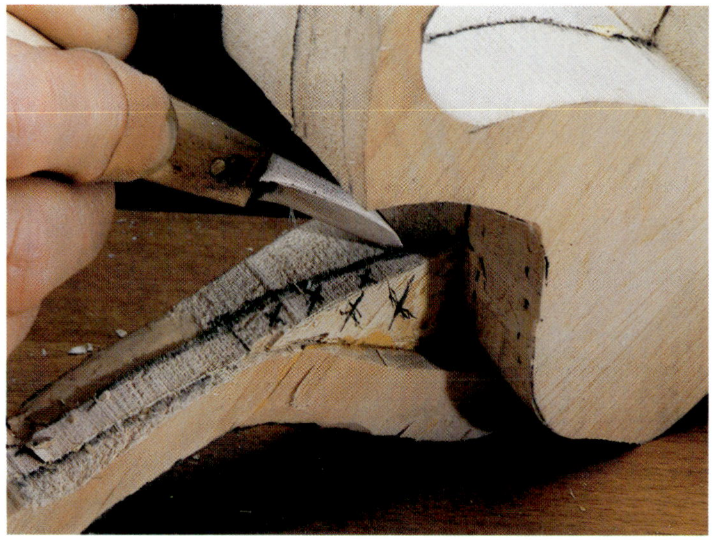

Still supporting the trailing leg, remove the excess wood from the front of the leg, revealing where the underside of the tail hangs below it. Scribe a stop cut line along the inside of the leg as well. The wood to be removed is marked with X's.

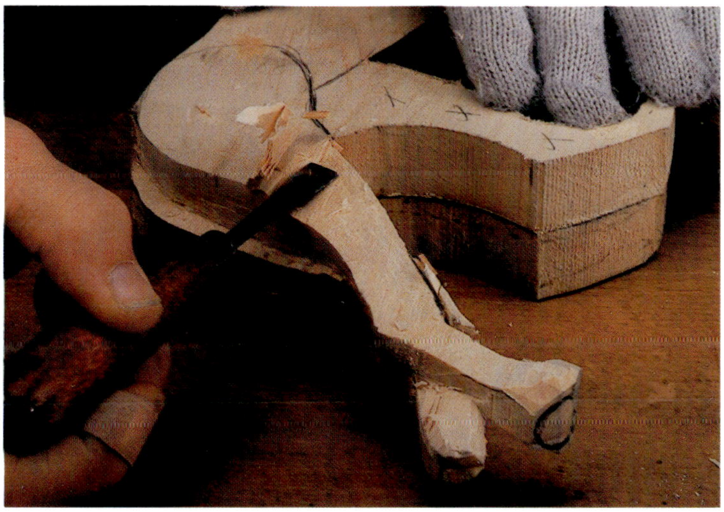

Using the square-nosed gouge, begin removing the excess wood. Start at the foot and move on up the leg. Thin the legs on both sides up into the body. However, don't thin them so far that you leave them too fragile.

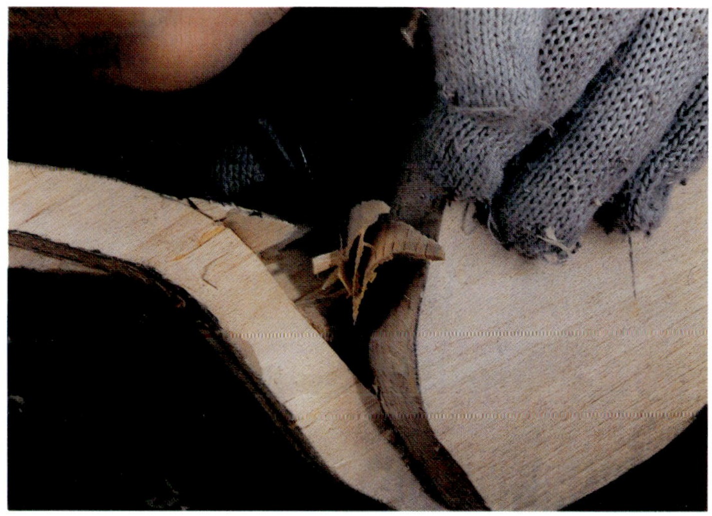

Remove the excess wood with the square-nosed gouge.

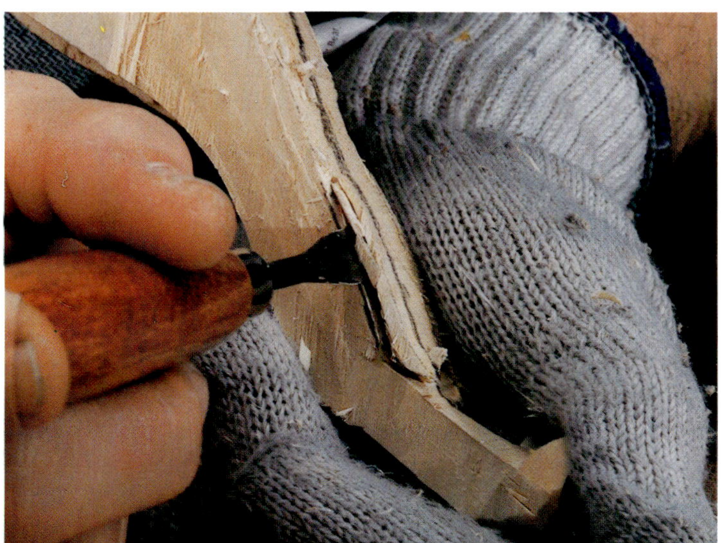

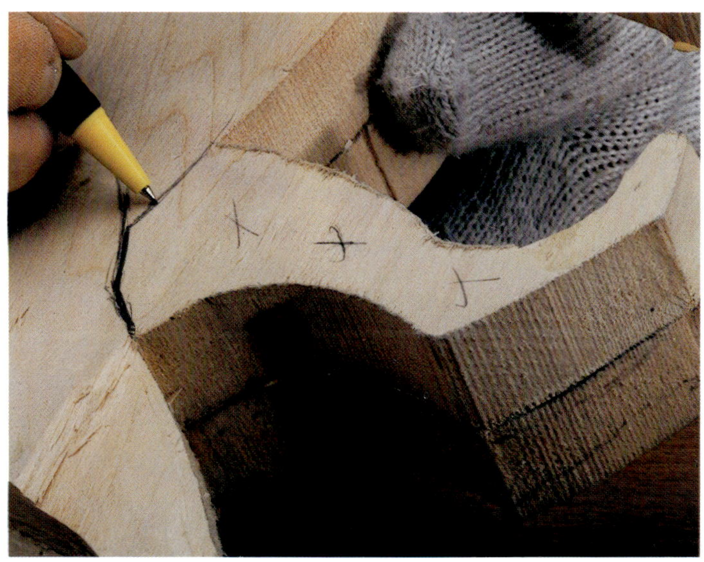

Sketch in the location of the front of the trailing rear leg and the belly. Now we will prepare to remove the excess wood indicated here with X's.

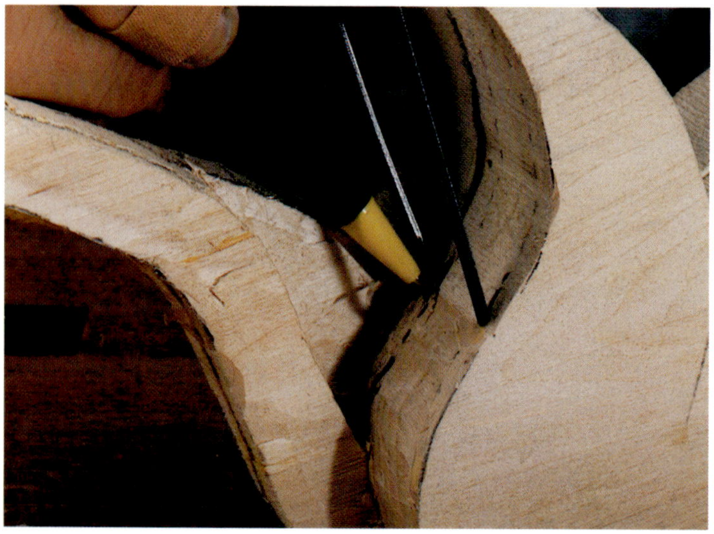

Use proportional dividers as shown to locate and size the leg properly off the center line before cutting away the excess wood and exposing the inside of the leading rear leg.

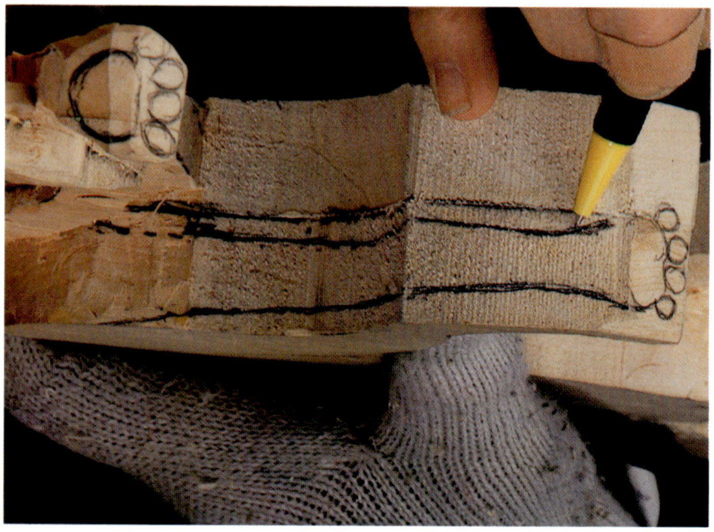

Draw in the measured leg lines to indicate the area of the leg.

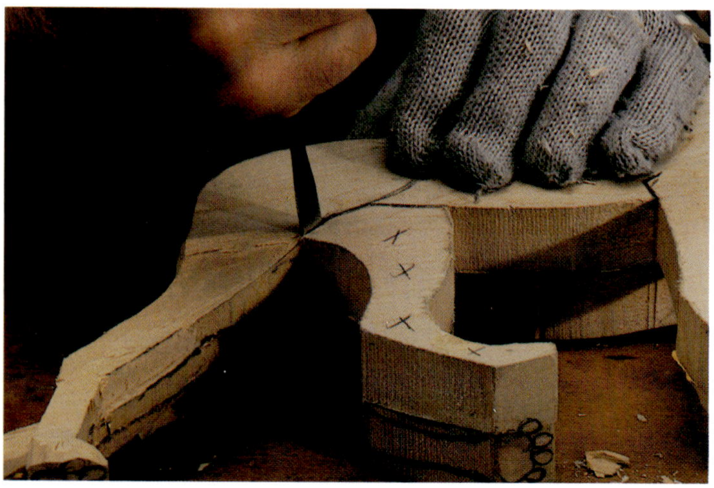

Remove the wood from the inside of the leading rear leg first so that the table can support the leg. This leg lies flat against the table while you work with a square-nosed gouge. Cut in the stop cut lines and remove the excess wood from the inside of the leg. The stop cut lines are being incised here with the square-nosed gouge.

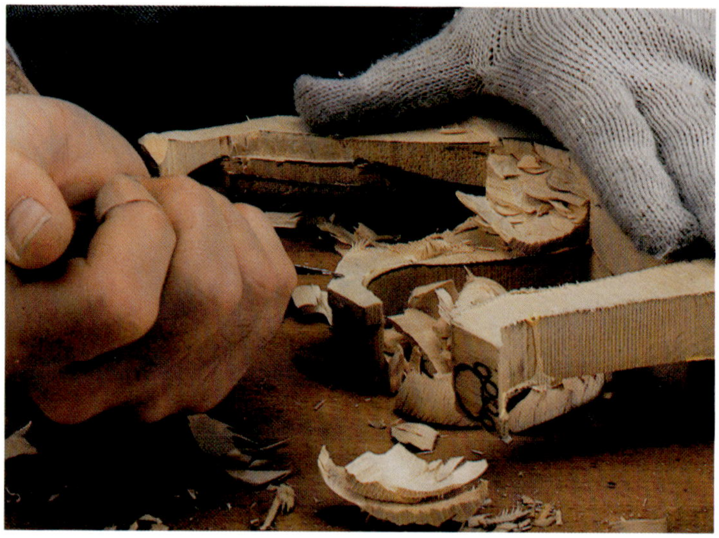

Remove the excess wood from the inside of the leg with the square-nosed gouge.

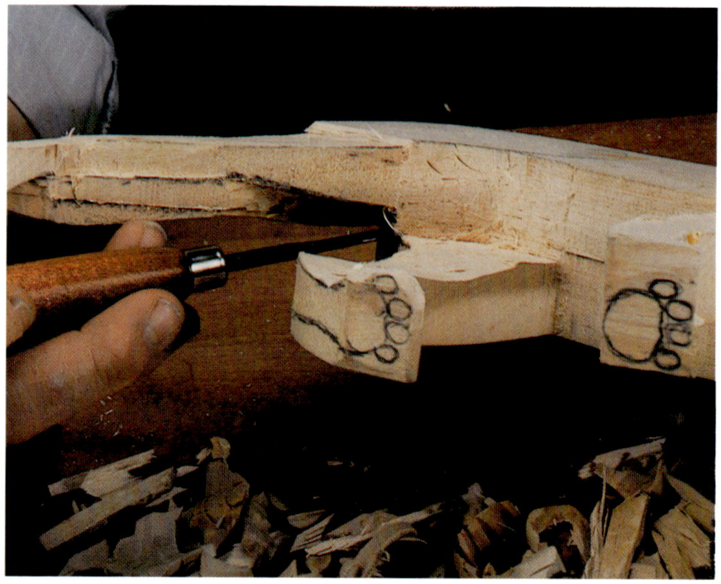

Now the insides of both rear legs have been cleared of excess wood. Final shaping will come later, after the body has been roughed out.

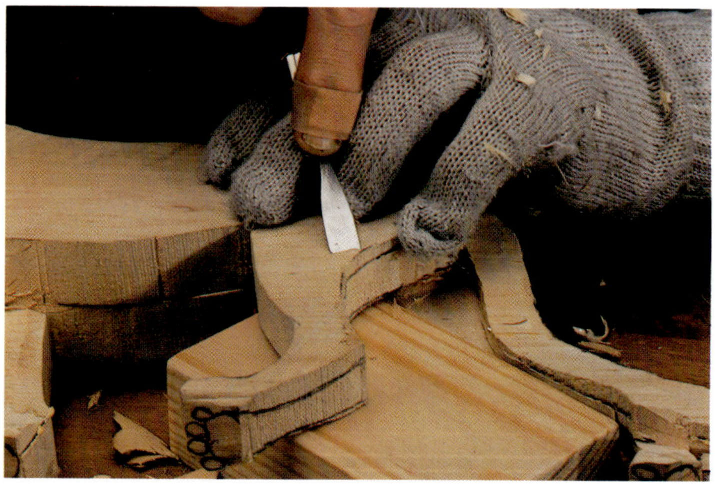

We are now ready to start clearing excess wood from the outside of the leading rear leg with the square-nosed gouge. I suggest you support the leg with a piece of scrap wood as you carve to prevent breakage.

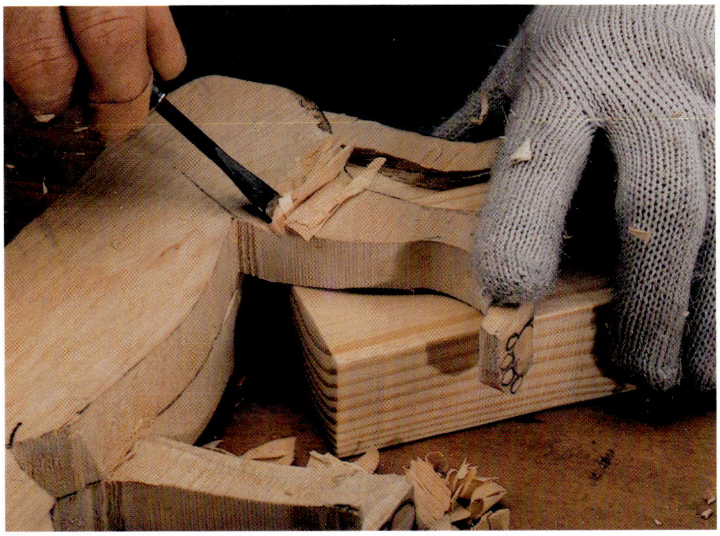

It might be helpful to mark the very top of your cut with a stop cut to prevent removing of too much wood on the flank.

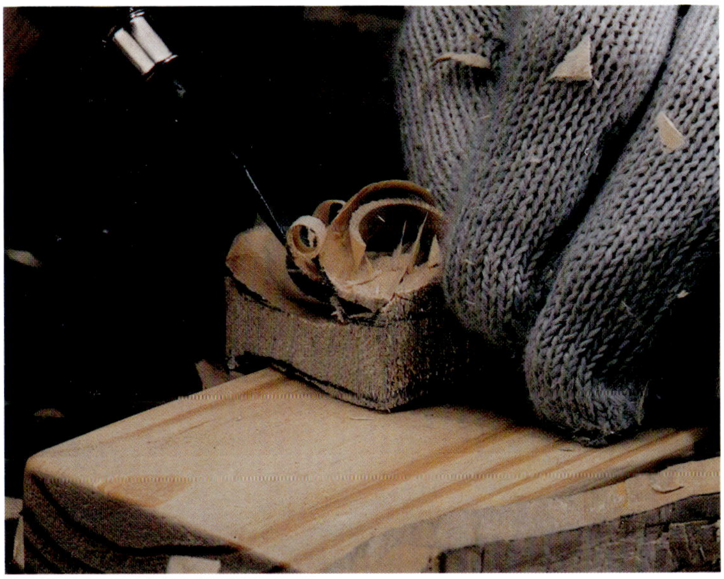

Remove the excess wood from the outside of the leading rear leg with the square-nosed gouge, beginning at the foot and working your way up to the stop cut line at the flank.

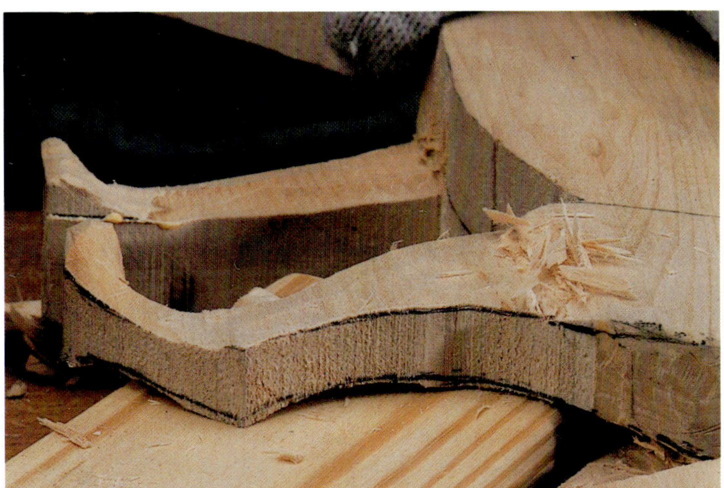

Here is how the outside of the leg should appear when you are finished.

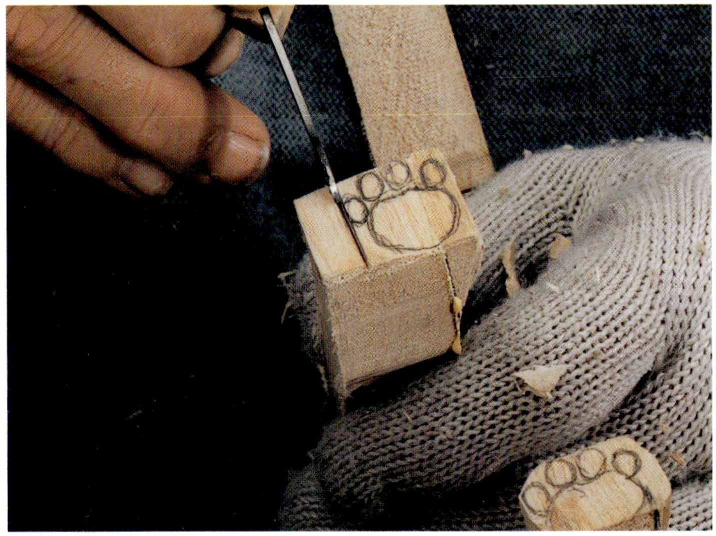

Moving to the front legs, again starting to work from the foot area up the leg on both front legs, remove the excess wood from the outside of the legs. Use a block of scrap wood again to support the legs. First scribe a stop cut line, beginning along the side of the foot and working up the leg.

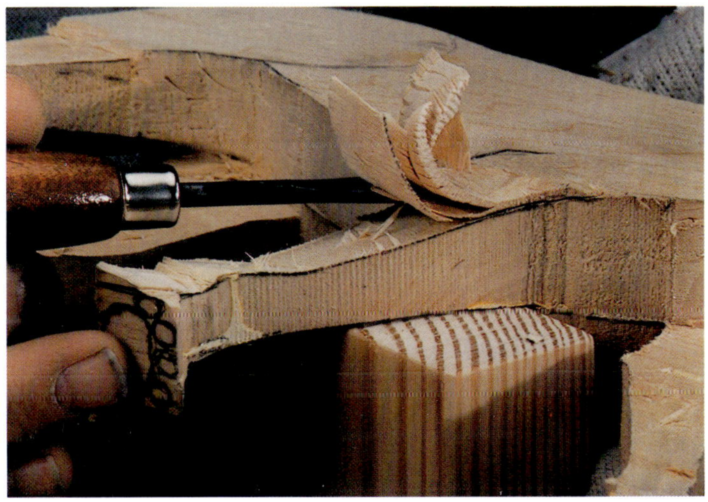

Remove the excess wood along the outside of the front legs with the square-nosed gouge.

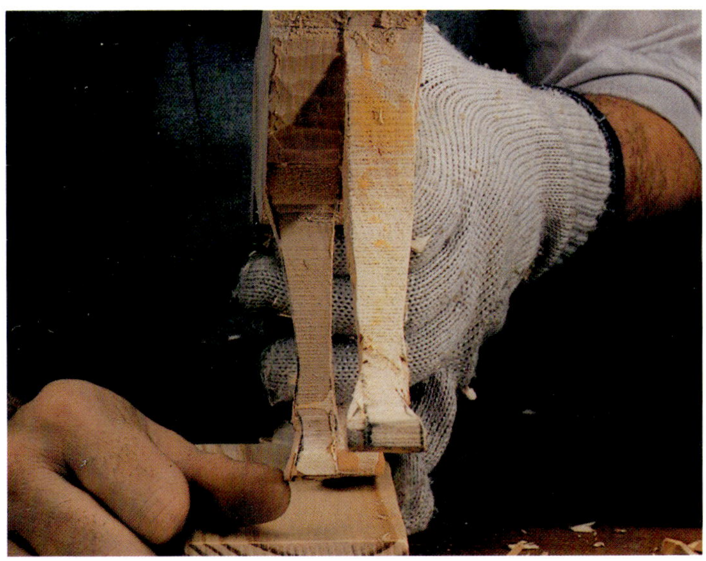

Both front legs have been cleared of excess wood.

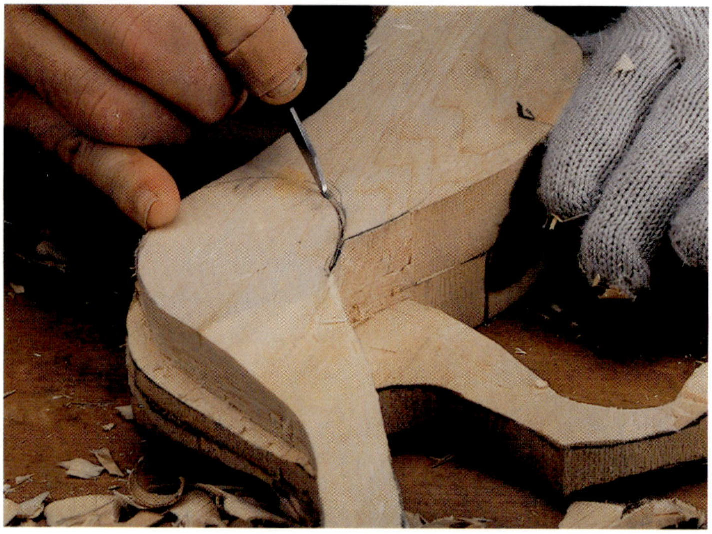

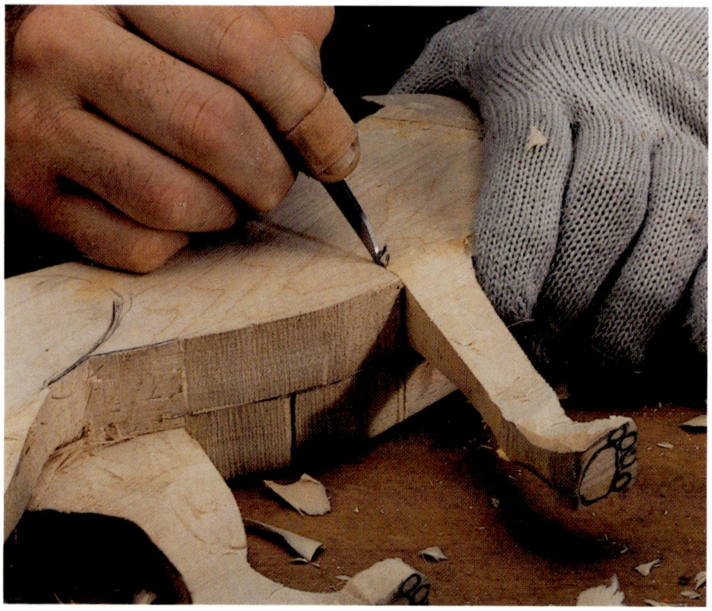

We are going to cut in the front and back edges of the legs on both sides so that we can round the upper body. Scribe in the lines in front of the flanks and behind the front legs prior to starting to shape the body.

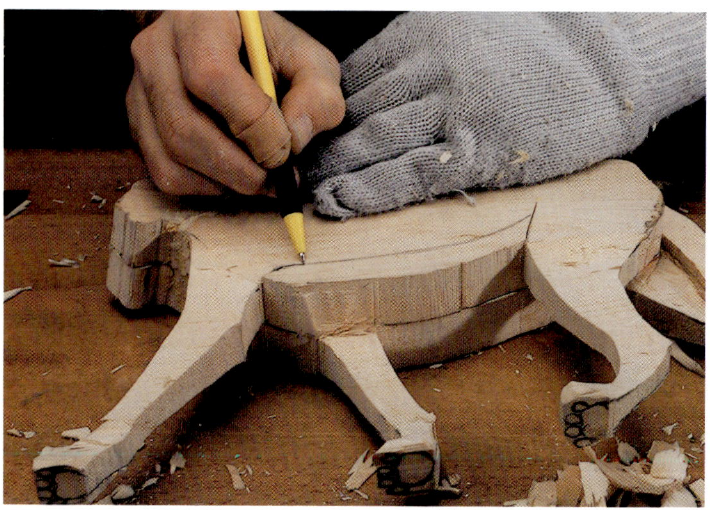

Sketch in a line from the point where the front leg connects to the body to the front of the rear flank approximately 1/2" up from the edge of the belly.

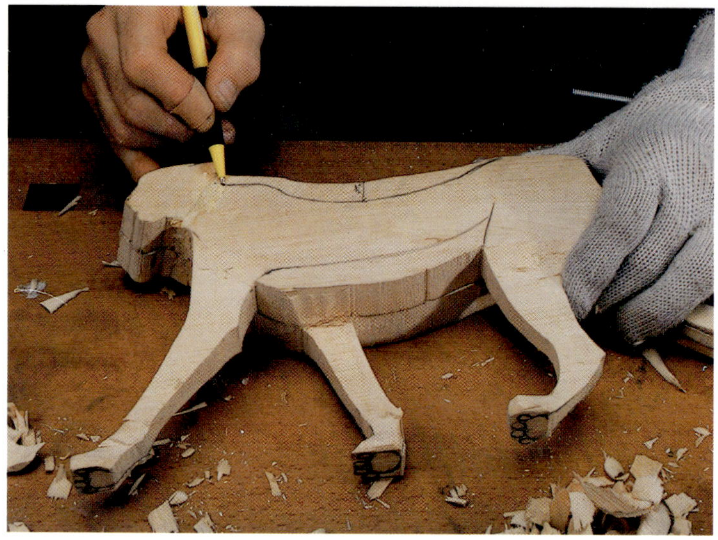

Draw a line along the upper back that is, at its widest point, 1/2" below the upper edge of the cheetah.

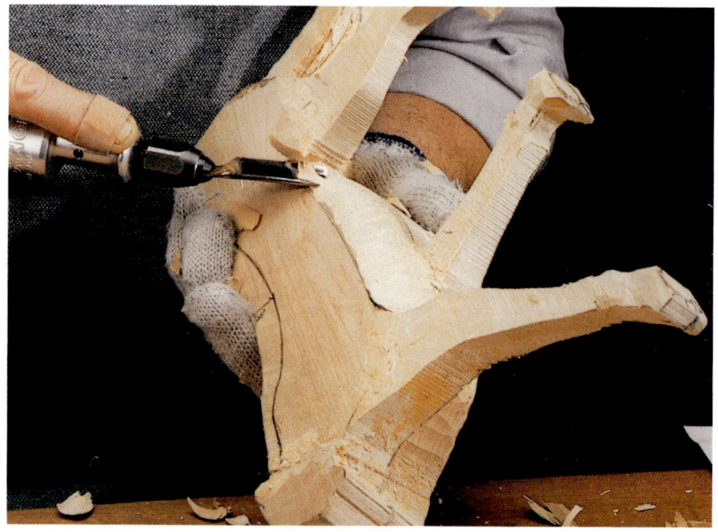

Using the power chisel with its wide gouge, round from the sketched line to the underbelly center line in a gentle arch that frees the belly of excess wood.

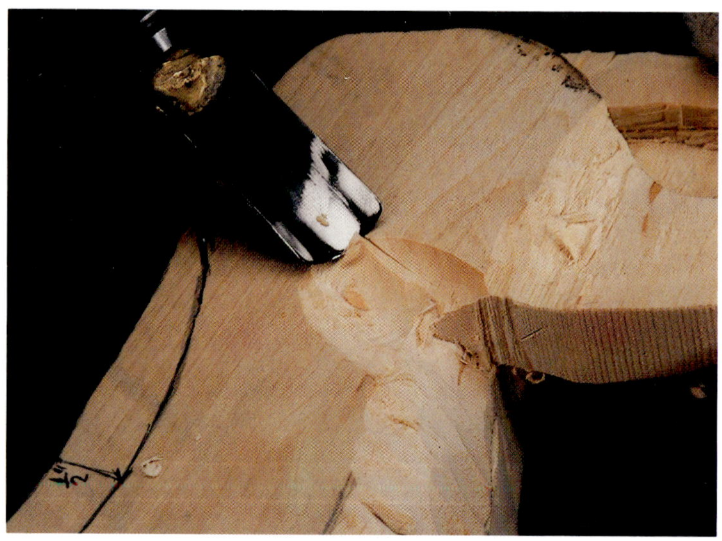

Along the leading edge of the rear flank, where it meets the side, remember there is a web of skin fastened to the side and the front of the leg. Make sure you leave ample wood for this web.

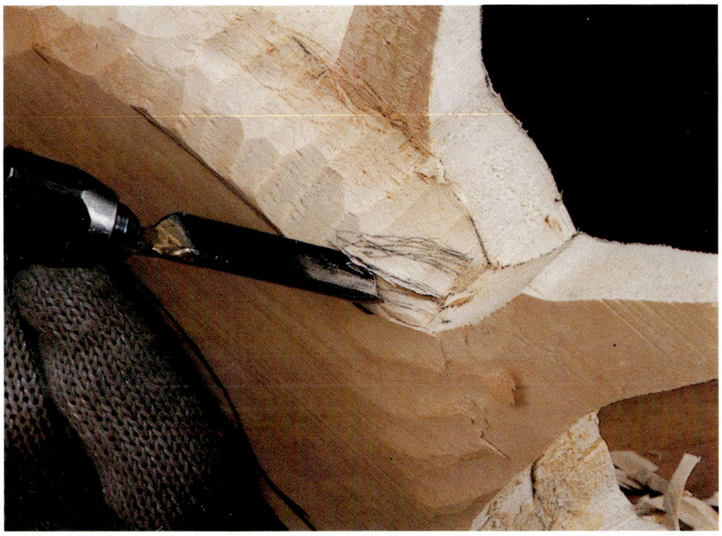

We're now forming the web of skin that extends from the ribs to the front legs. This also helps to define the brisket. This web is formed by cutting out a very shallow V right here. When we shape the front leg this web will become more evident.

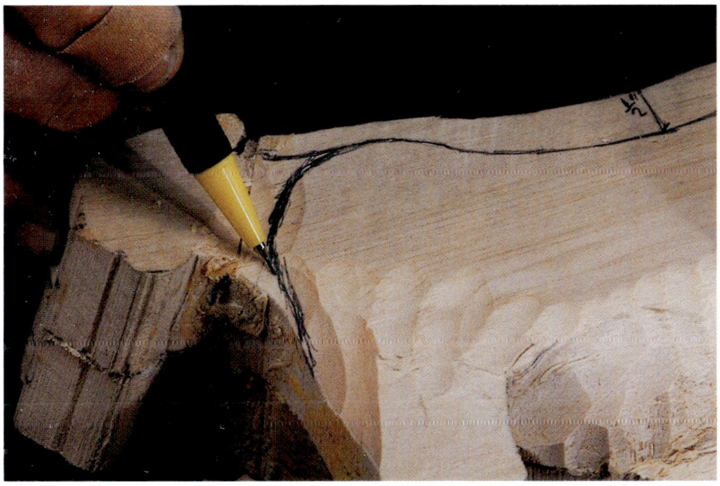

At this time it is helpful to sketch in the line of the front shoulder where it lies up along the neck.

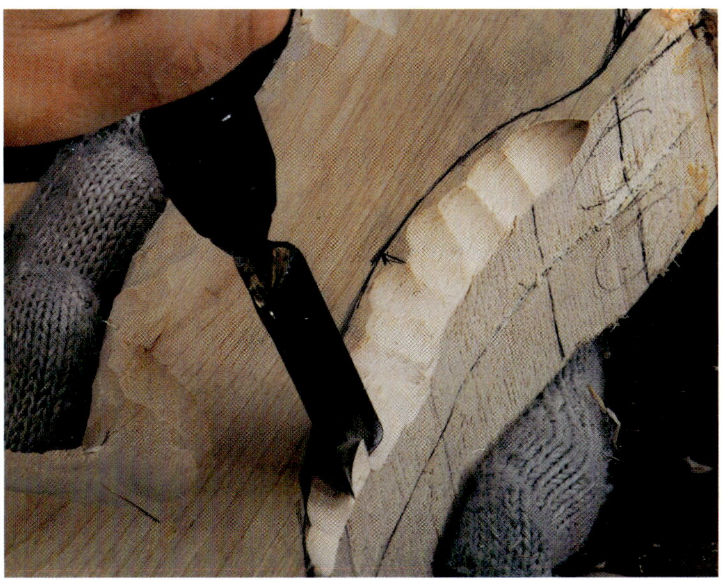

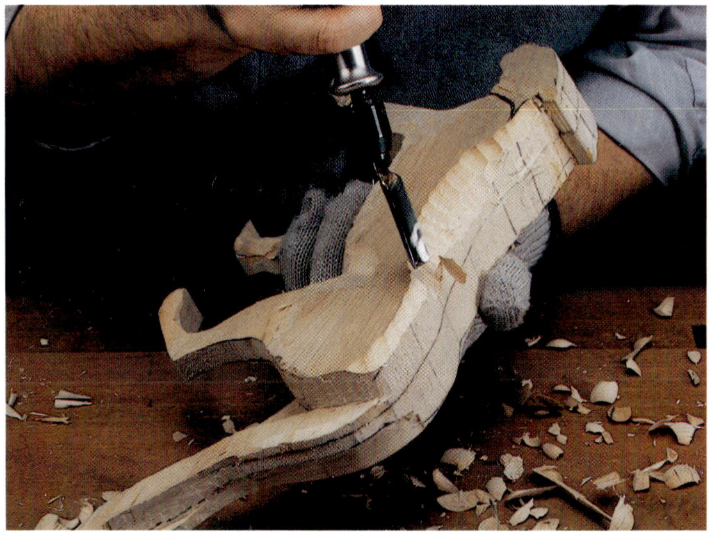

Round up the top of the back toward the center line, being careful not to round too far up along the hips and shoulders.

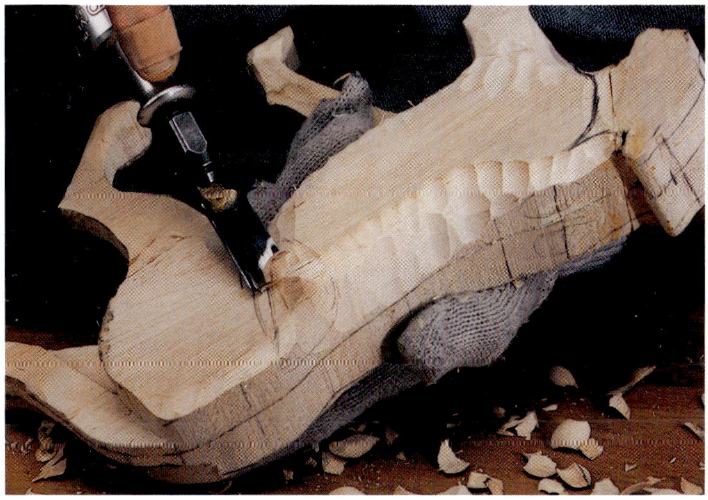

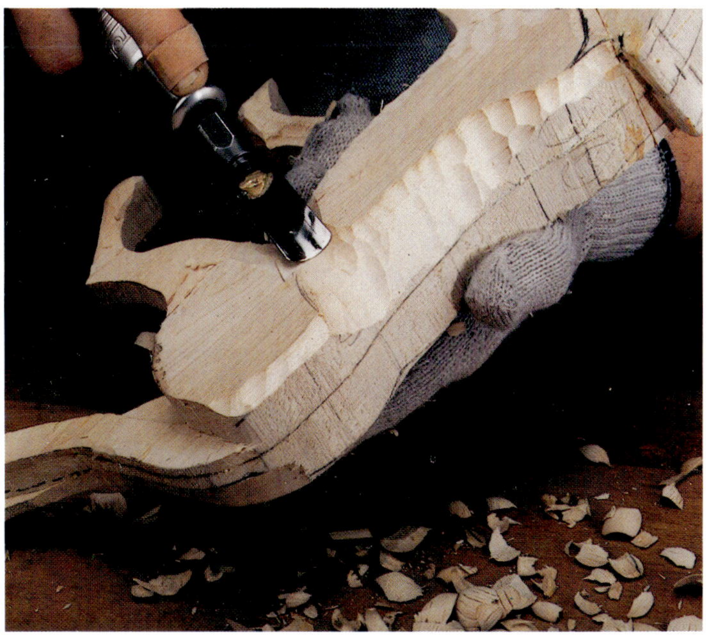

Sketch in and carve the hollow that forms behind the rib cage and in front of the hips. Here is the hollow as it is being carved and after it has been completed.

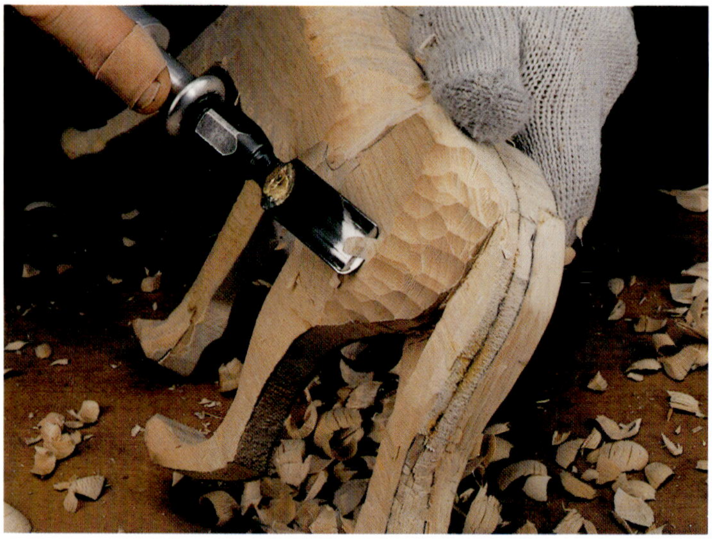

Round down the back of the flanks now. They are very thin at the tail.

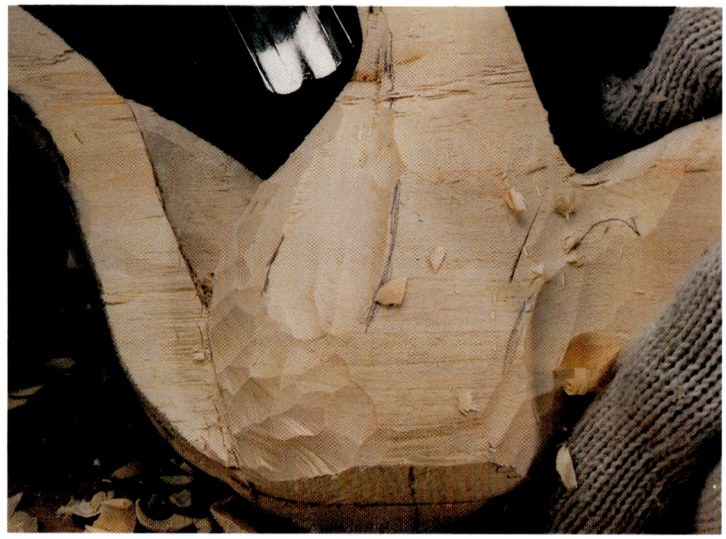

The valley defined.

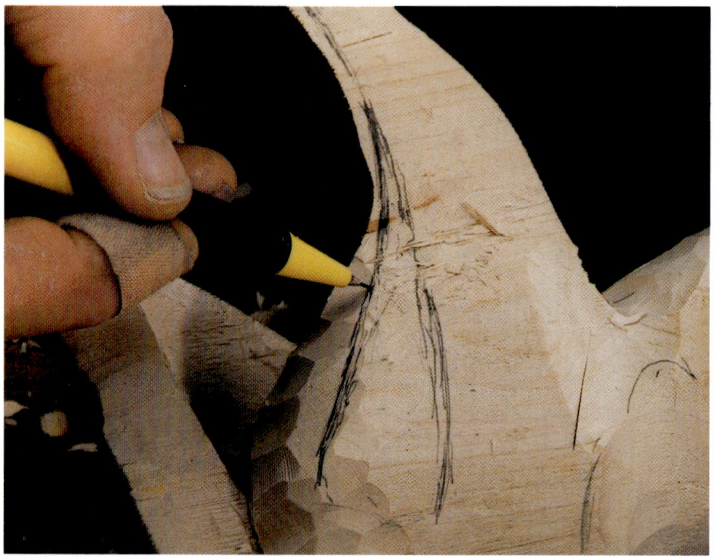

We will now round this area to indicate a valley between two large muscle groups. This valley is very shallow at the front and works deeper to the back.

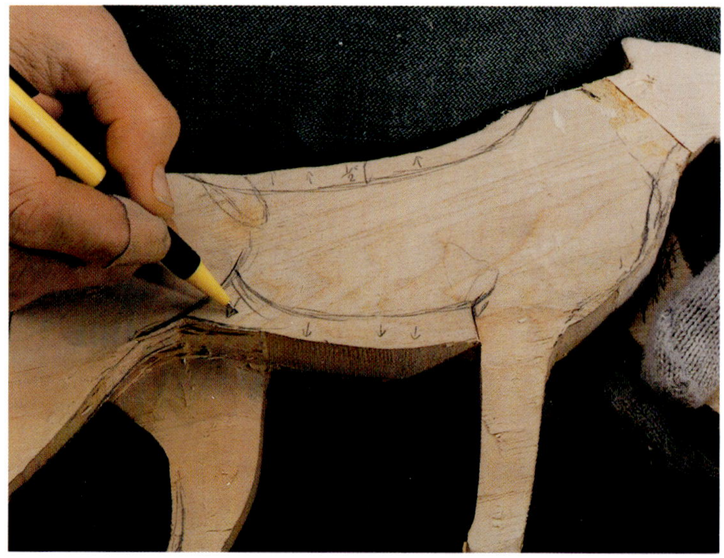

As we did on the other side, draw a line from the back of the front leg to the front of the rear leg to indicate where we will start rounding off on the side and belly.

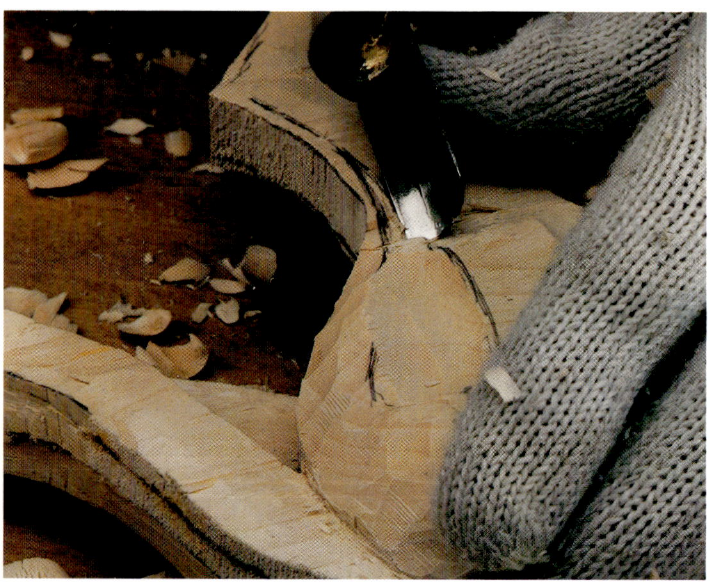

Define the valley with the power chisel.

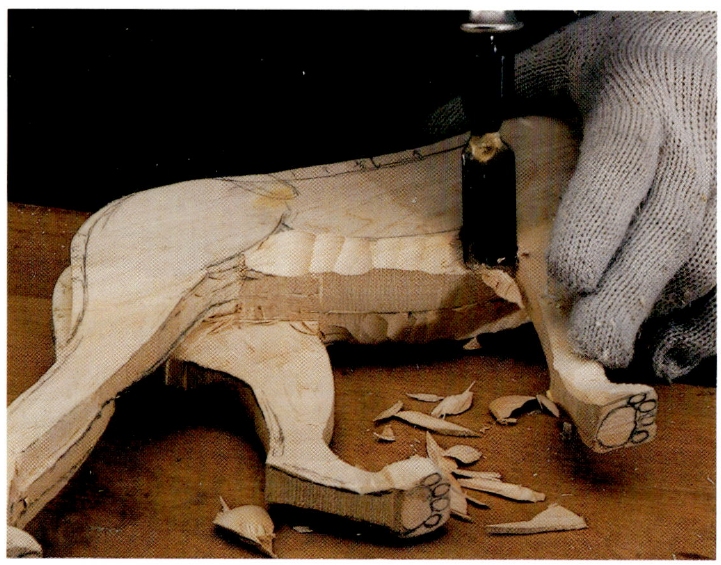

Rounding the belly from the sketched line on the side down to the underbelly centerline.

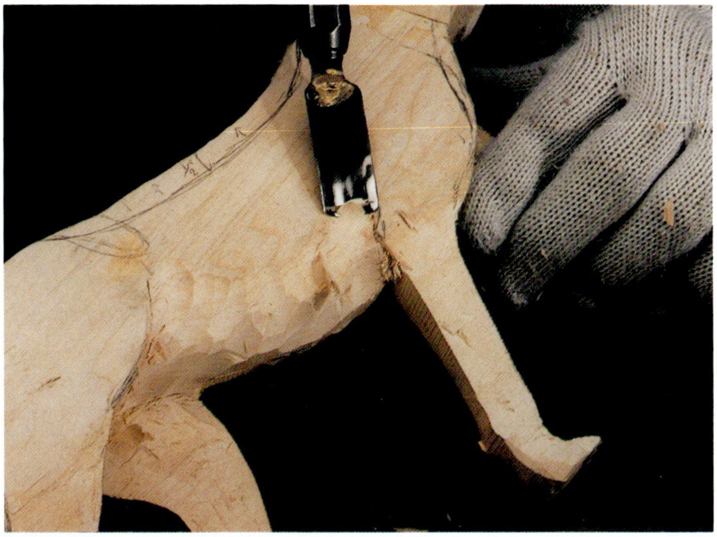

Remove some of the excess wood from the behind the front leg to free it.

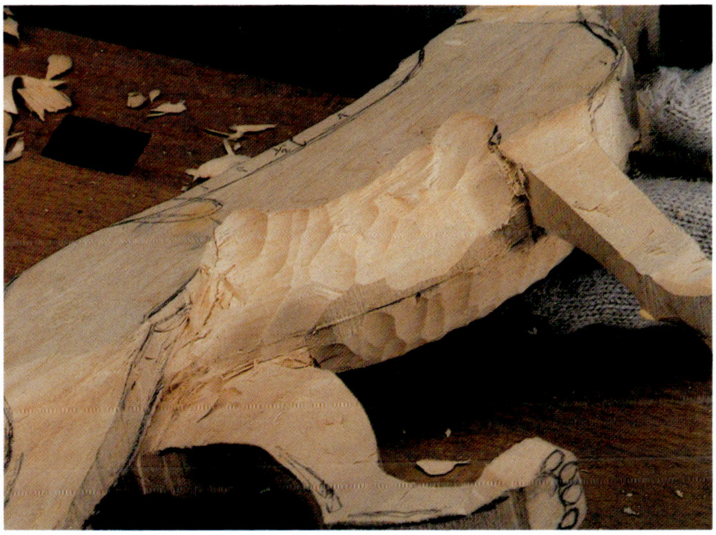

The rounded lower side and belly.

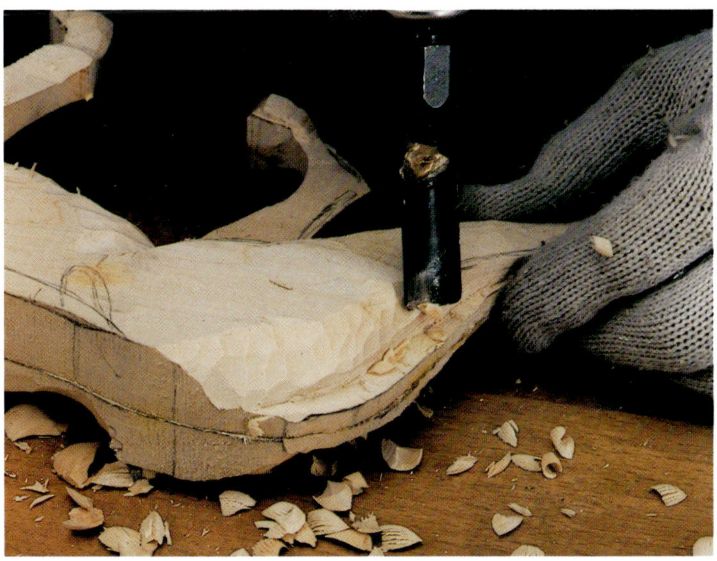

Round the back of the flank down in an ever decreasing arc toward the tail. Note that on this side the rear flank has very little muscle mass showing. It appears relatively flat. We will do further rounding and final shaping later on.

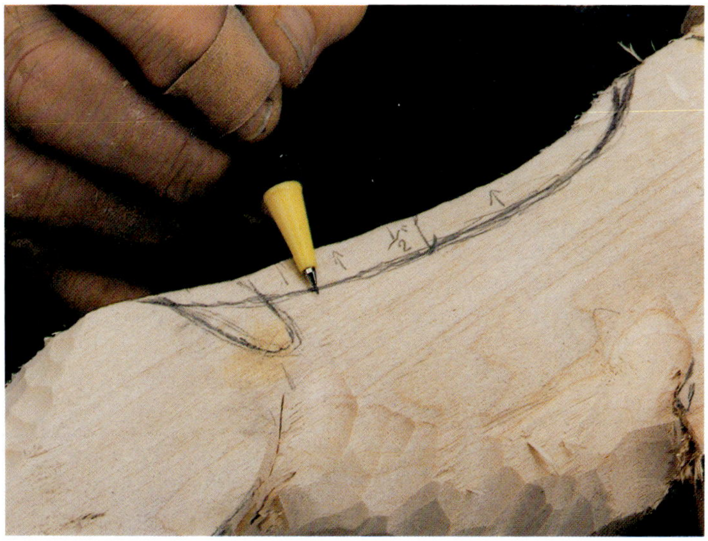

Draw a gentle arc as shown from the front right shoulder to the right rear hip. As on the left side, the deepest part of this arc should be 1/2" down from the back. Indicate the hollow that forms between the front of the hip and the back of the rib cage as well.

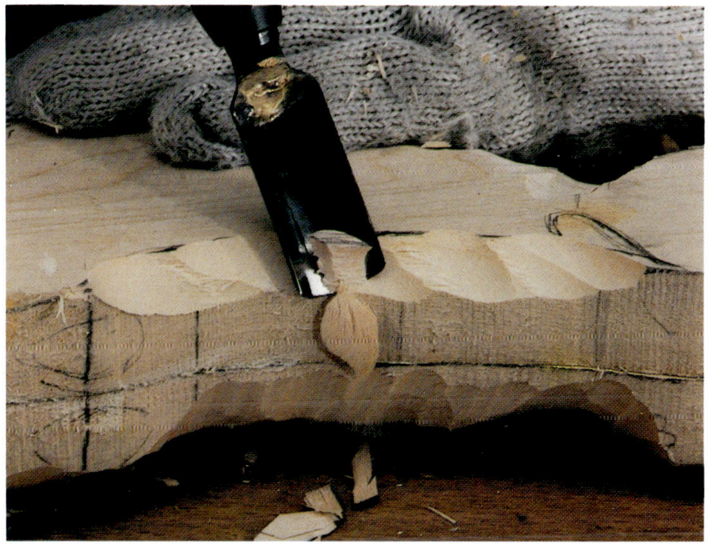

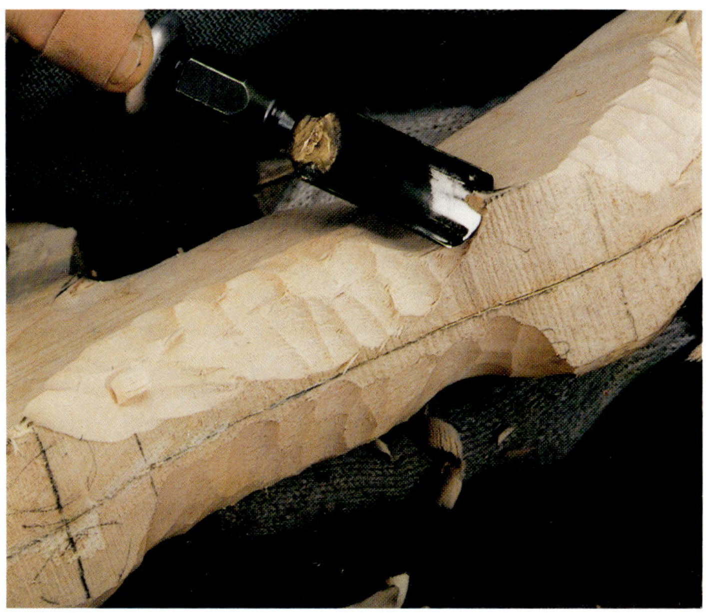

Round the back along the sketched lines up to the center line.

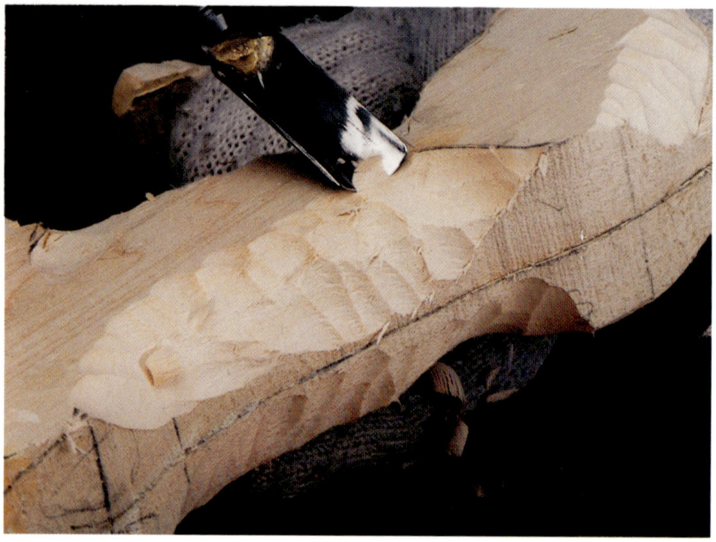

Rounding out the hollow between the hip and rib cage.

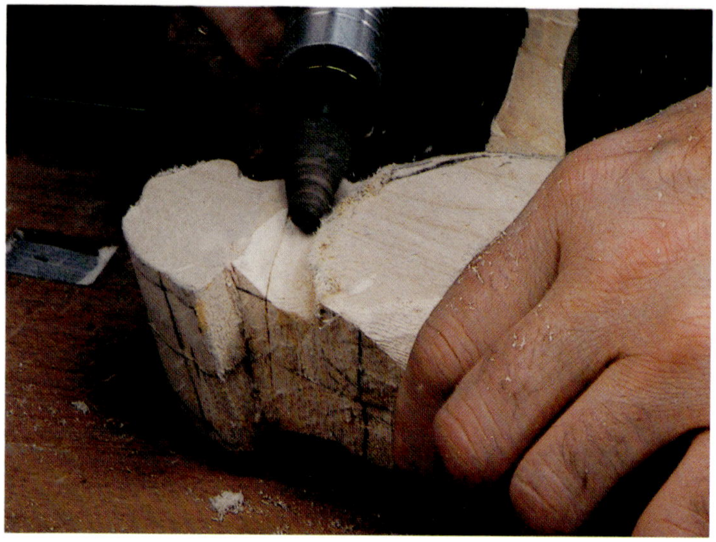

This is a good way to open up the area of the neck between the front of the shoulder and the back of the head as well.

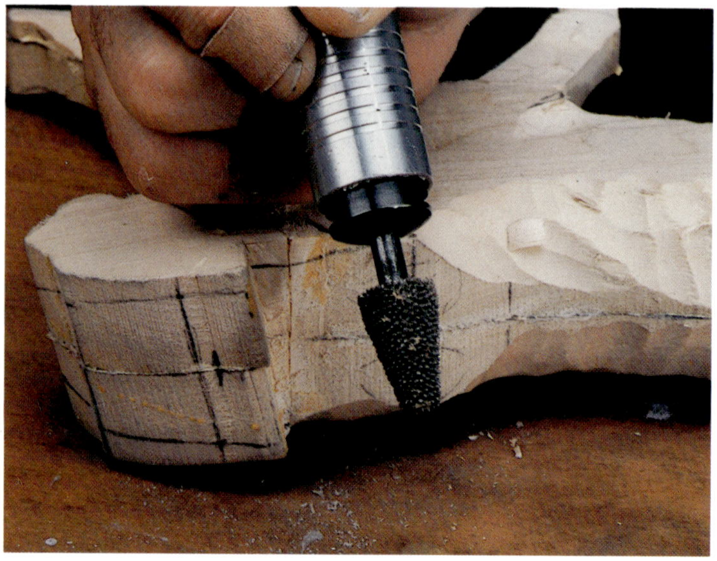

Change tools, fitting your Foredom flexible shaft machine with a "Christmas tree" shaped Kutzall bit.

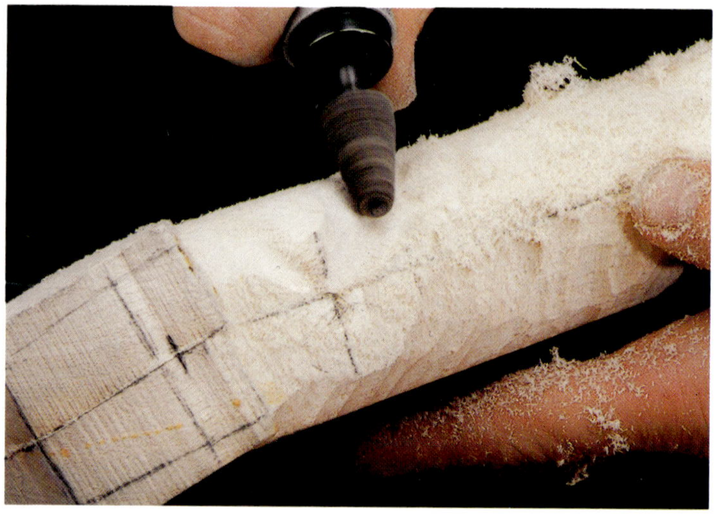

Round up around the shoulder to get it to show.

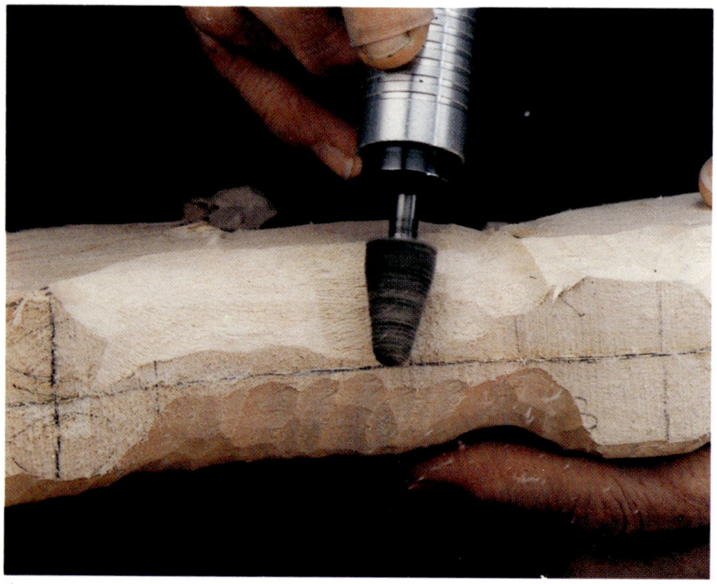

We are now smoothing out chisel marks and rounding off the cat to give it a smooth but muscular shape.

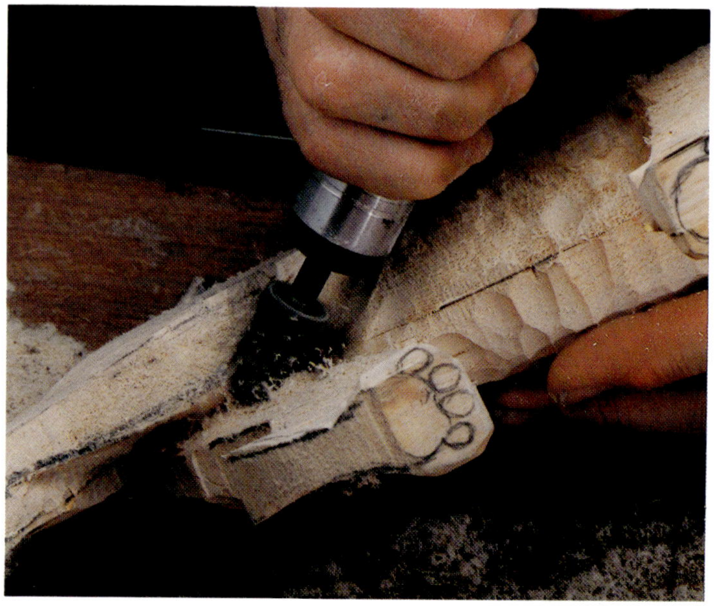

Work the belly area in beside the rear leg where the skin would be stretched out.

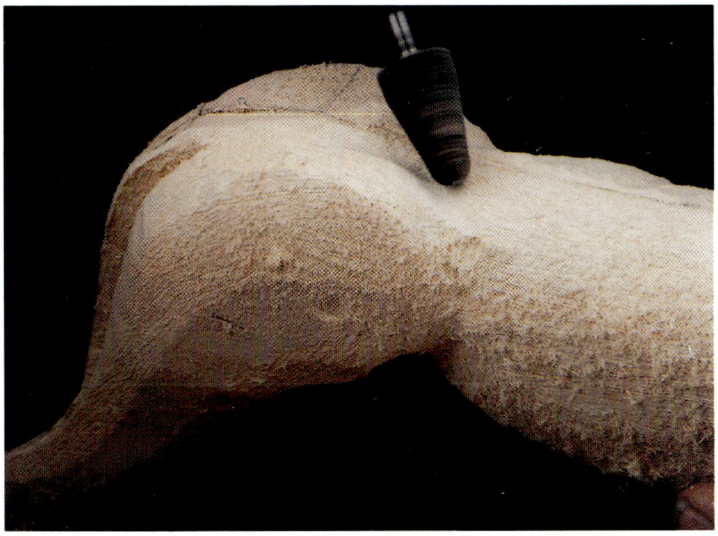

Indicating the hip bone, the pelvis sticks up as cheetah's walk.

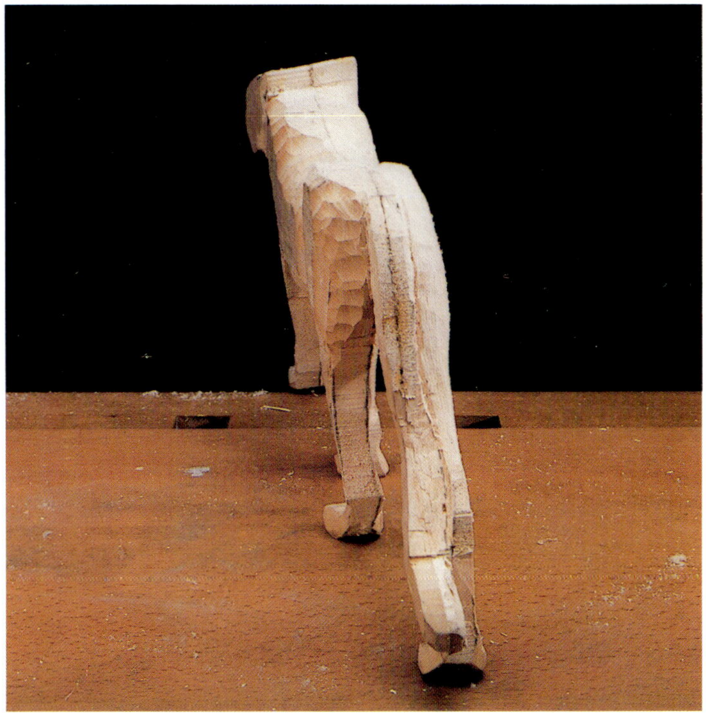

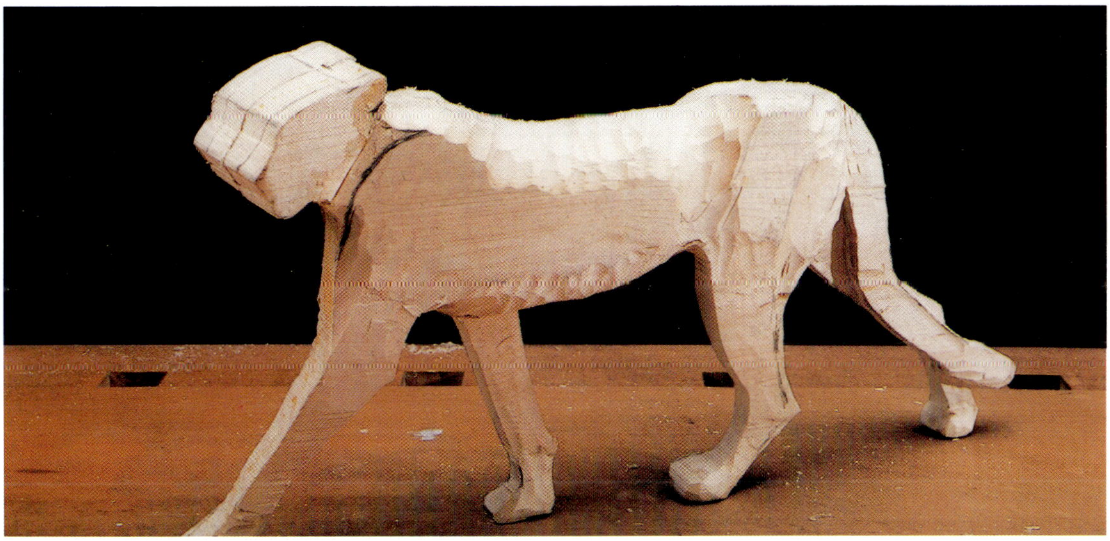

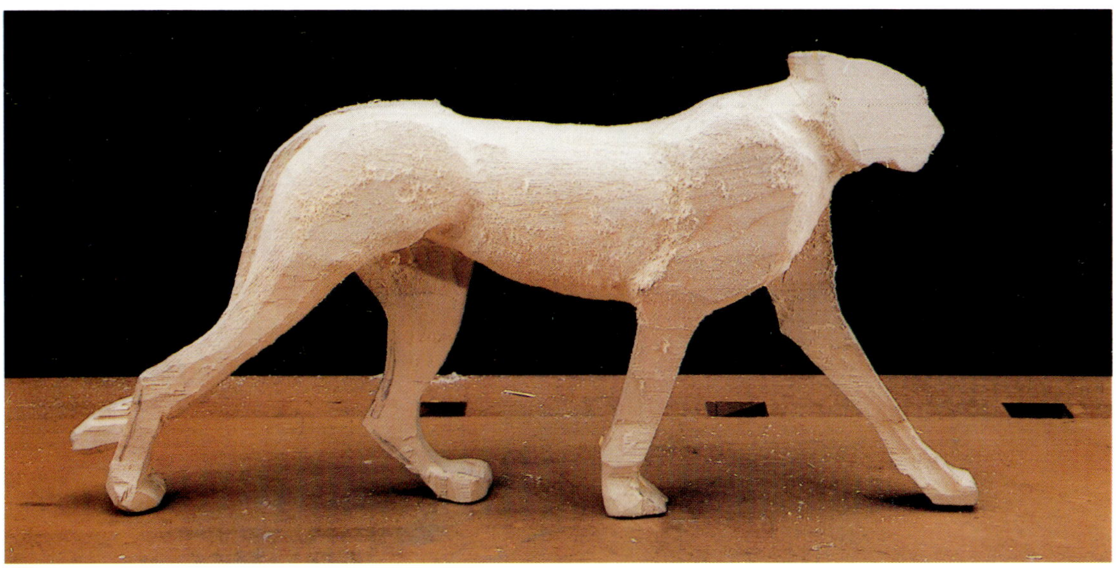

Here is how the half rounded cat looks so far.

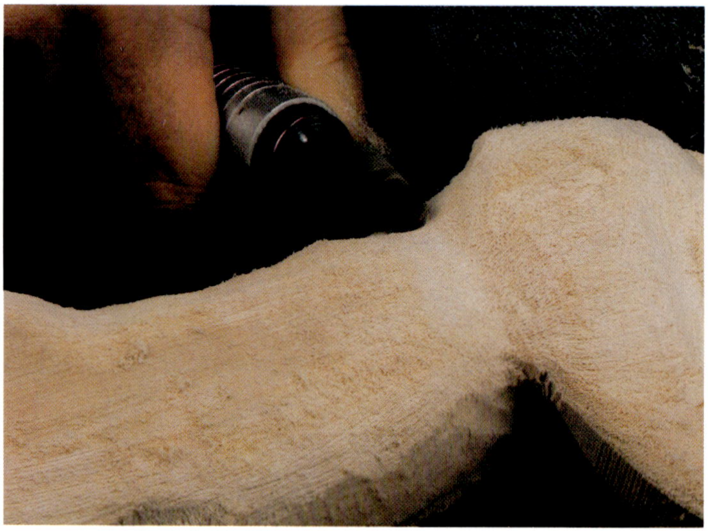

Smoothing out all the chisel marks in the hollow between the rib cage and the back.

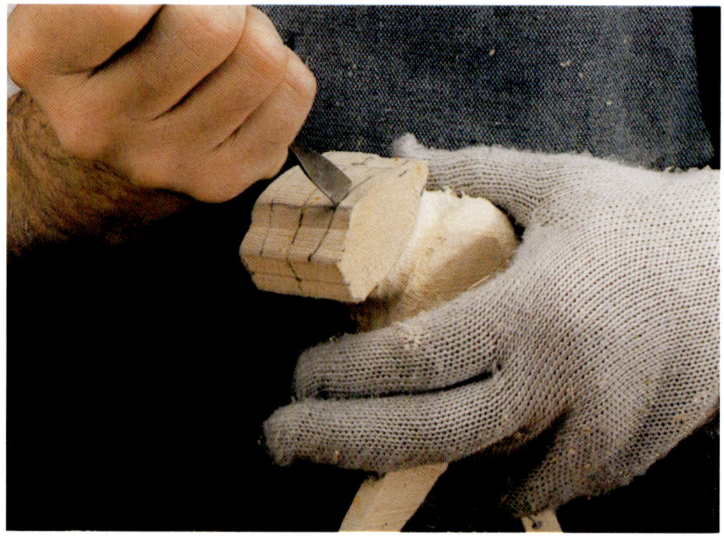

Moving to the head, scribe in the line on both sides of the head with a square-nosed gouge to avoid chipping away too much wood.

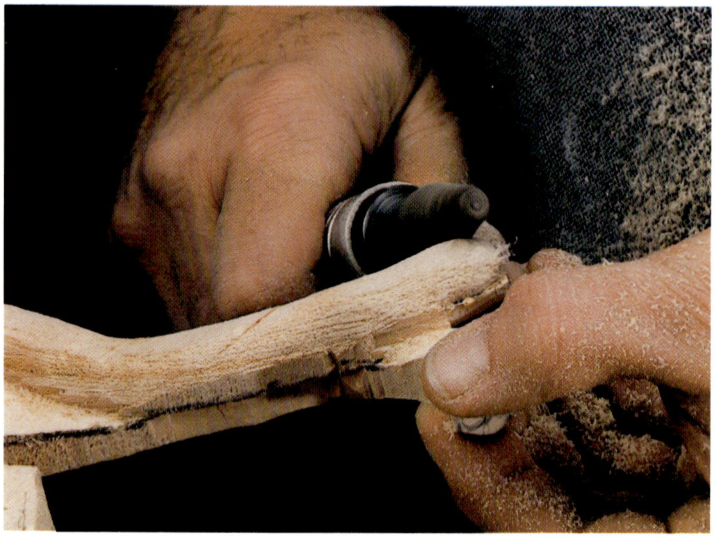

Round and smooth the tail. A word of caution, the tail never has any flat spots. Work all around the tail to avoid these.

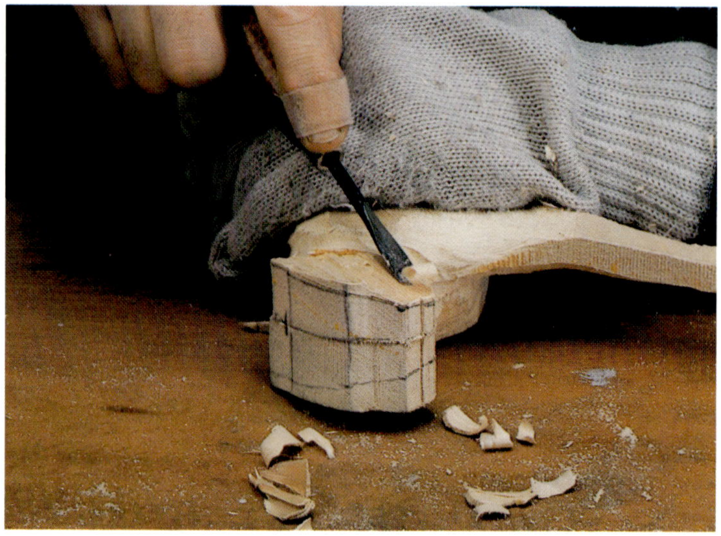

Remove the waste wood from each side of the head, making a gentle V shape out of the head.

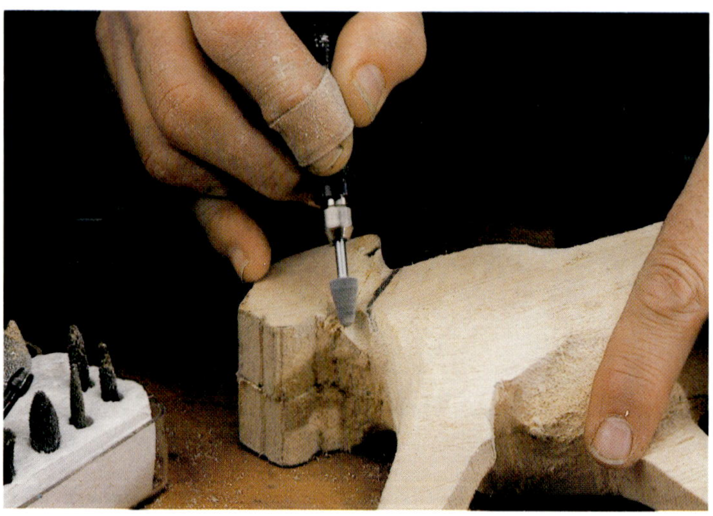

Changing tools again, switch to a Optima 2 high speed grinder with a small "Christmas tree" Kutzall bit. This will work in muscle groups and refine the legs and feet. First clean out some of the excess wood on the neck between the head and shoulder. Be careful not to make a sharp edge on the shoulder.

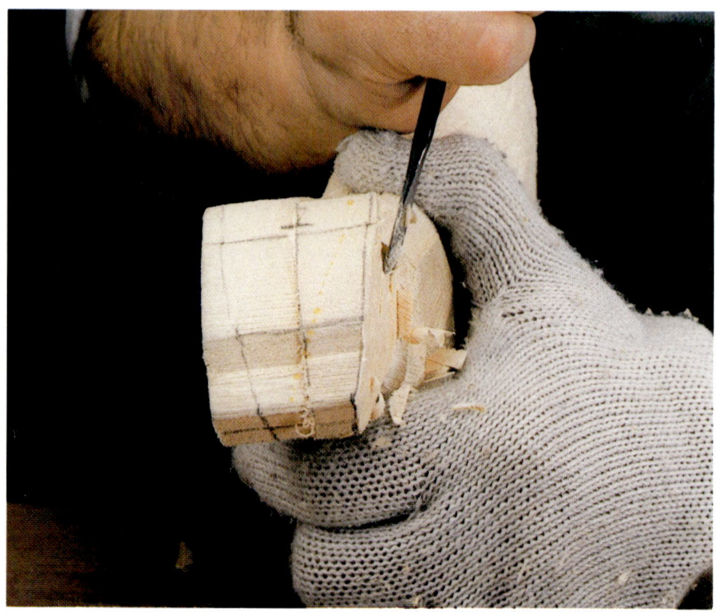

Half of the head has been shaped.

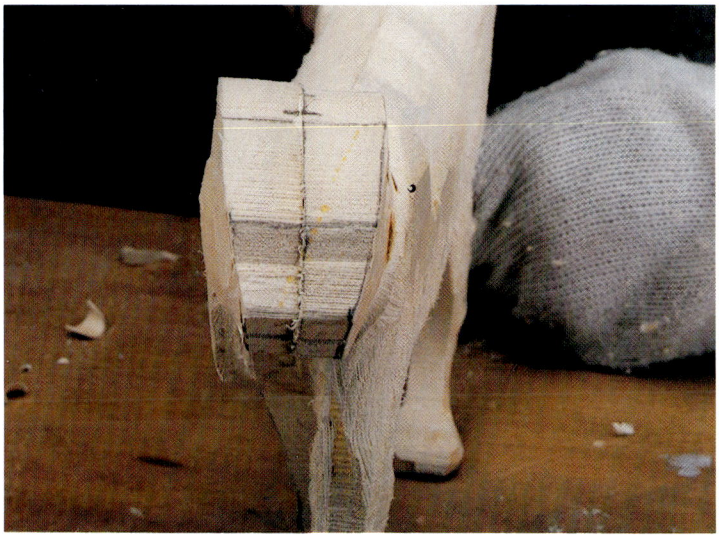

The head has been shaped. The reason we cleaned the head off now is to gain access to the neck.

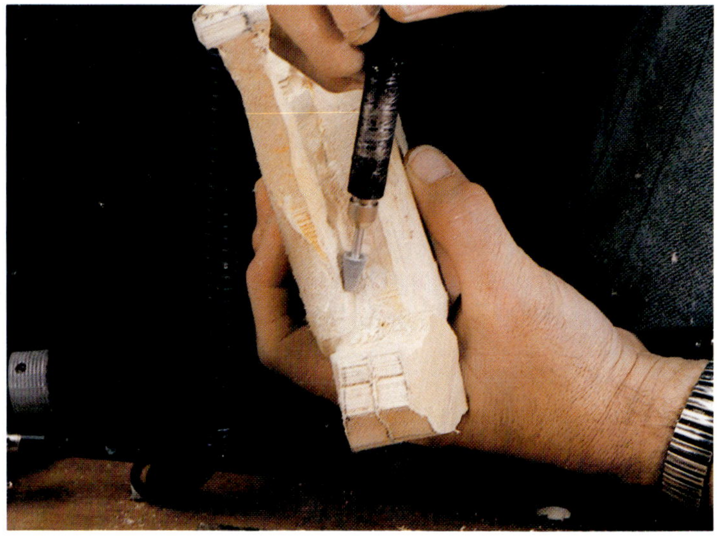

Work down the inside of the neck where the front shoulder is pushed forward in its stride.

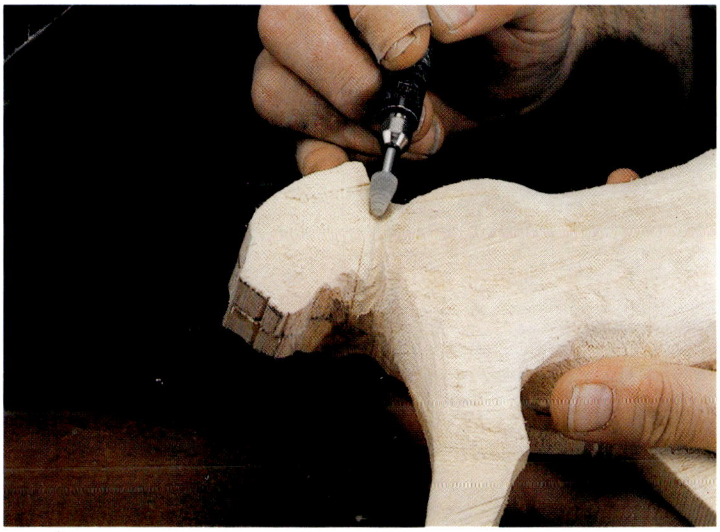

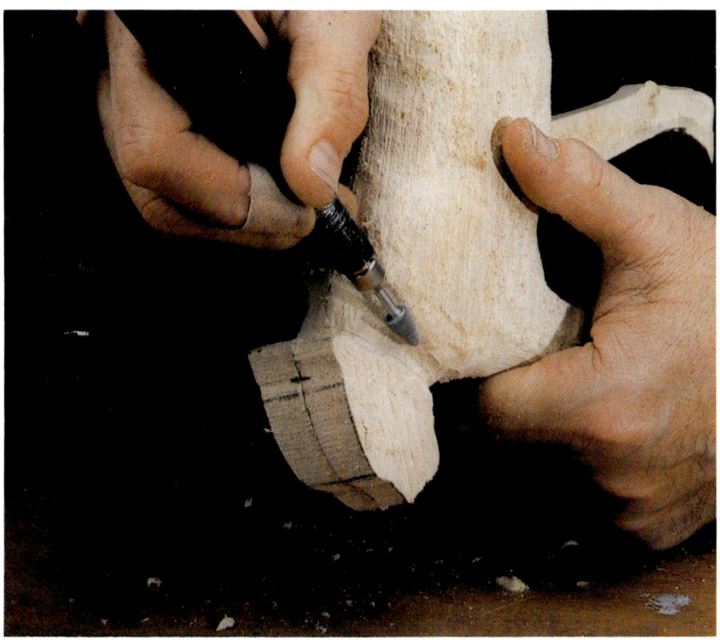

Work the neck again with the high speed grinder and "Christmas tree" shaped Kutzall, putting in the details of the muscles where the head is turned toward the shoulder.

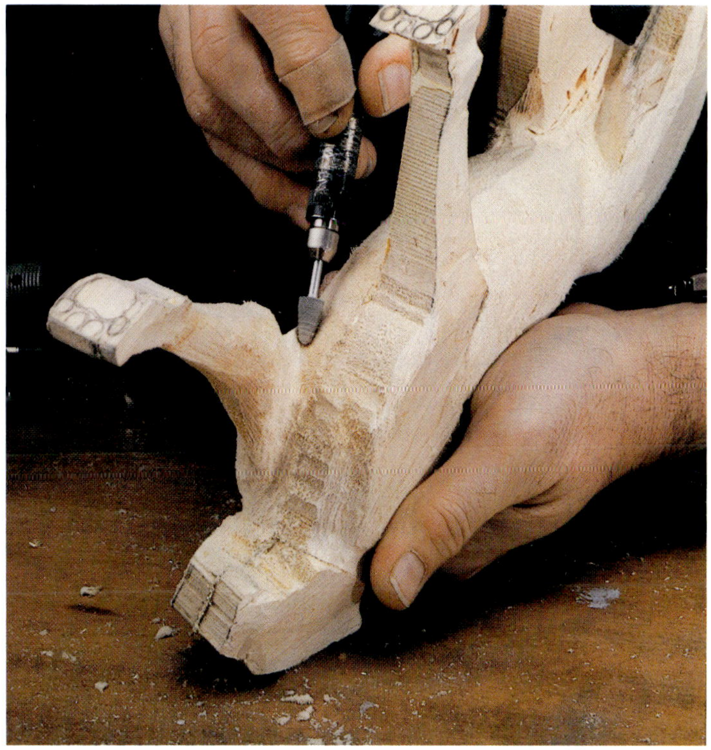

Work on around the leading front leg to form the armpit.

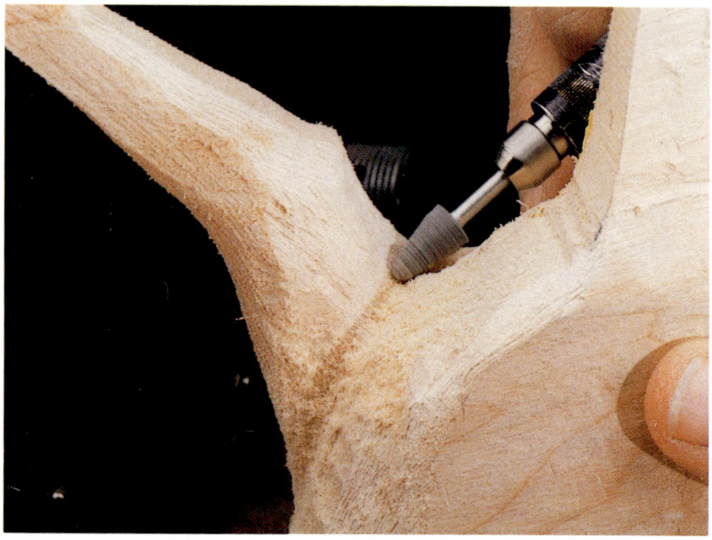

Start defining line of the tendon that attaches at the elbow.

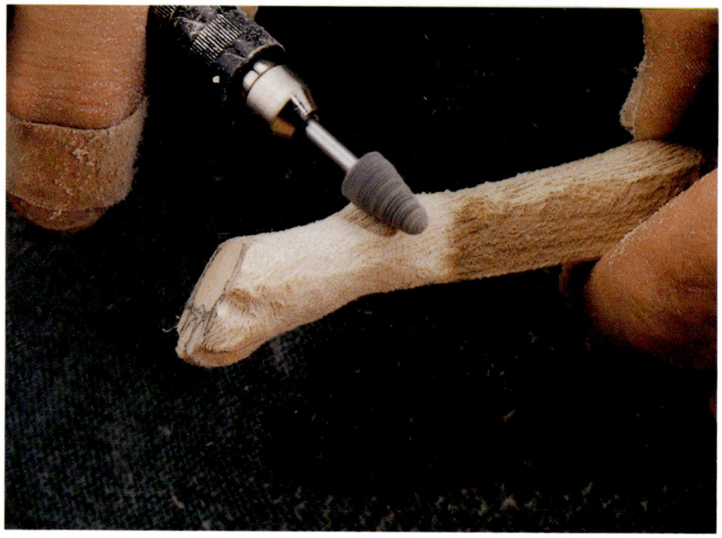

Start rounding the lead foot and shaping the back of the leg all the way to the elbow. Both front legs are rather flat on the outside and rounded on the inside.

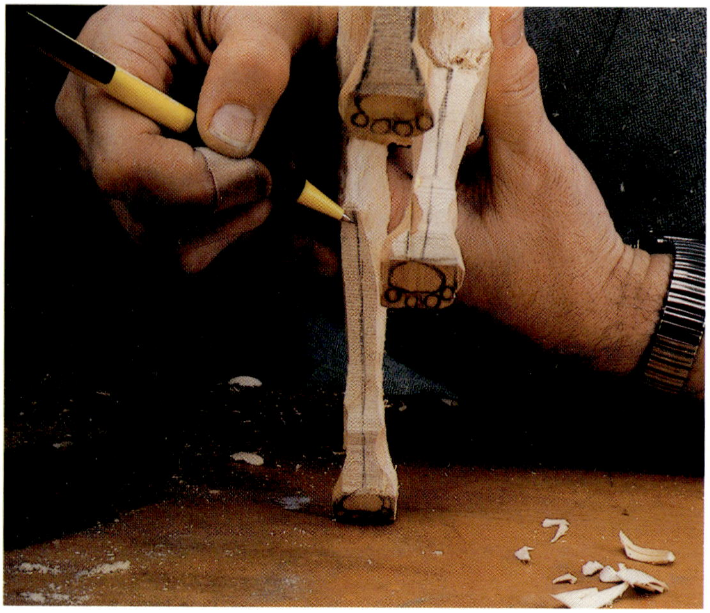

Draw a center line down the back of both front legs.

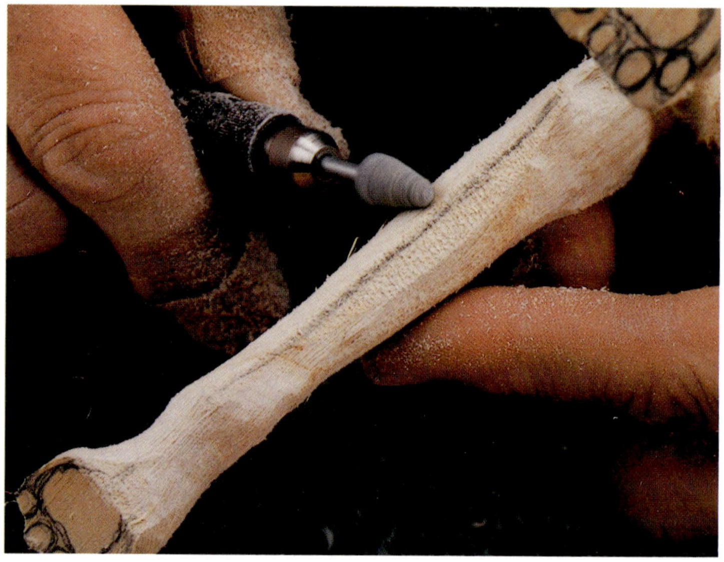

Rounding the outside of the leg back to the centerline. More wood is left along the insides of the front legs, the major muscle groups are located here.

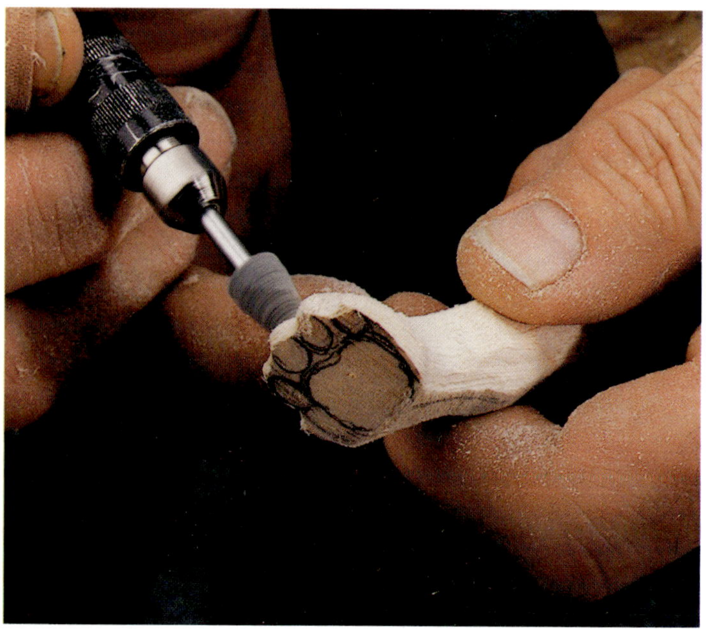

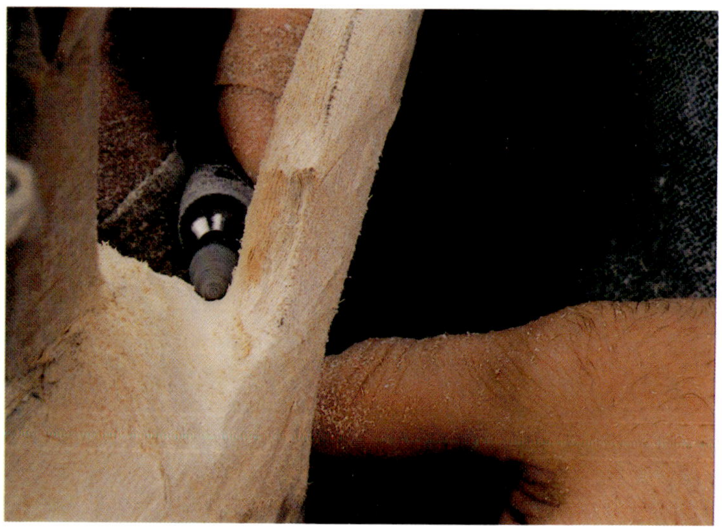

The rounded back of the leg.

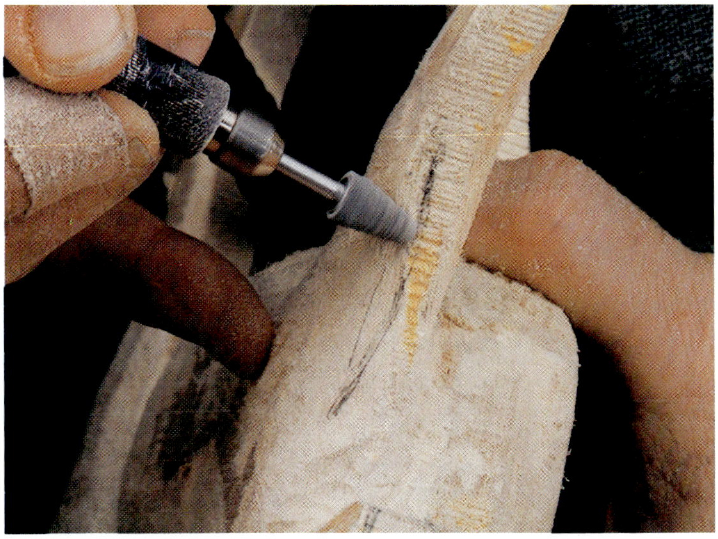

Moving to the front of the leg, accentuate the valley between two muscle groups outlined here in pencil.

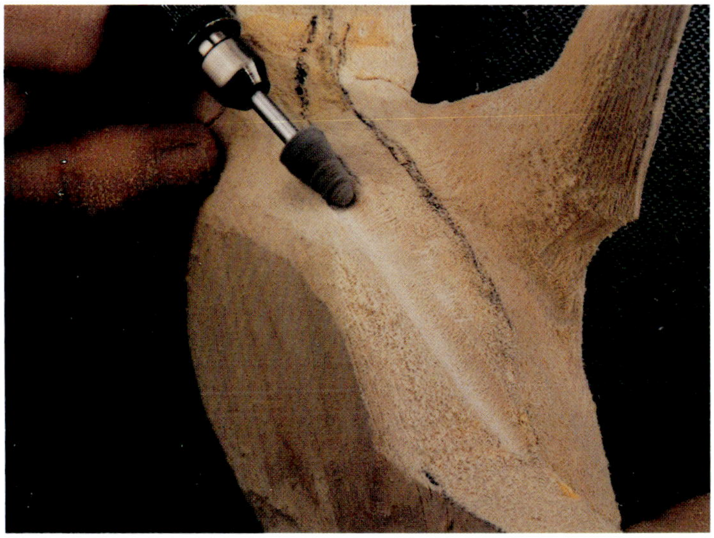

Open this area up with the Kutzall to add definition between the muscles of the shoulder and the chest.

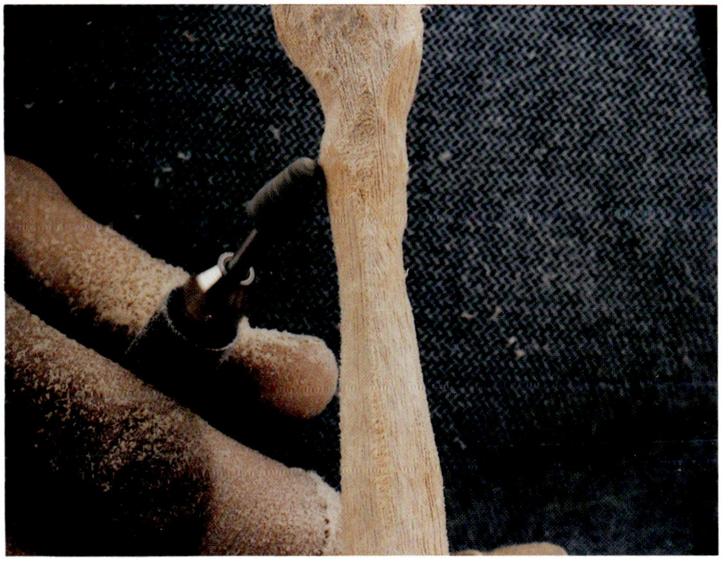

Below the knee the front of the leg becomes quite narrow and rounded, tapering down to the ankle bone.

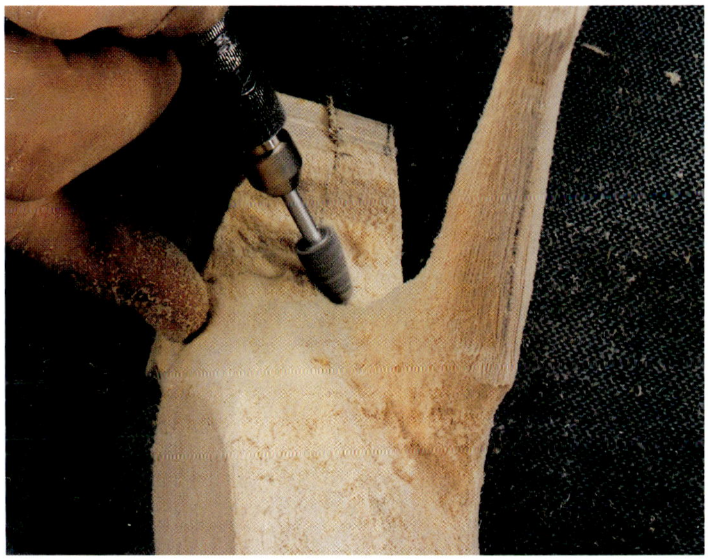

Repeat along each side of the muscle group.

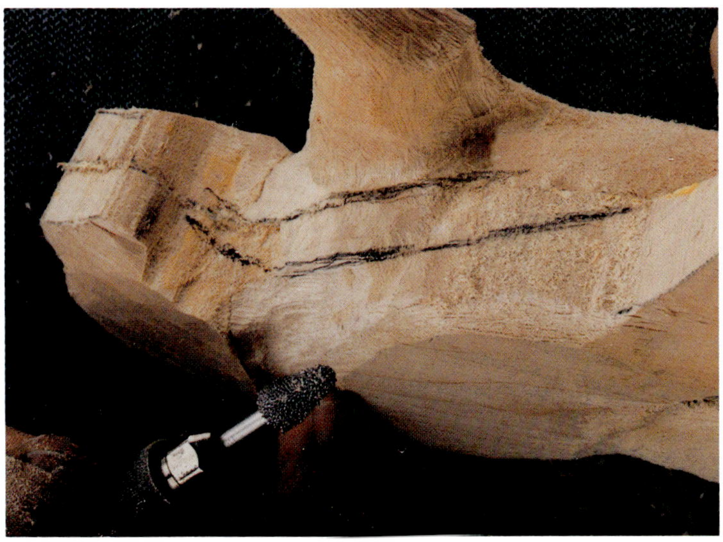

These lines indicate the muscle group running from the throat down through the neck.

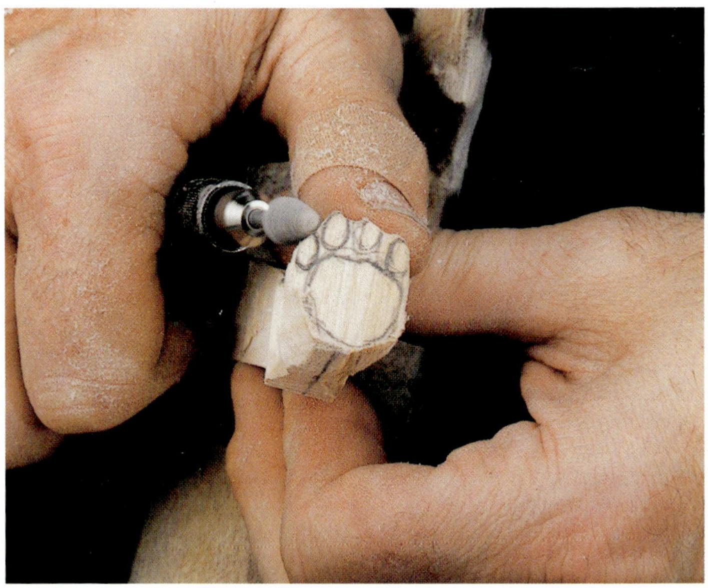

Continue on to define the trailing front foot.

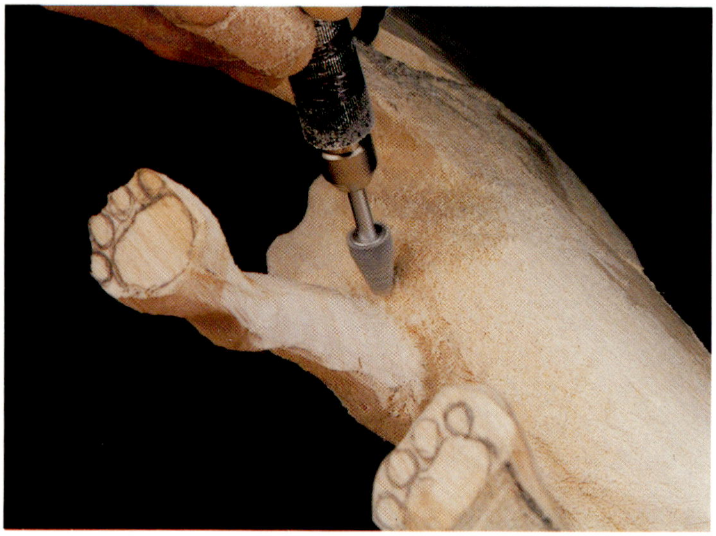

Separte the leg from the chest cavity by creating a fold with the Kutzall.

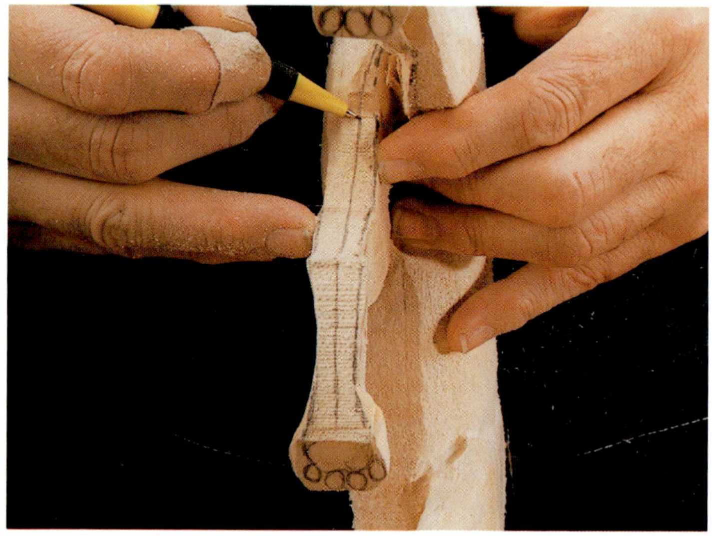

Moving on, draw in the center line on both back legs.

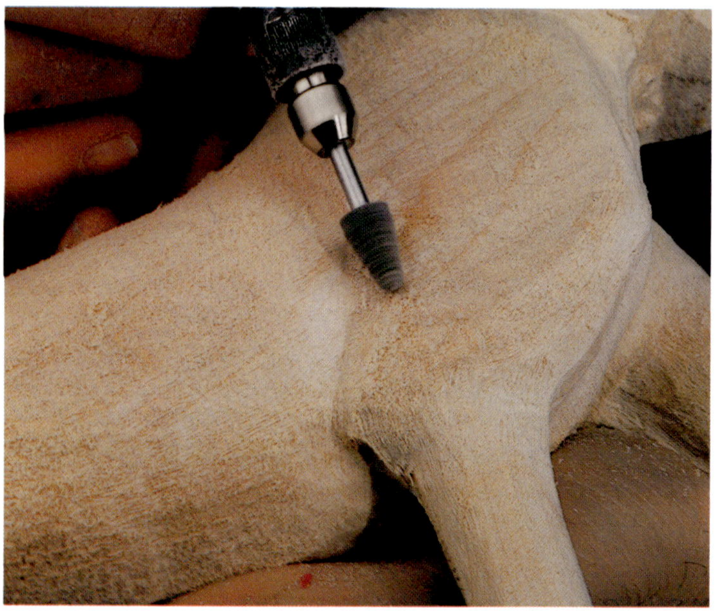

Further define the hollow between the chest and the trailing edge of the leg on the outside as well.

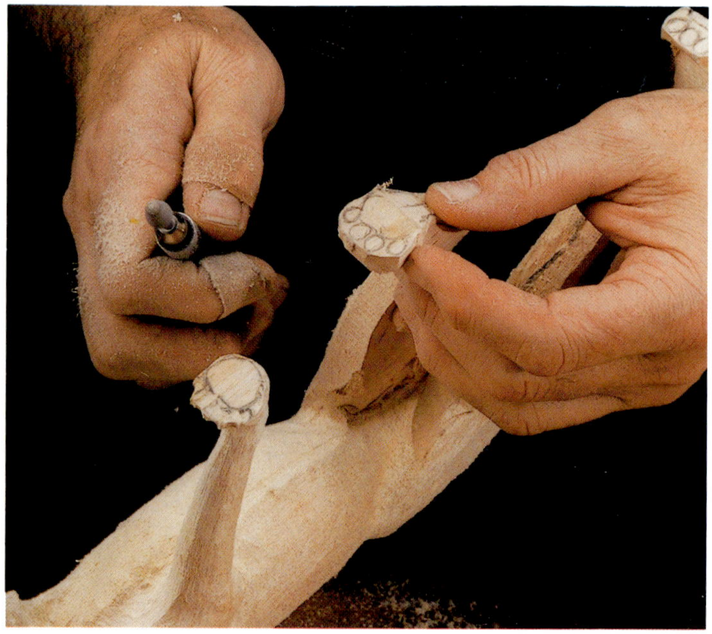

Start at the feet, rounding them first with the high speed grinder and the small "Christmas tree" shaped Kutzall.

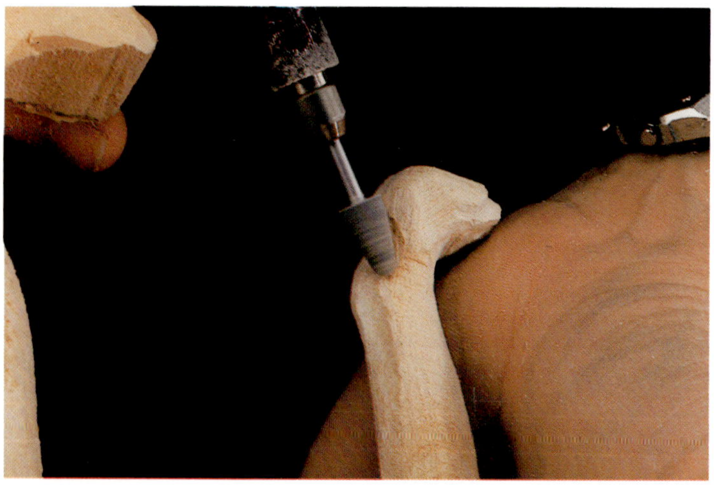

Carefully create a shallow depression indicating a tendon that connects to the ankle and is partially exposed on the inside of both front legs.

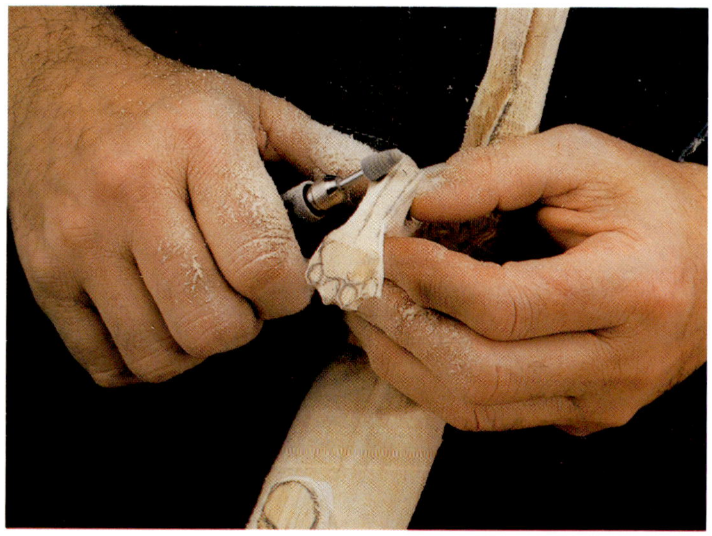

Begin rounding up the back of the leg on the outside.

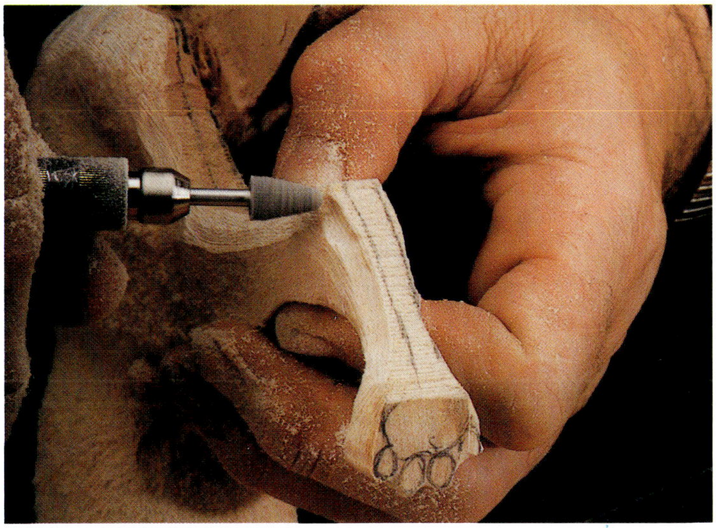

Note that a tendon runs from the heel of the foot to the ankle, forming a very narrow line.

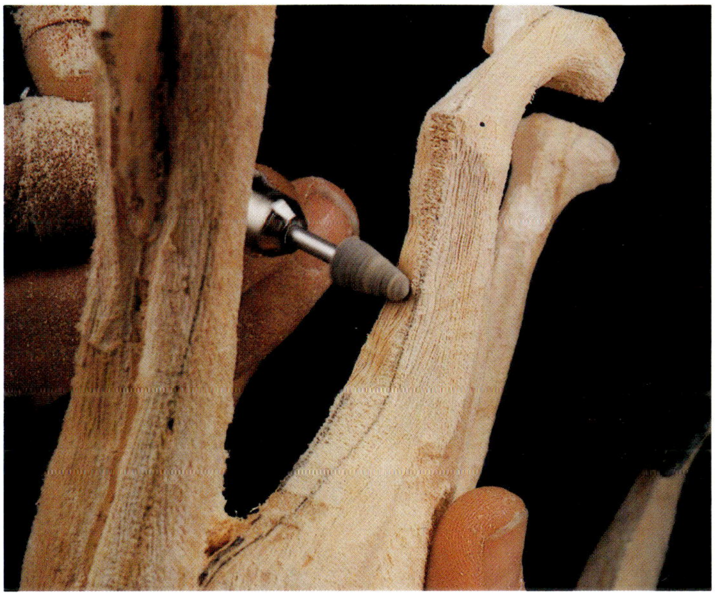

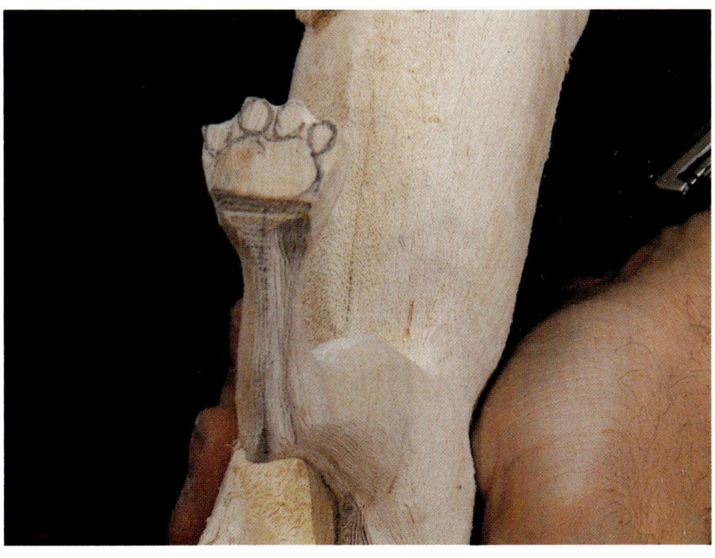

In laying in the back of the rear legs, the tendon that appears between the knee and the upper muscle group is broad and forms an almost flat shelf. Where the tendon goes on up into the large muscle and under the tail, the back of the muscle comes to a fine edge.

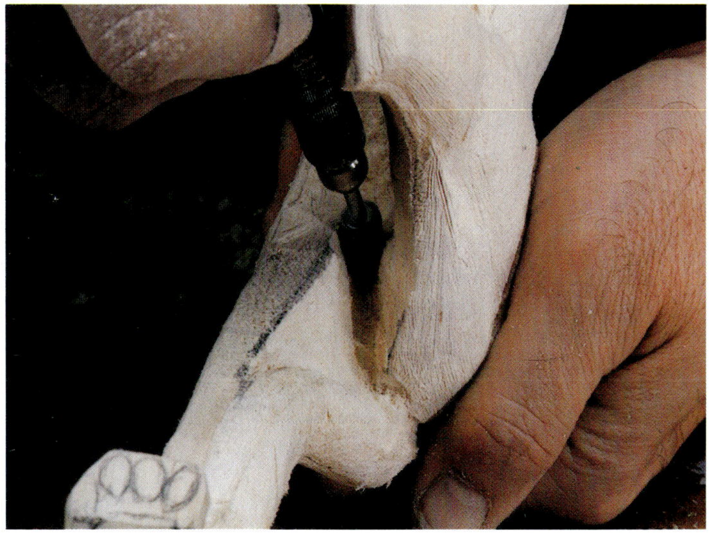

At this time you can clean out between the back legs with the high speed grinder.

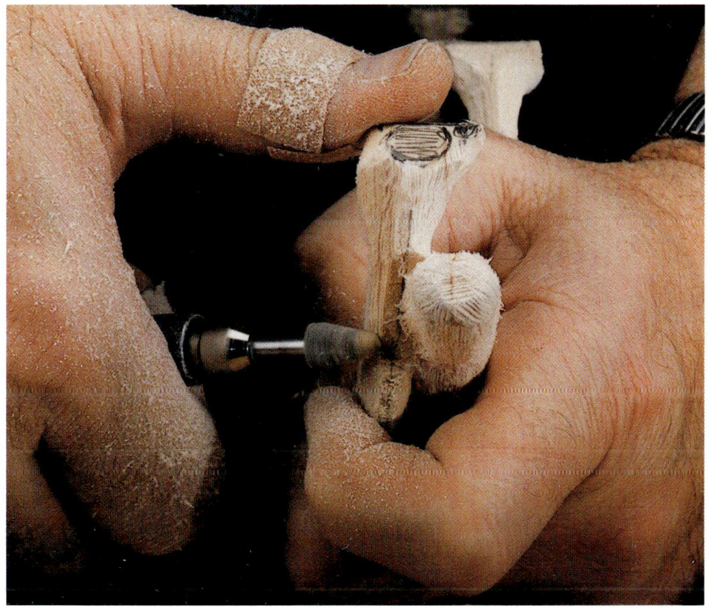

The trailing rear foot is a little different. The pad is showing. This cheetah is up on his toes on this foot; the tendon in the back will not be as prominent as on the others. It is pulled tight to lift the foot.

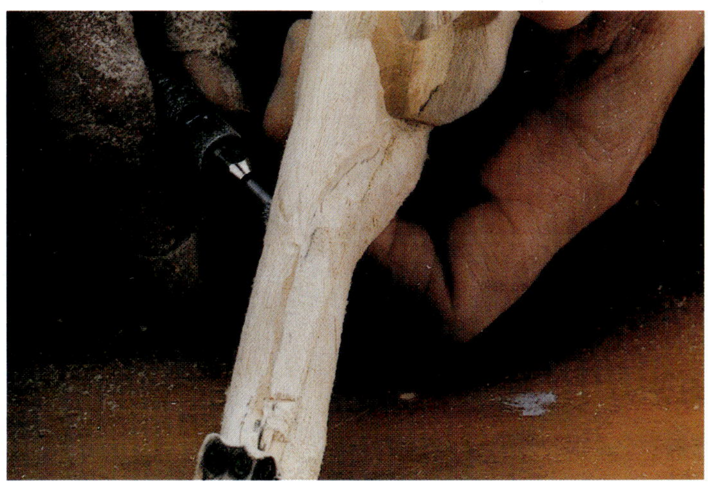

The front of the cheetah's rear legs are flat on the outside, bulging on the inside and rounded across the front where the muscle pulls.

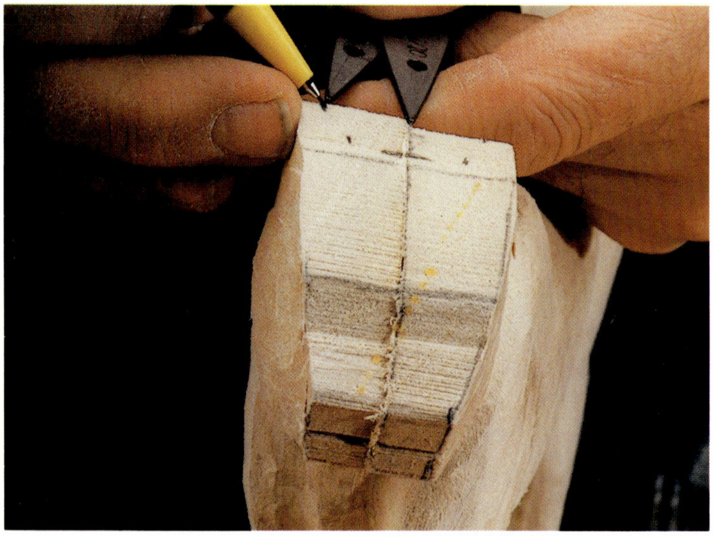

It is time to begin defining the face. Start at the back of the head and work forward. First locate the upper inside edge on both sides for the back of the ears. Measure out from the centerline.

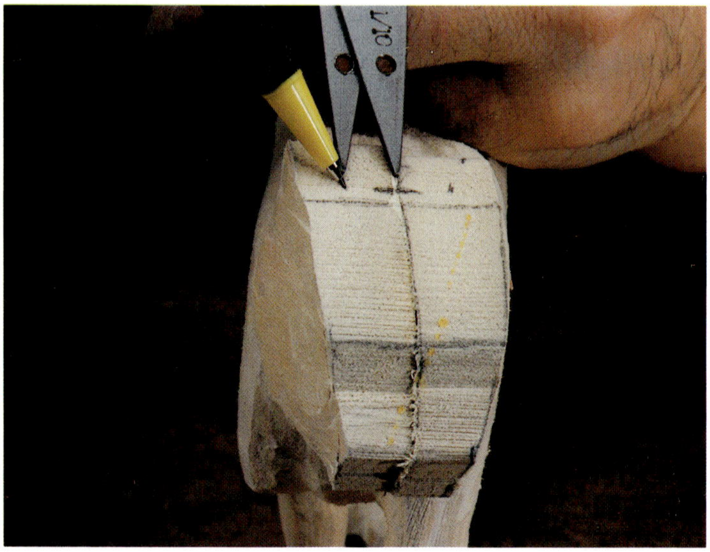

Locate the point for the base of the ears as well.

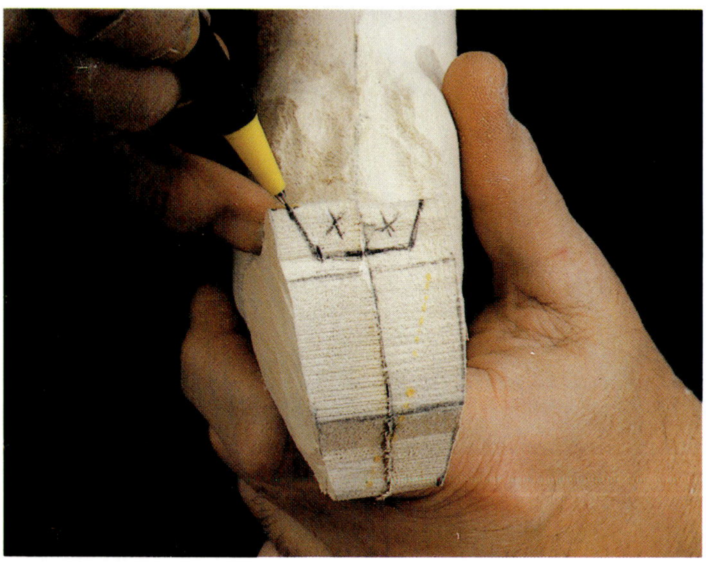

Connect the dots. The X's indicate the material that is to be removed between the ears.

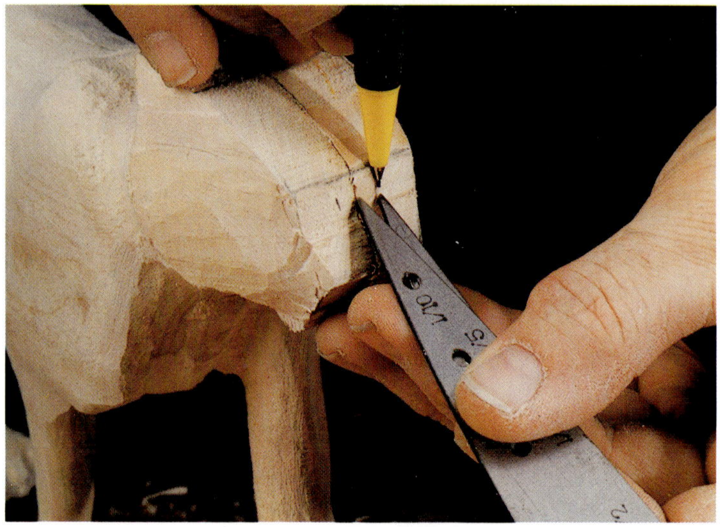

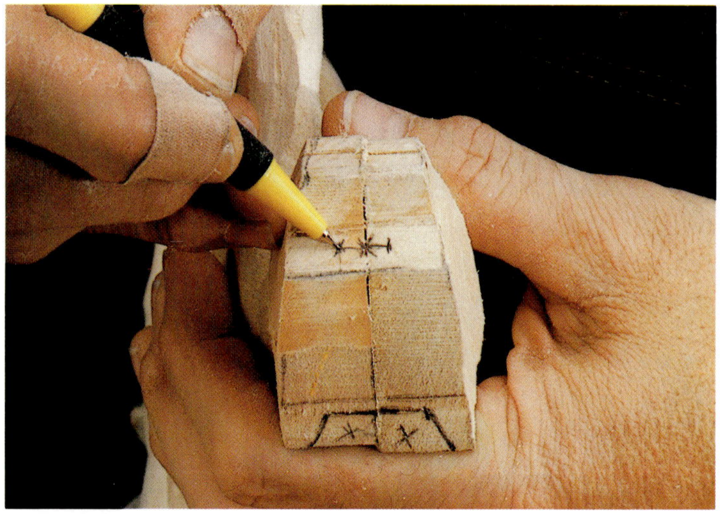

To locate the inside corners of the eyes, measure out 3/16" in either direction. The distance out from the centerline to the inside corner is equal to the distance between the inside and outside corner of the eye or 3/16".

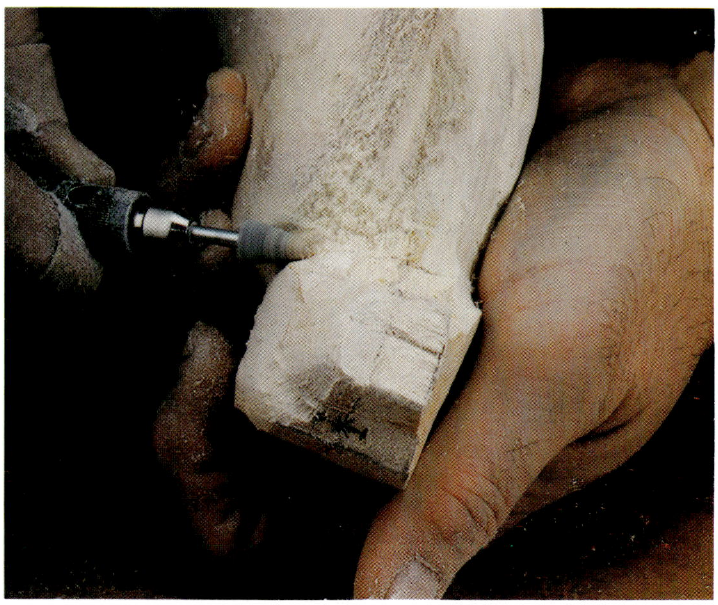

Round down the face on both sides with the high speed grinder. Make sure that when you cut in for the eye, you leave that area flat. A predators eyes face straight ahead.

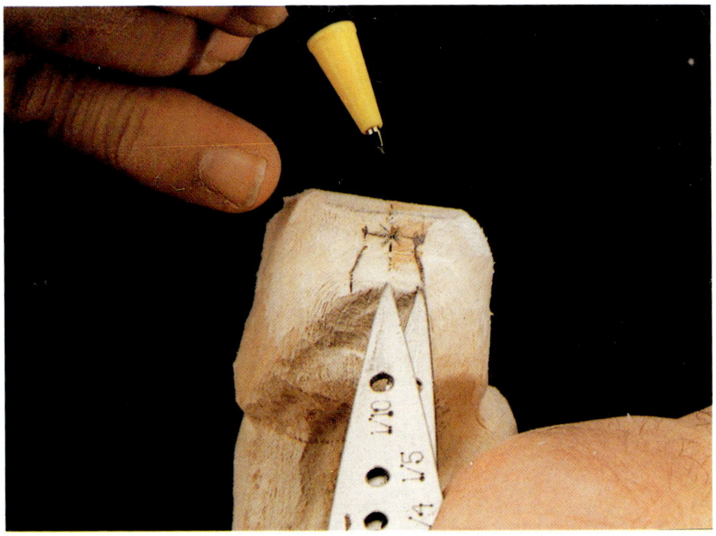

The measurement for the width of the nose is the same from the centerline out as it is to the inside corner of the eyes, 3/16".

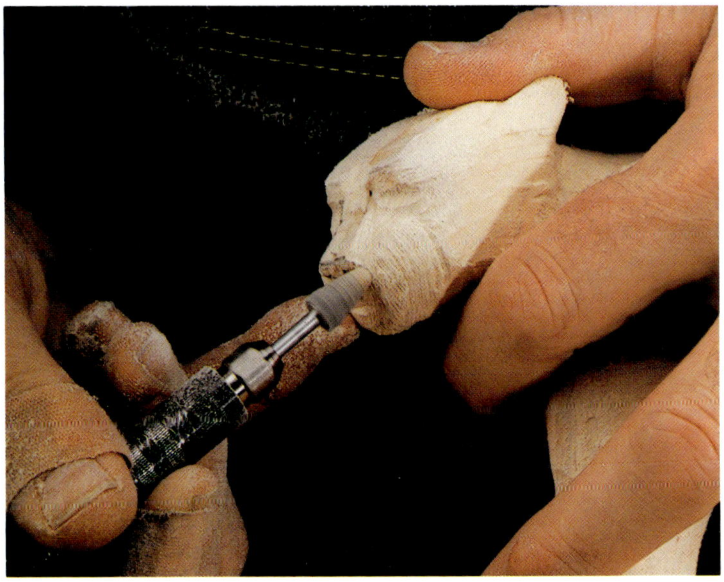

Cut down along the outsides of the lines for the nose to define the nose.

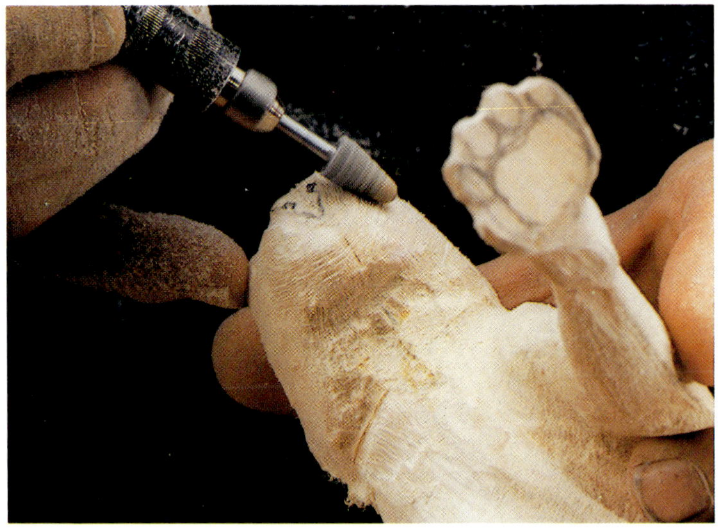

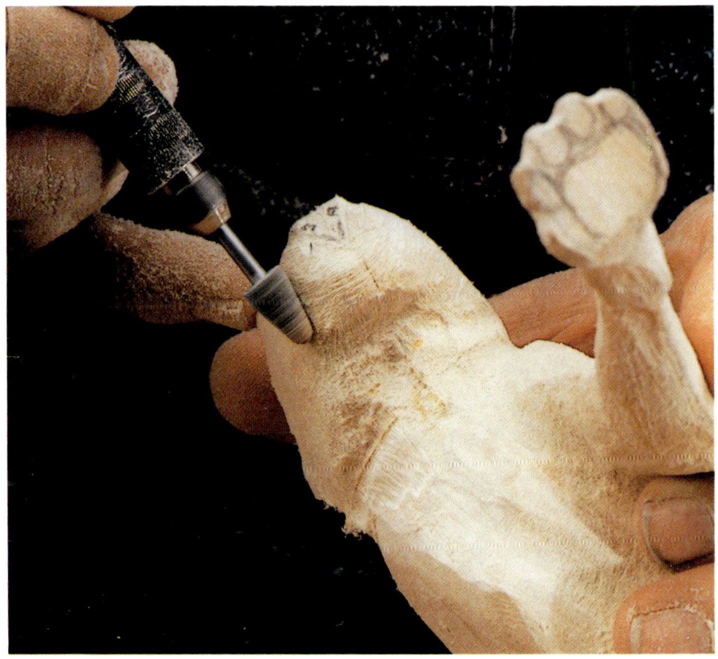

Round the front edge of the muzzle from the center line out in both directions, making sure you do not leave a flat area on the front of the face.

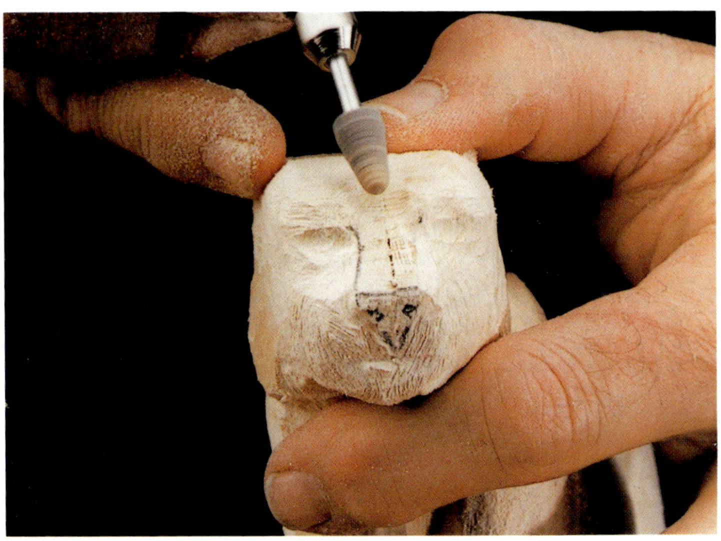

Make a slight hollow between the eyes, creating a smooth transition between the forehead and the bridge of the nose.

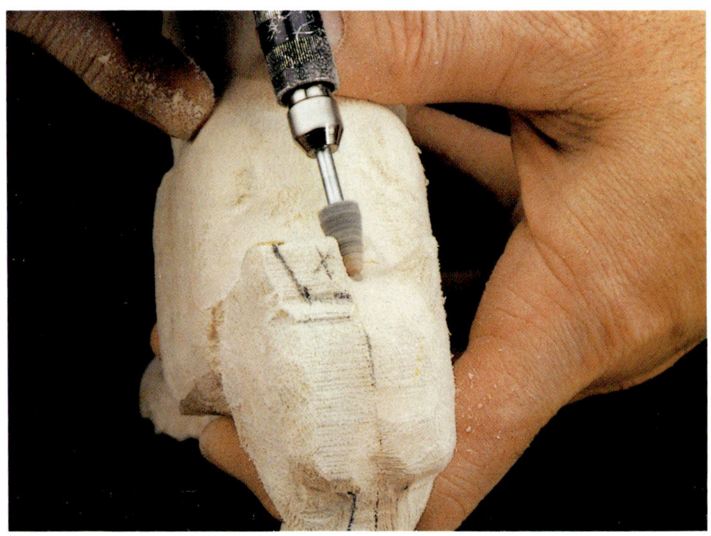

Clean out between the ears.

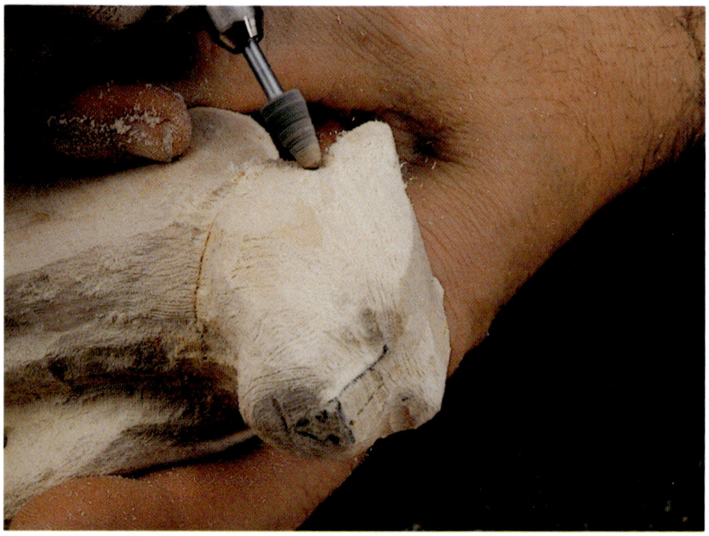

Sculpt in underneath the outside of the ears.

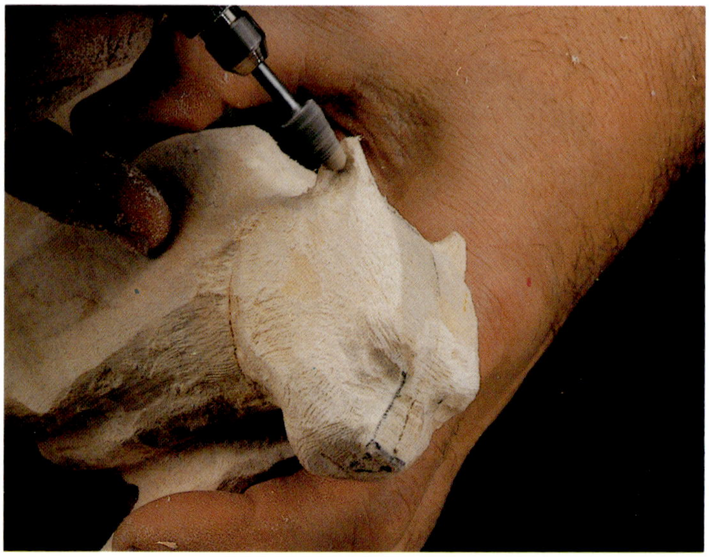

Sculpt out the insides of the ears before you finish the backs of them.

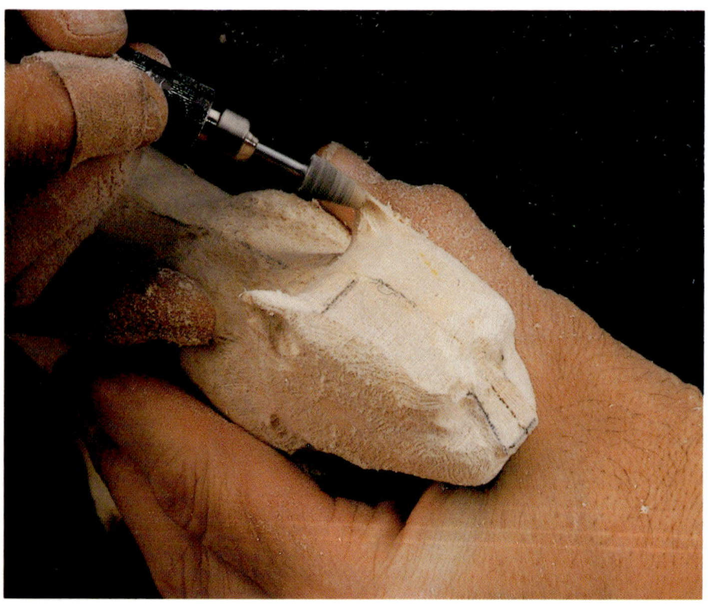

To define the outside of the ear make a little notch along the leading edge.

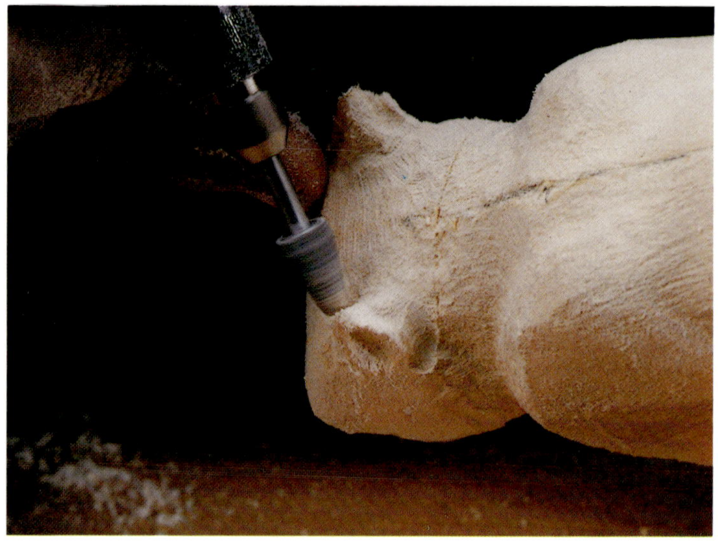

Make another notch along the trailing edge. Round the middle of the outer ear to create a sweeping cone shape.

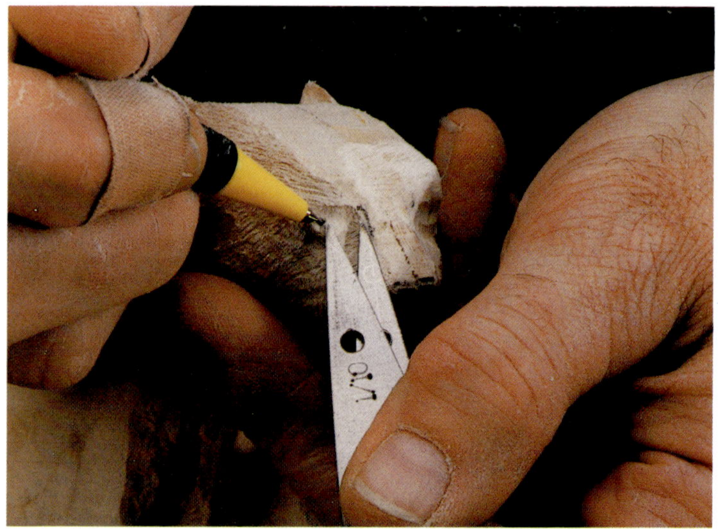

When drawing in the eye, it is the same measurement from the center line to the inside corner as it is from the inside to the outside corner of the eye itself, 3/16".

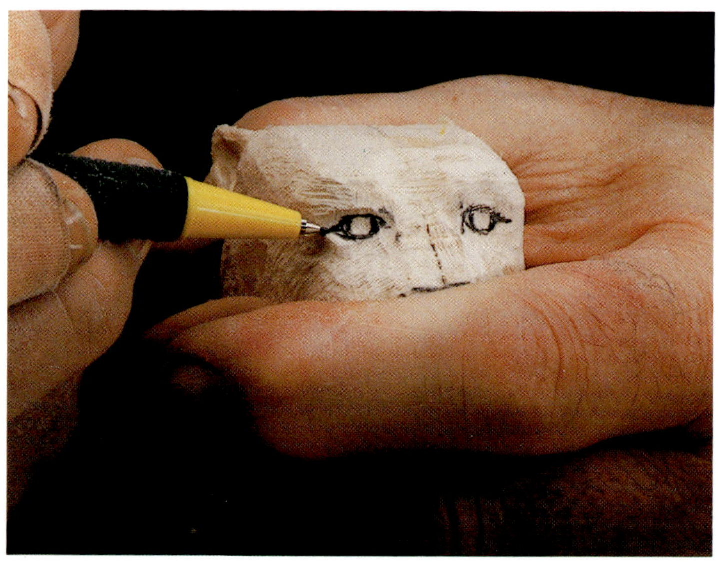

Draw in the eyes. Form a small circle that extends above and below the eyelids, that will be cut in later.

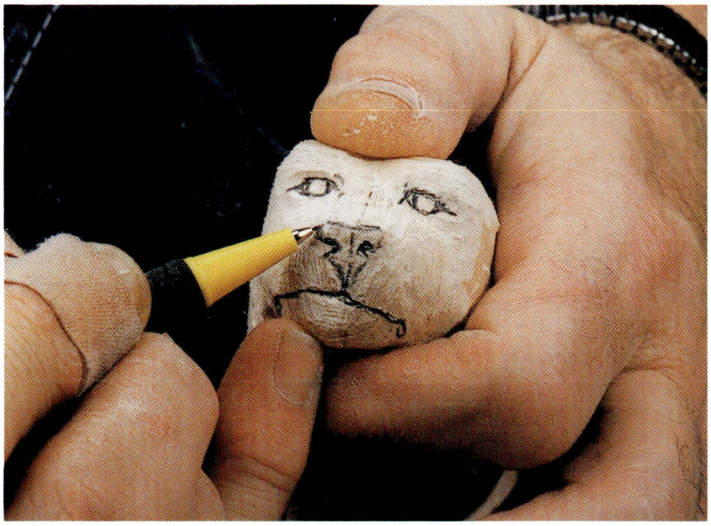

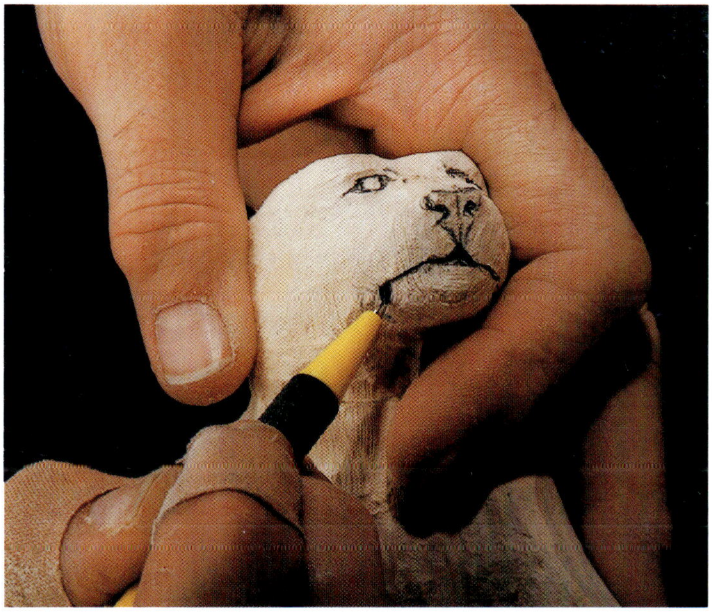

Draw in the nose and mouth.

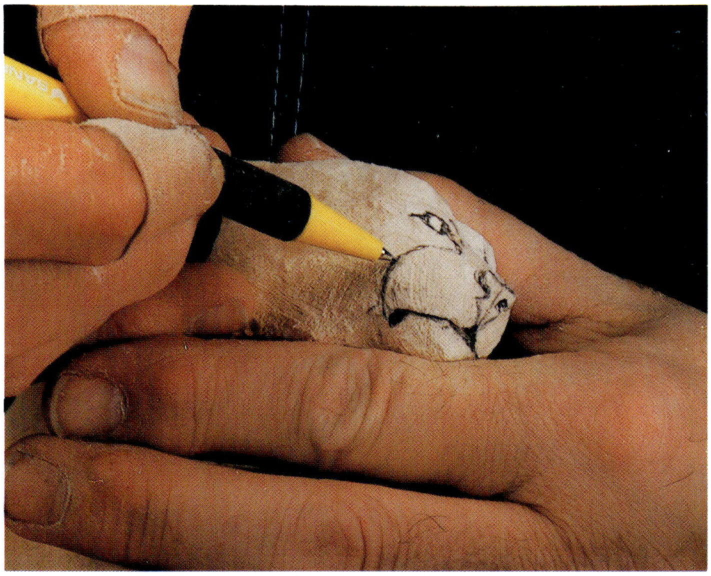

What defines a cheetah from other spotted cats are the unusual facial markings, dark lines running from the inside corners of the eyes down and looping out to the outer corners of the mouth.

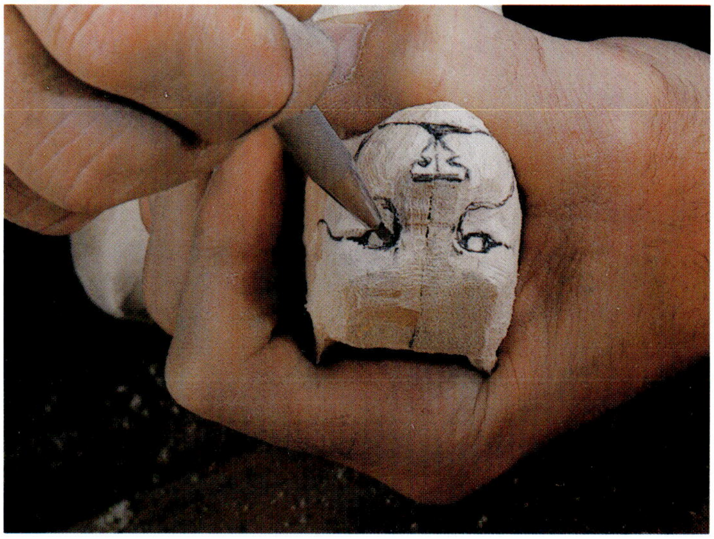

Time to carve the eye. Place the point of a small bench knife blade along the upper inside corner of the eye and press down, cutting into the eyeball.

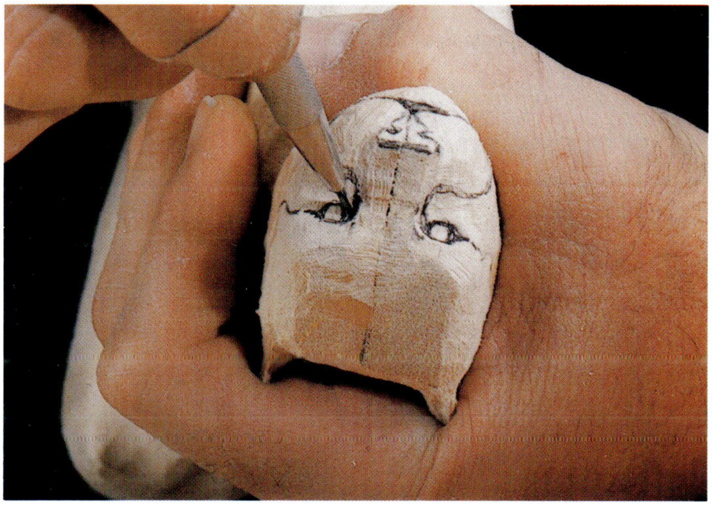

For the second cut place the point of the knife into the lower inside corner of the eye, pressing down toward the corner of the eyeball.

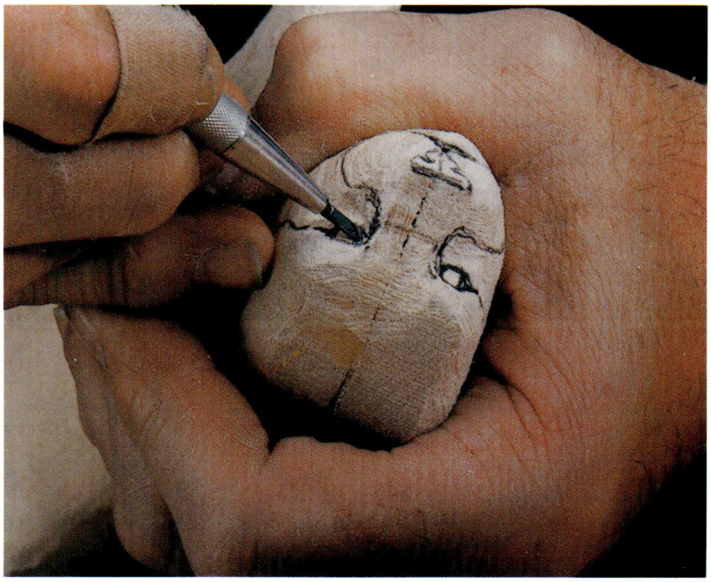

The third cut is made at a slight downward angle, pressing the blade against the pupil and pushing down toward the inside corner of the eye

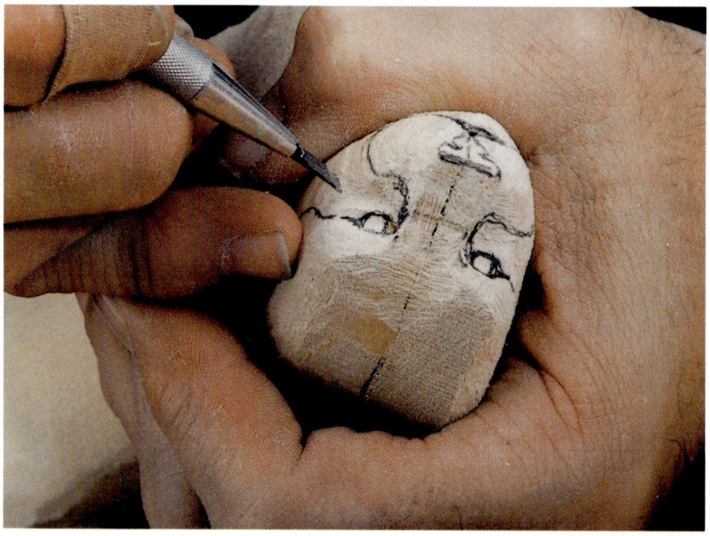

... popping out a small triangular chip. Repeat the same movement to create the outside corner of the eye.

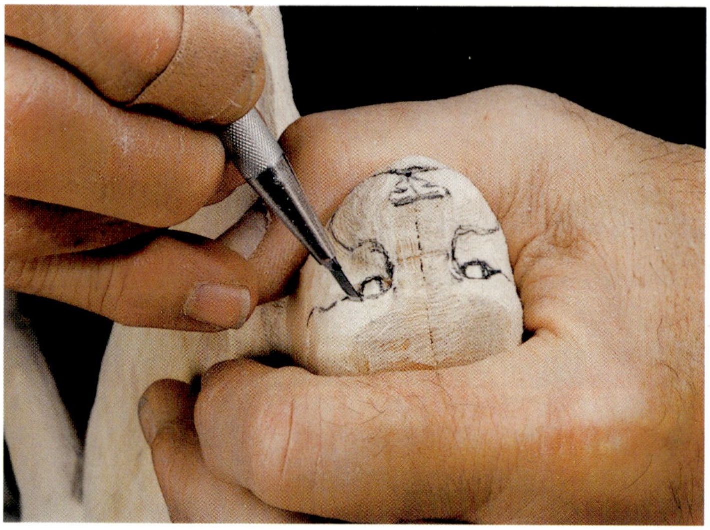

Pushing the knife in at an upward angle several times along the upper edge of the eye will create the upper eyelid.

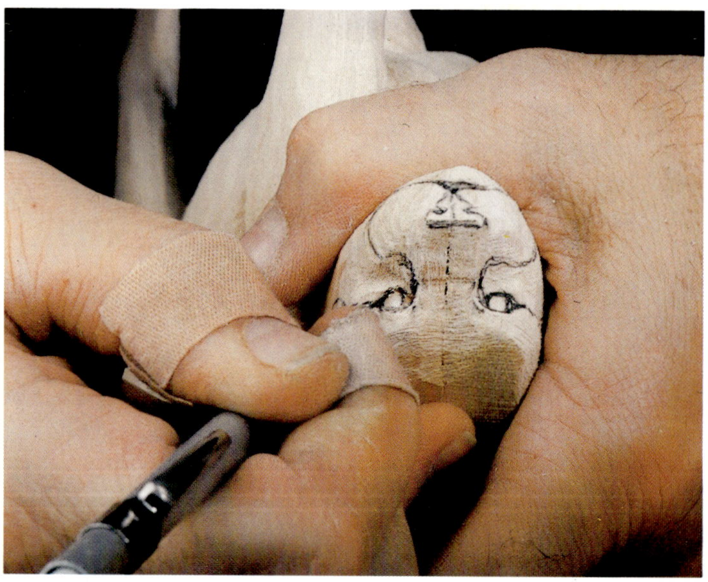

Repeat the process along the lower line to create the illusion of the lower lid. Repeat the entire process on the second eye.

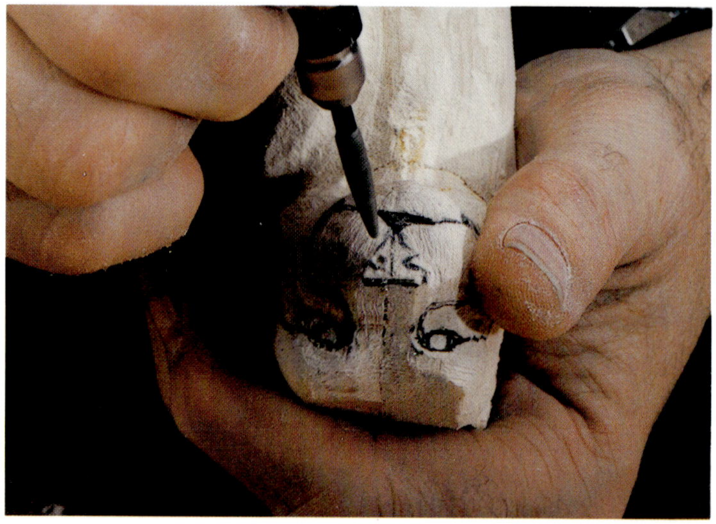

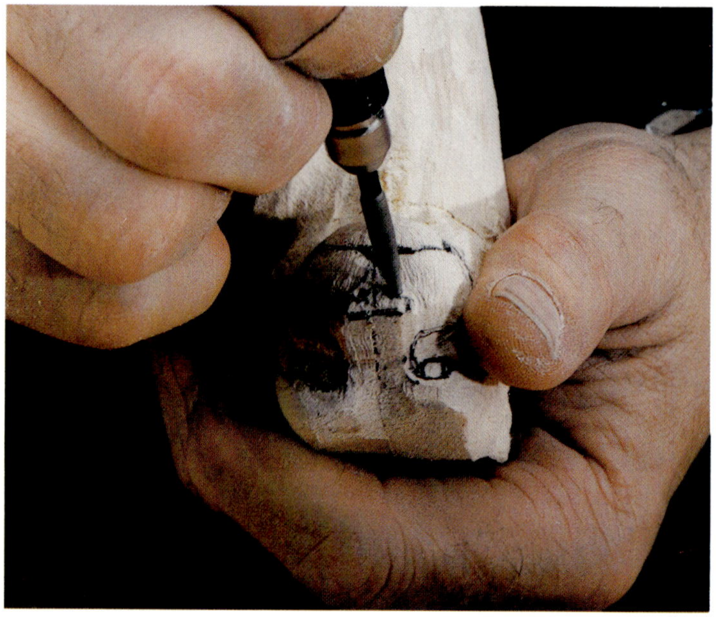

To form the nostrils, use the highspeed grinder and a small cone Kutzall. Cut in the nostrils, using a slight upward slant while creating the hole.

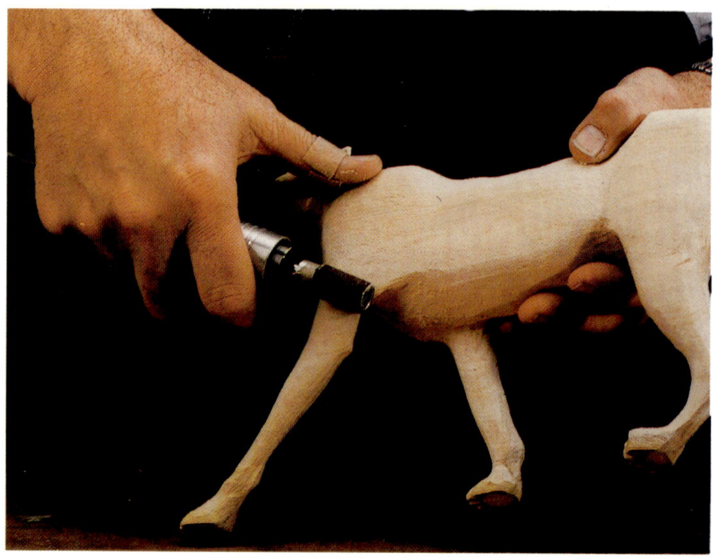

Sand the cheetah with the small 1" Soft Sand, using 150 grit sandpaper.

Here is how the carved cheetah should look. Ready to give him some spots?

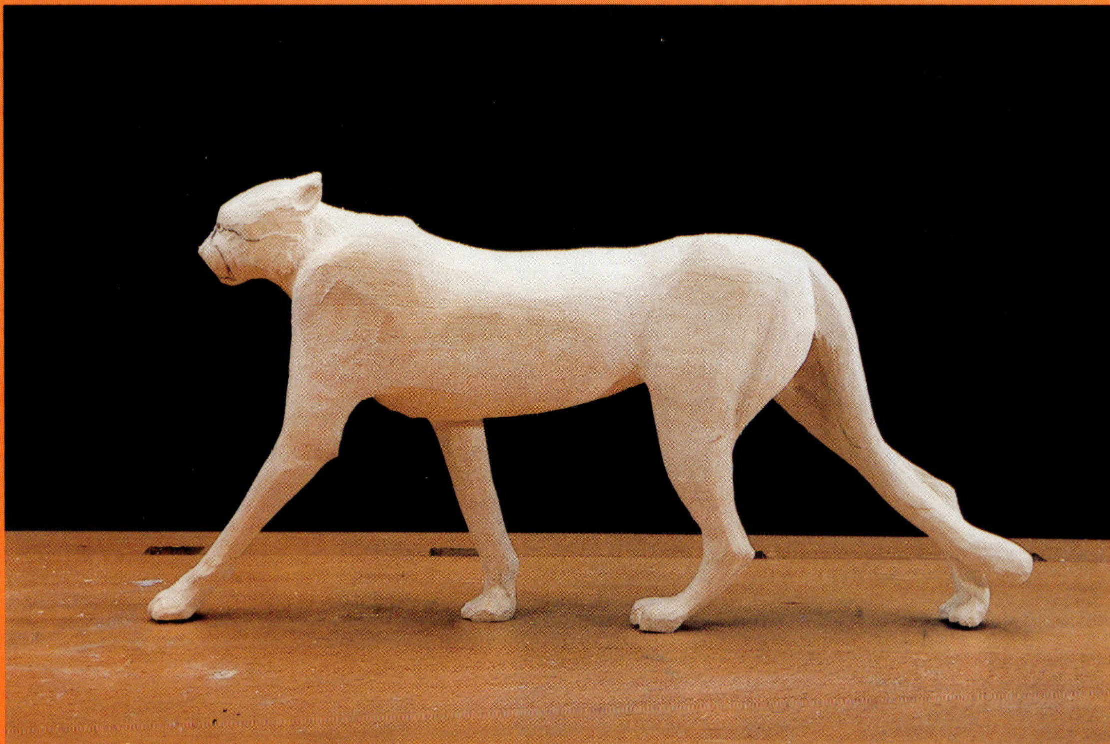

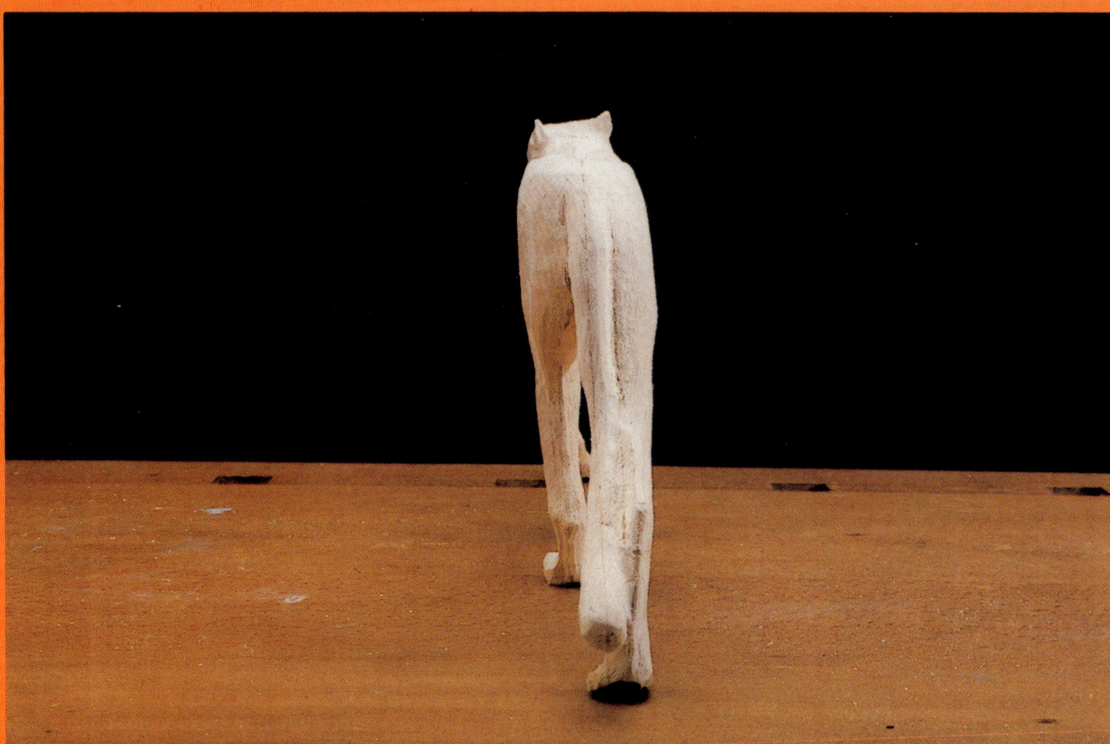

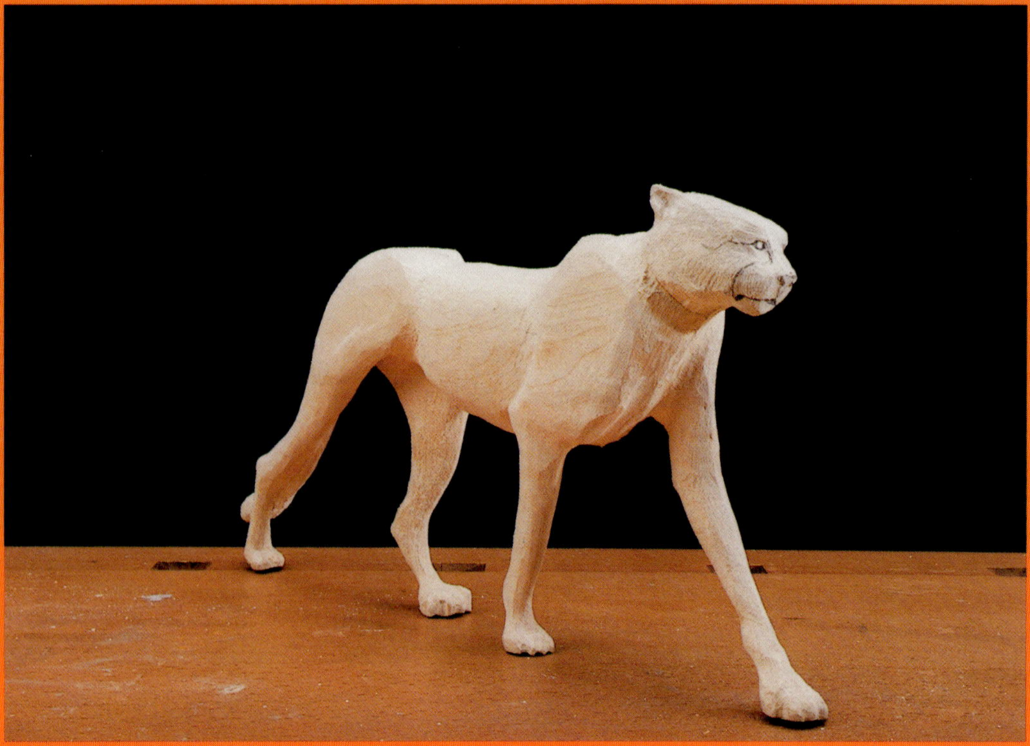

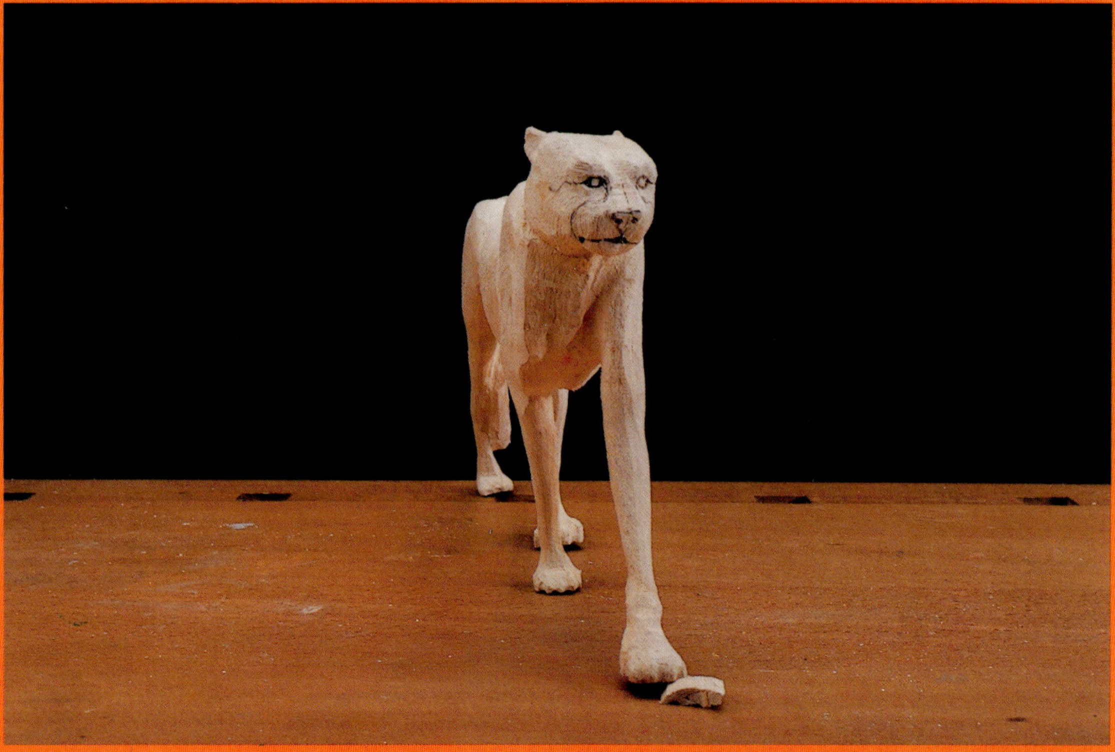

Burning the Cheetah

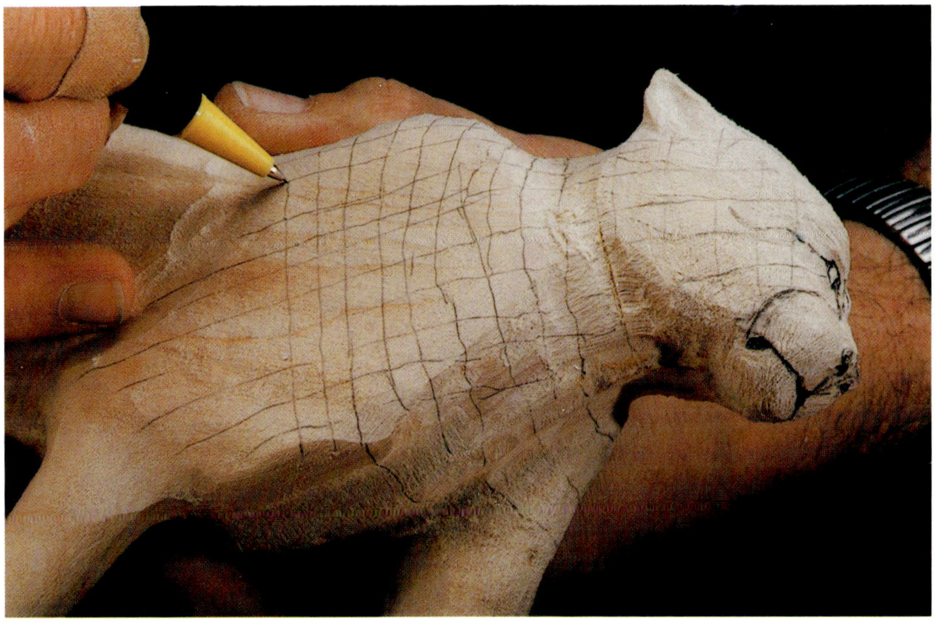

Let's burn in the spots on the cheetah. First draw a checkerboard pattern all around the head and body of the cheetah, the lines spaced about 1/8" apart.

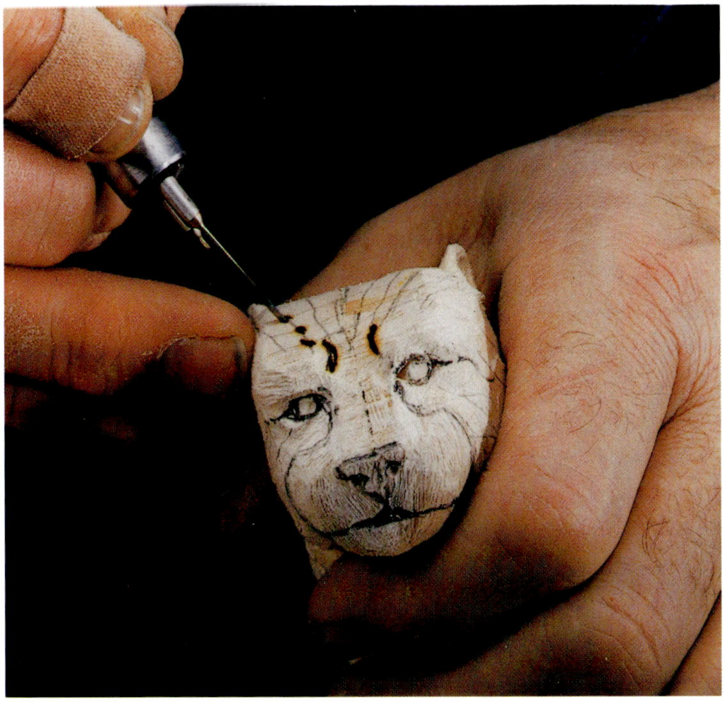

Starting at the forehead, first burn in these two lines of the brow and then start making spots, working out in a radiating pattern along the intersecting points of the checkerboard.

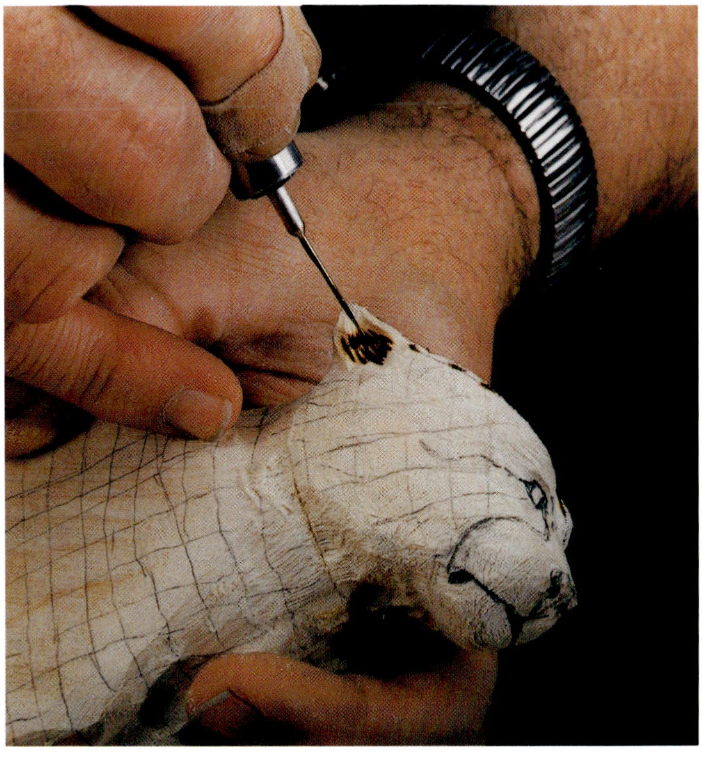

Burn hair into the ears as long as you're here.

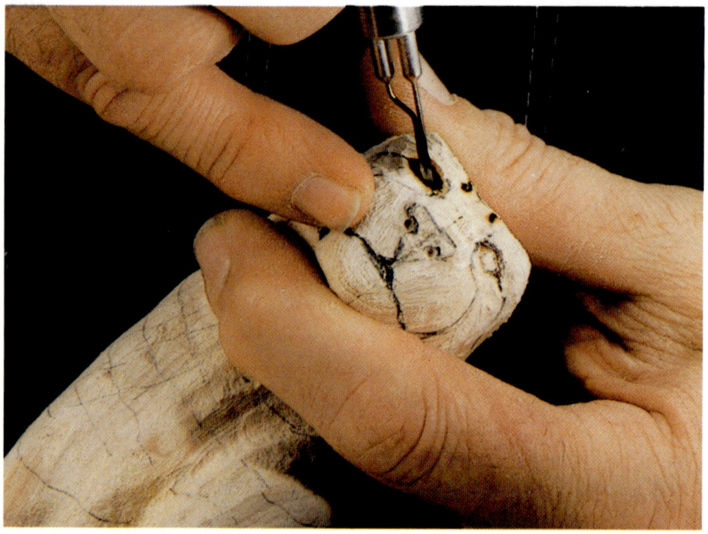

Leaving all those spots behind for a moment, place the wood burner in the same positions you used to make the cuts for the eyes and burn in the pattern of the eyes.

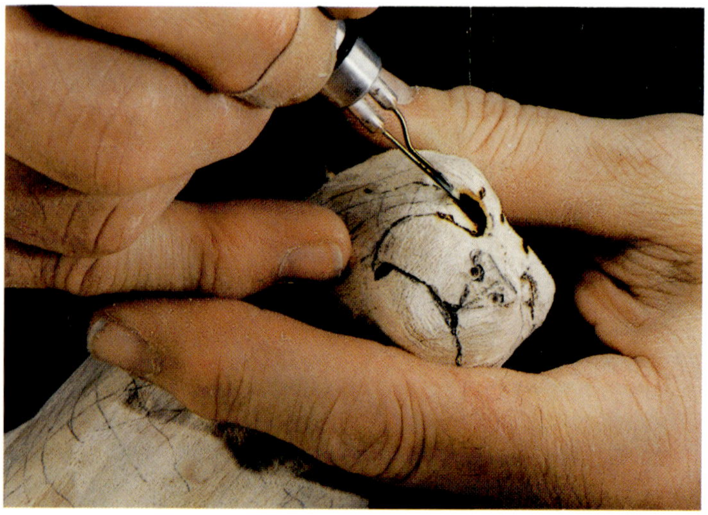

Then darken the pupil.

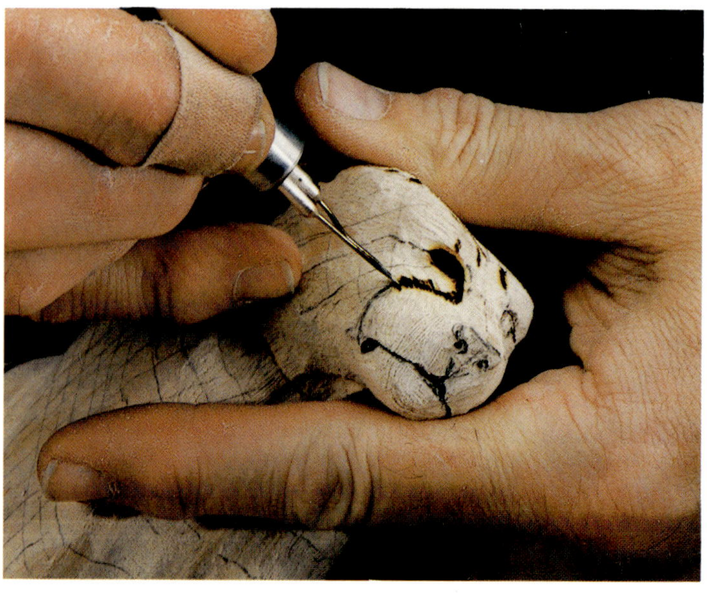

Burn in the unusual markings all cheetahs have on their muzzles in close, short strokes. Make them appear to be almost black. They end at the corners of the mouth.

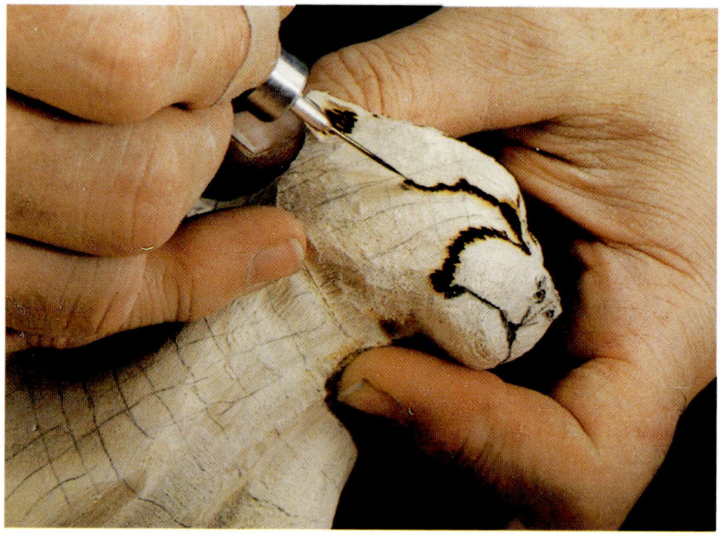

On some cheetahs there are lines known as tear lines extending from the rear corners of the eyes.

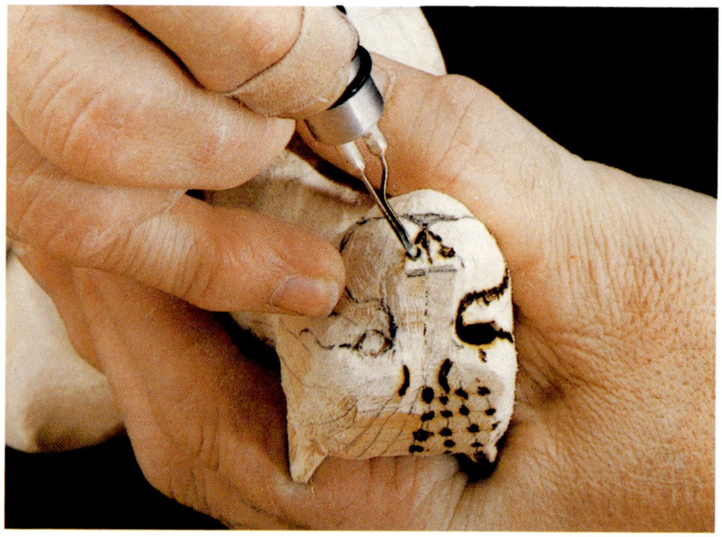

Burn the nostrils and the small lines that run from the sides of the nostrils around the edges.

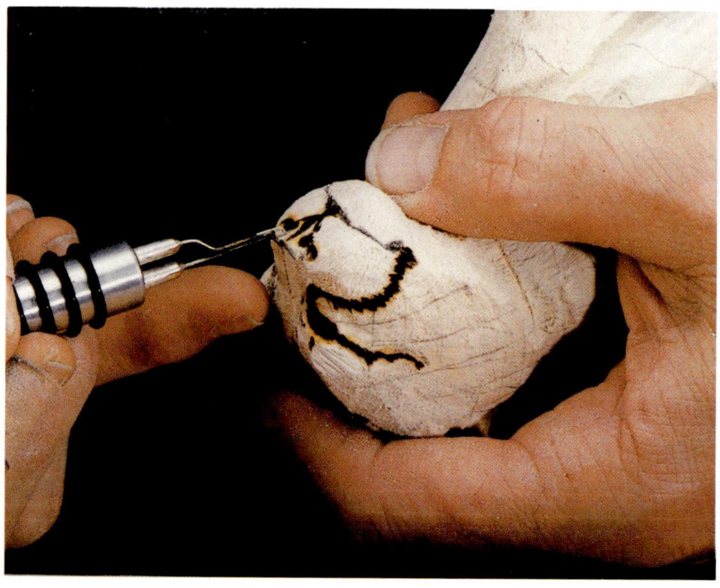

Cheetahs, like other cats, have a line directly down the middle of their noses that connect with their mouths.

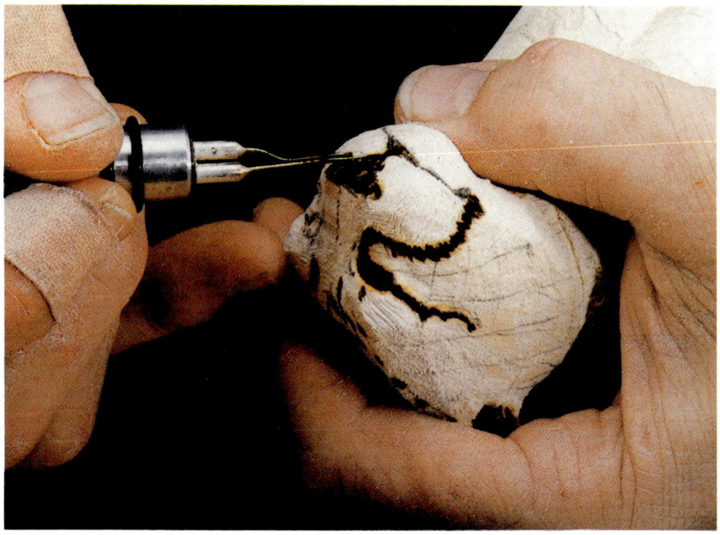

Use the flat edge of the burning tool to darken the nose.

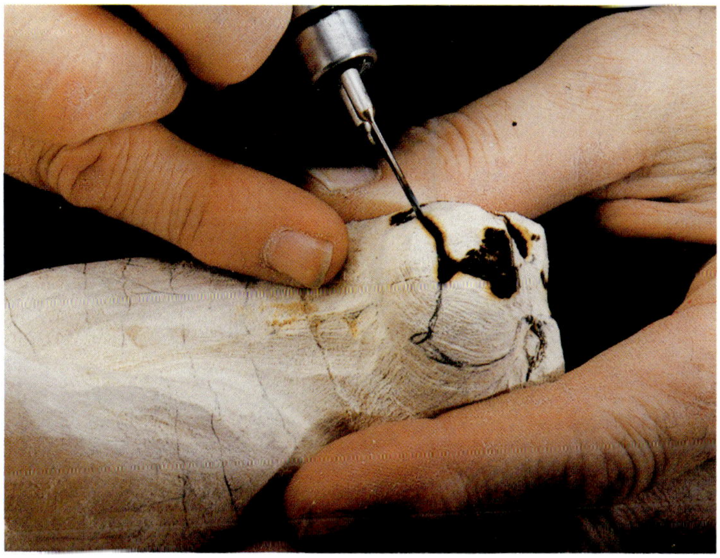

Cheetahs have dark lips, so burn them in.

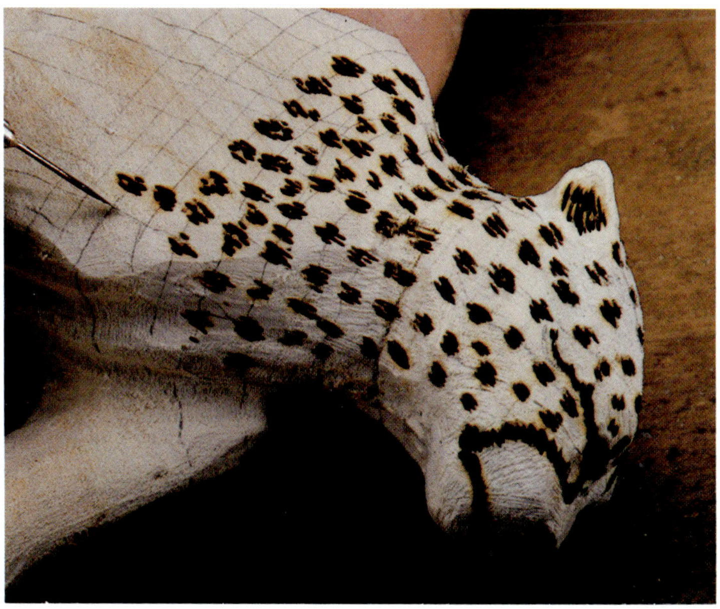

Back to the spots. Continue adding spots to the cheetah. In any large gaps, fill in small spots between the intersections.

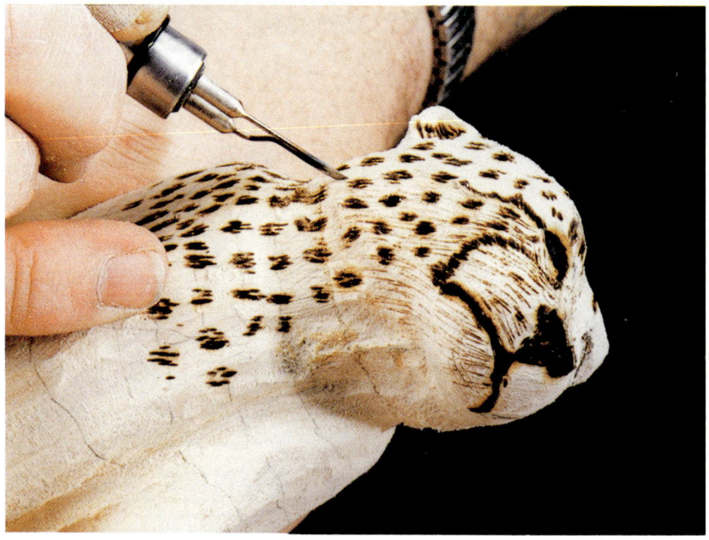

To make the cat appear to have hair, make a series of small rapid cuts. Rapid cuts keep the hair from getting too dark. The resulting marks show both the hair and the direction it is growing.

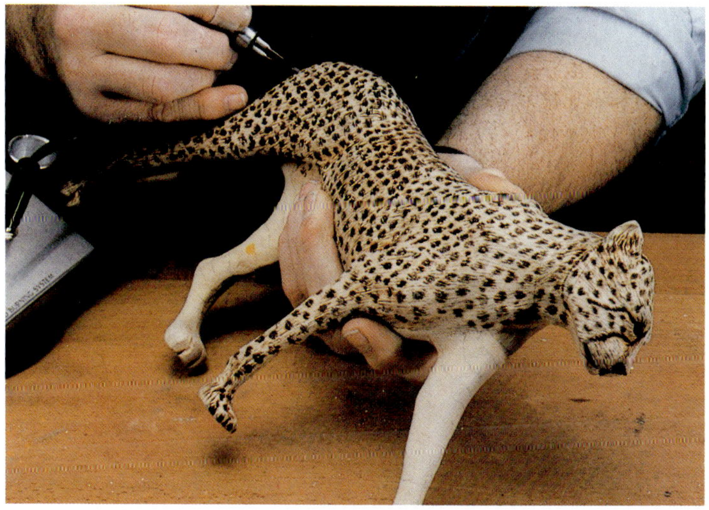

One side of the cheetah is burned in.

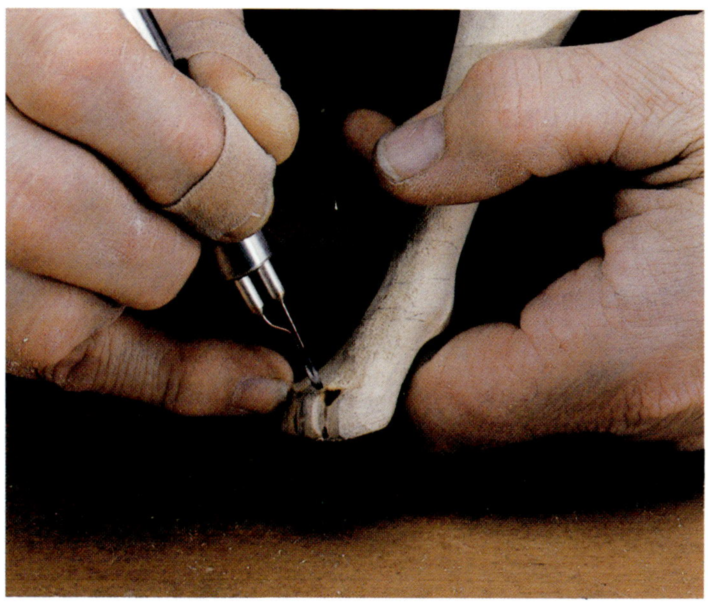

By pressing straight down and straight in with the wood burner, the toes appear separated.

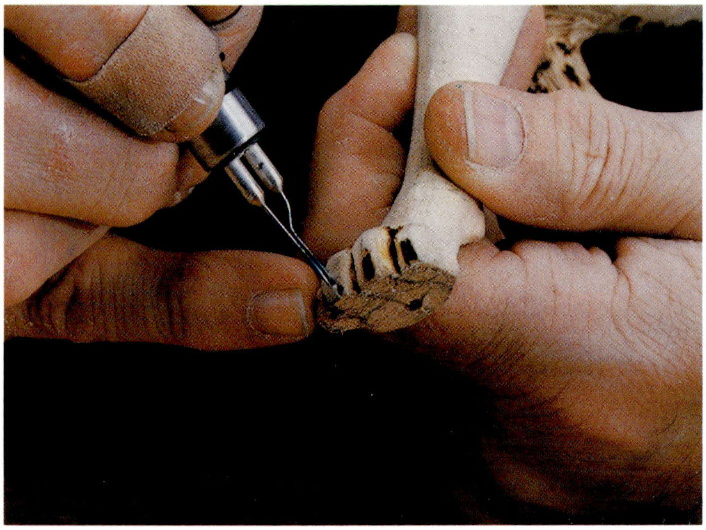

Burning double lines in the front of each toe creates the illusion of the toenails.

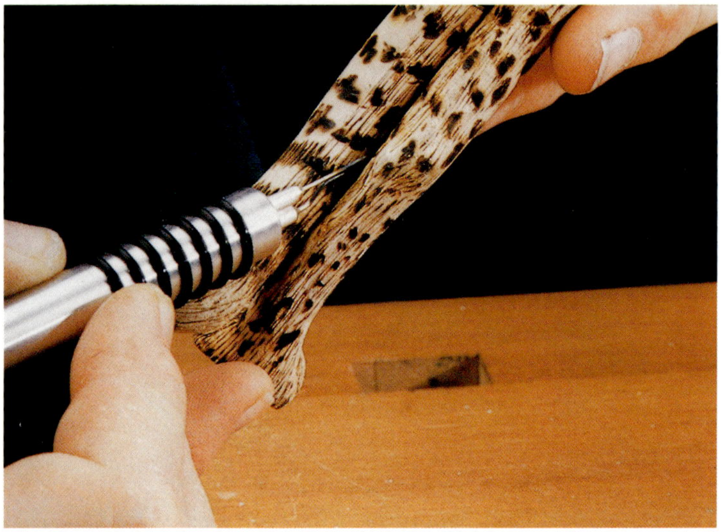

Remember to burn a good deep line beside the tail to make it appear separate from the leg.

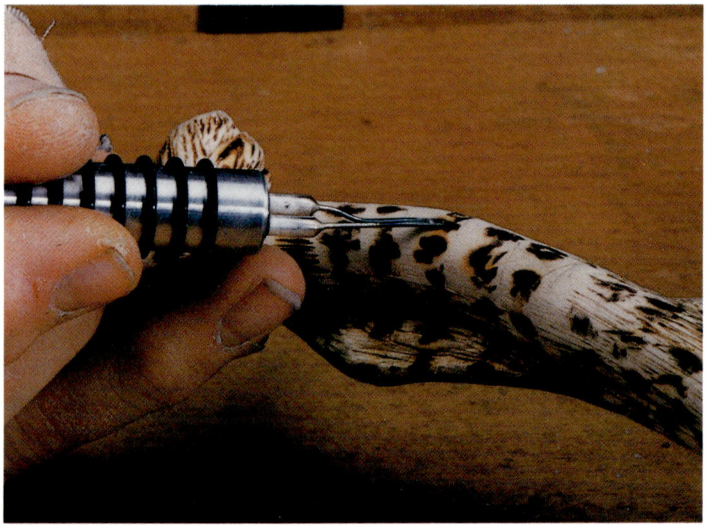

As you continue down the tail, the spots get closer and closer together, almost forming rings.

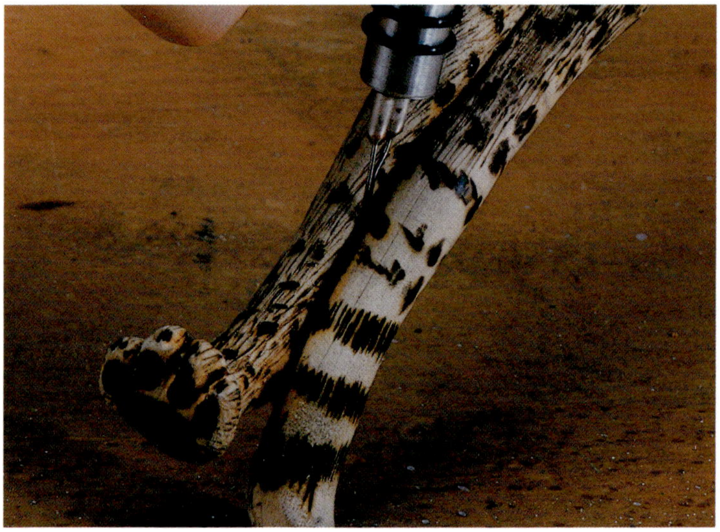

Repeat that line between the underside of the tail and the leg.

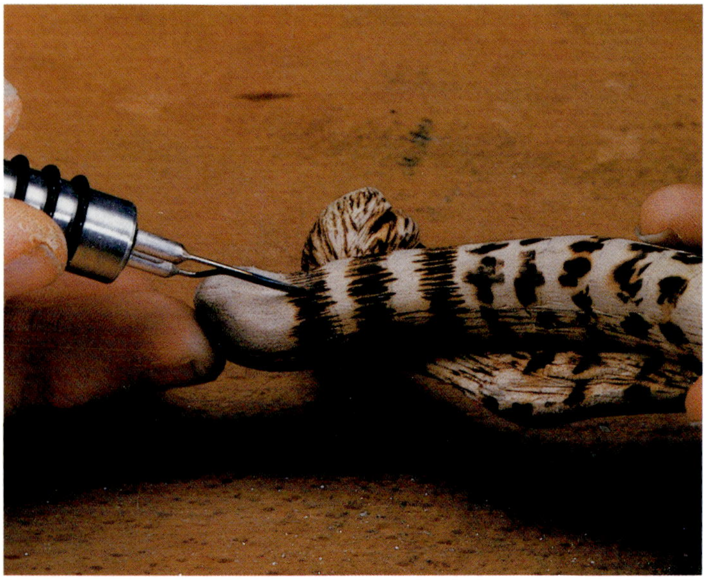

The last three strips around the tail from complete rings. These are the only stripes you will find on the cheetah.

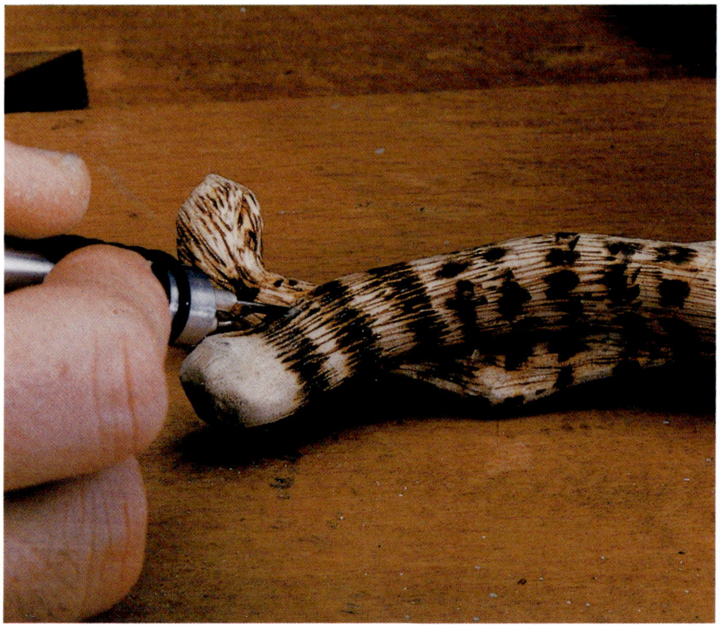

Remember to burn in the hair on the tail as well.

Burned in all around.

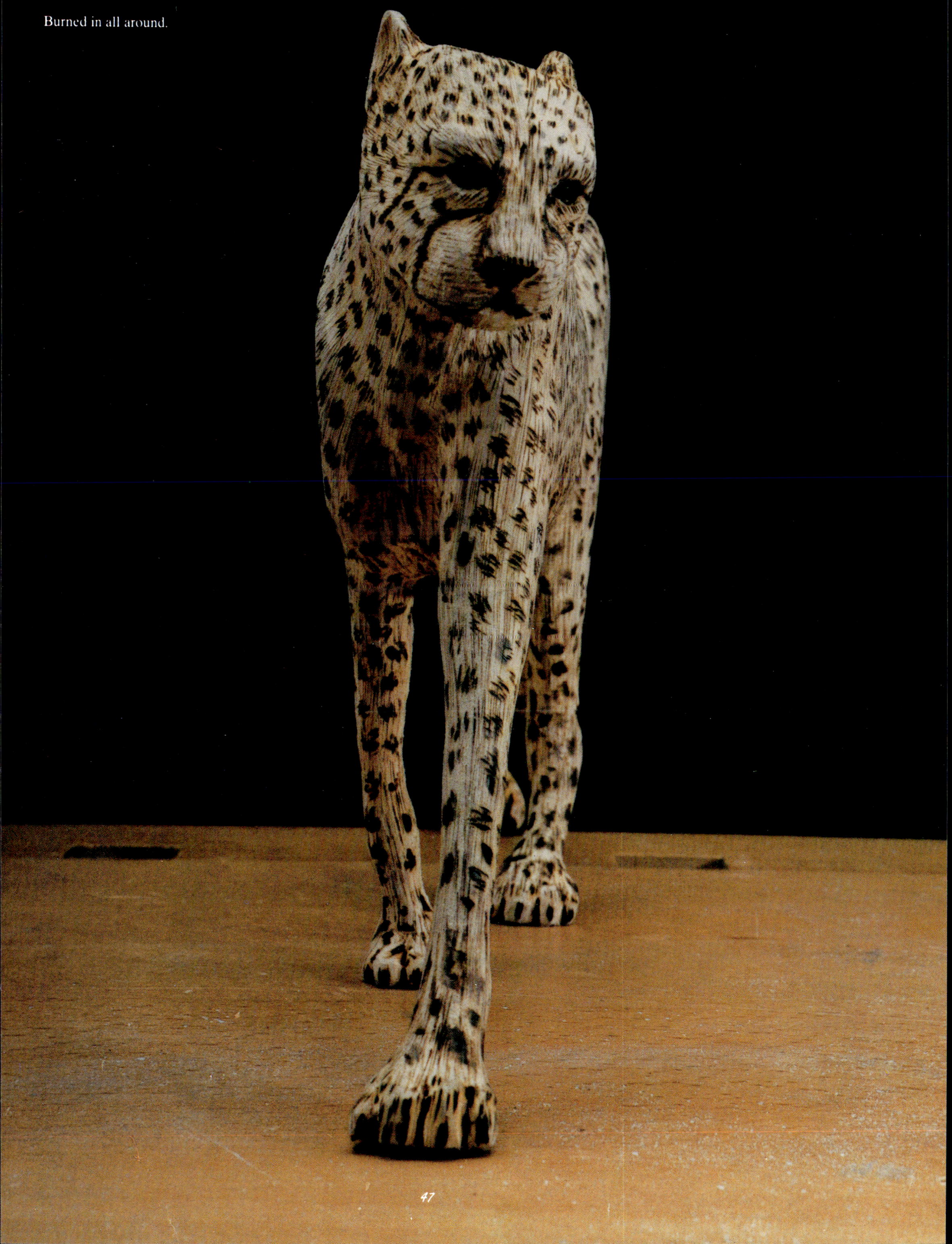

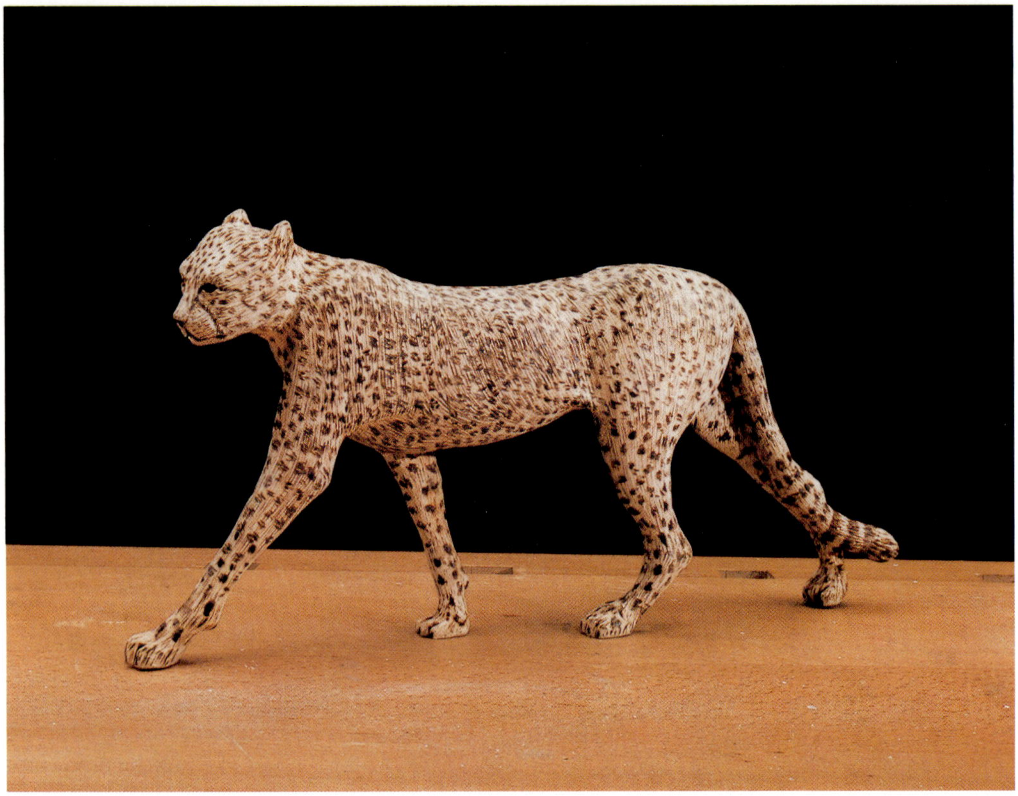

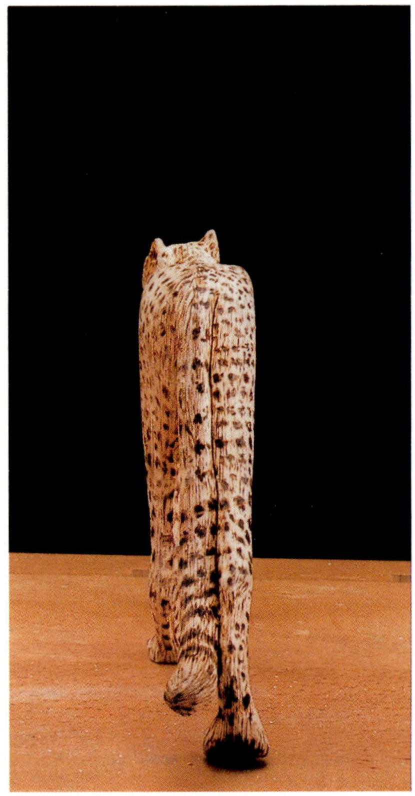

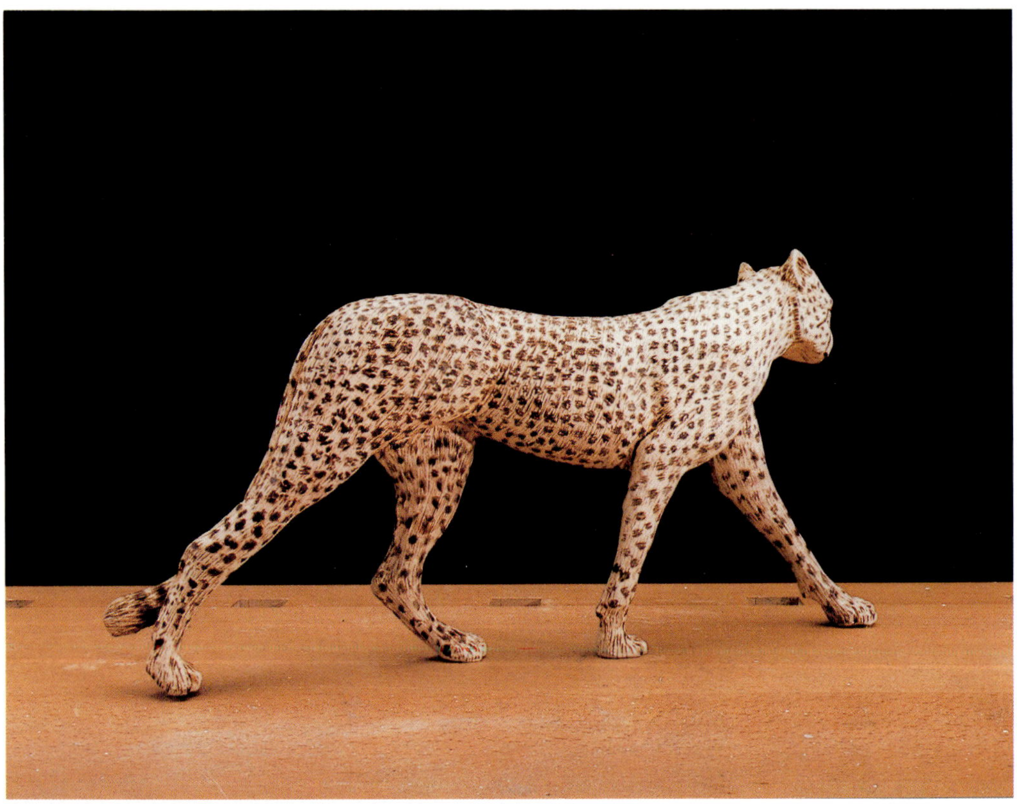

Painting the Cheetah

Cheetah painting time. We will be using white, yellow ochre and a small amount of black acrylic paint to color the cheetah.

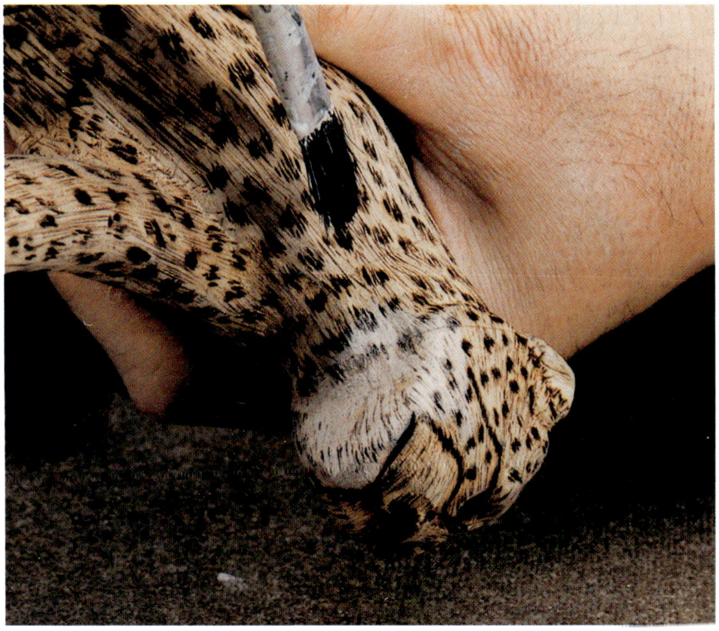

First apply watered down white (which will not leave a hard line) under the chin and on around to the lower part of the face.

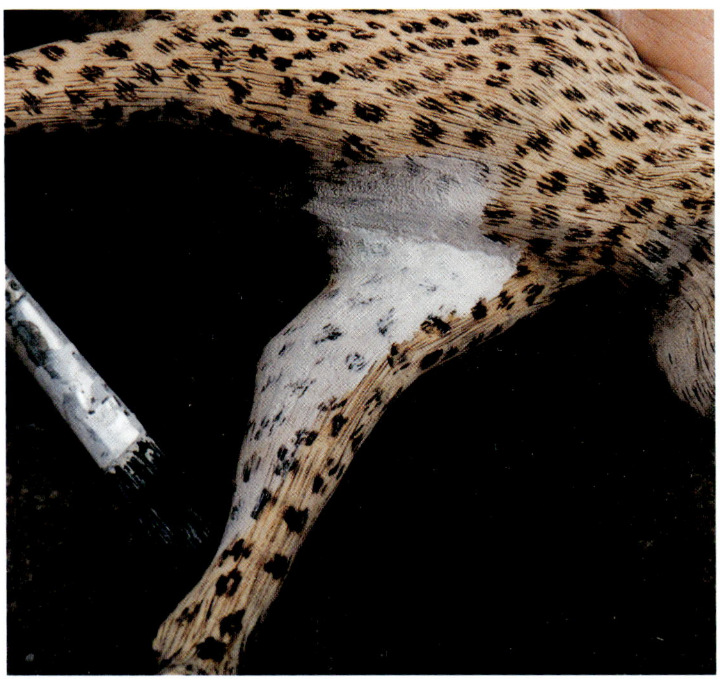

Now work on the cheetah's chest and down the insides of his front legs to the ankles.

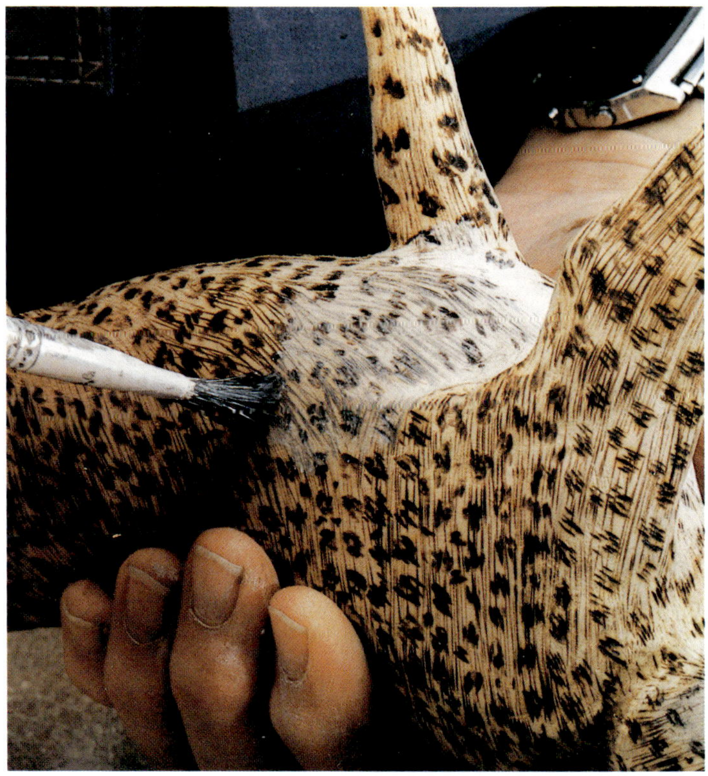

Blend out all the hard edges, using a brush dipped in pure water as your blending tool.

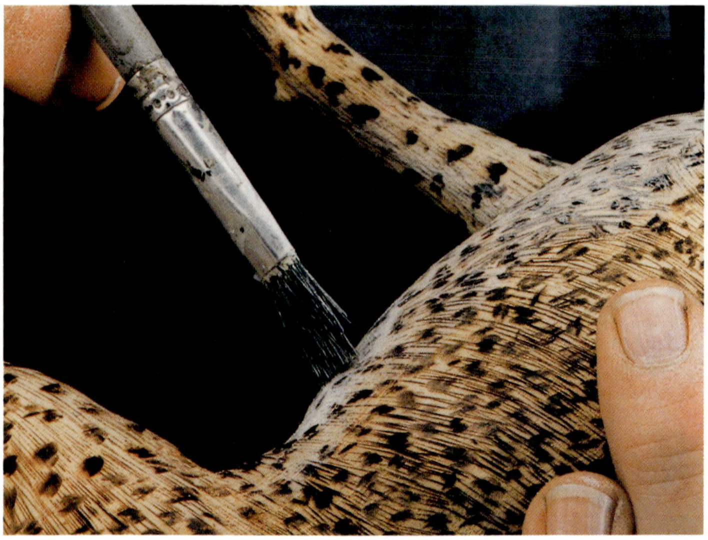

The white only comes up as far as the rounded sides of the cheetah.

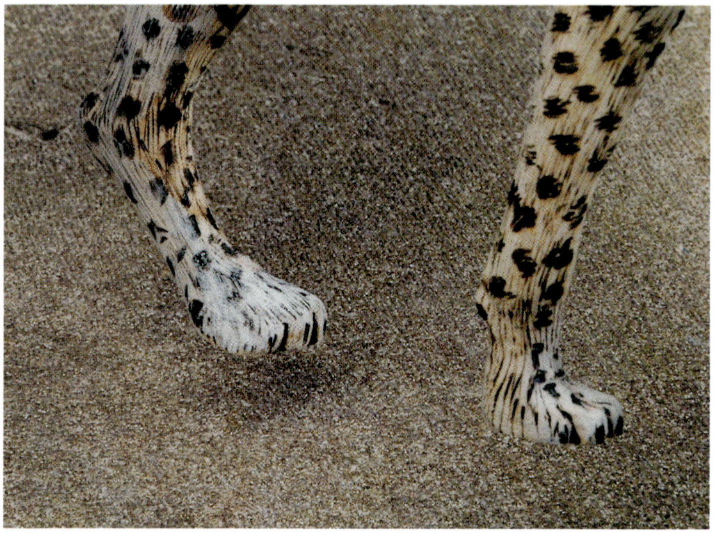

The tops of the feet are white.

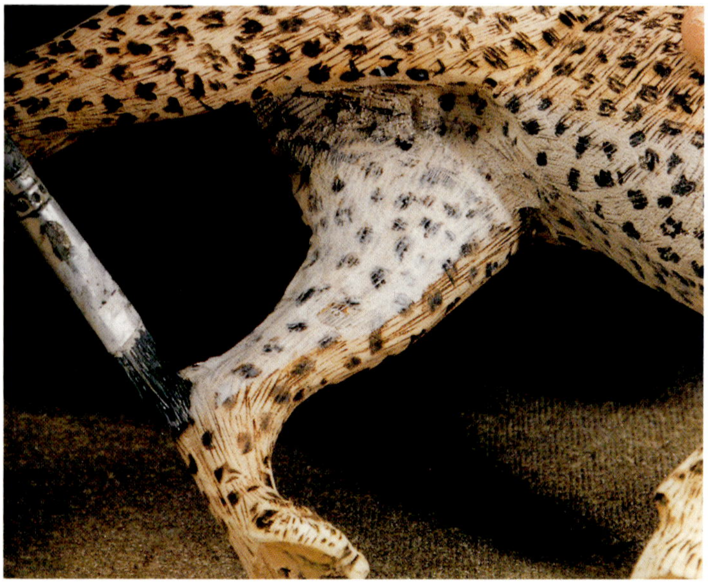

Extend the white down the inside of the back legs to the ankles.

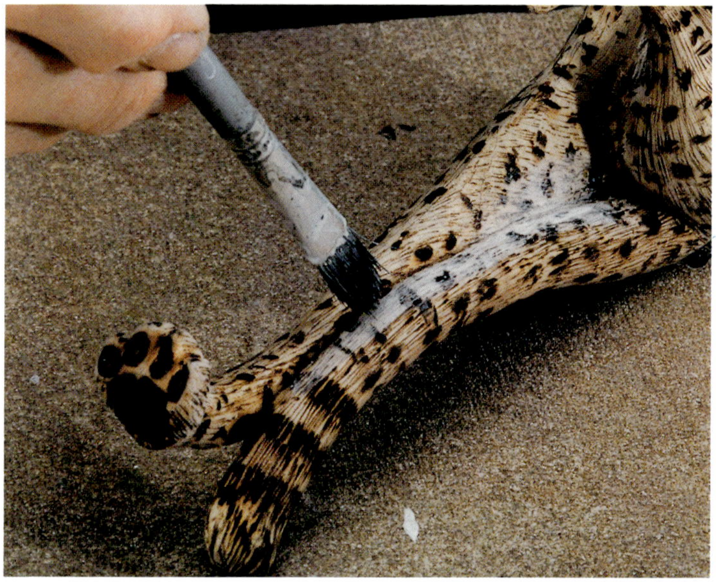

The inside of the back leg and the underside of the tail are white.

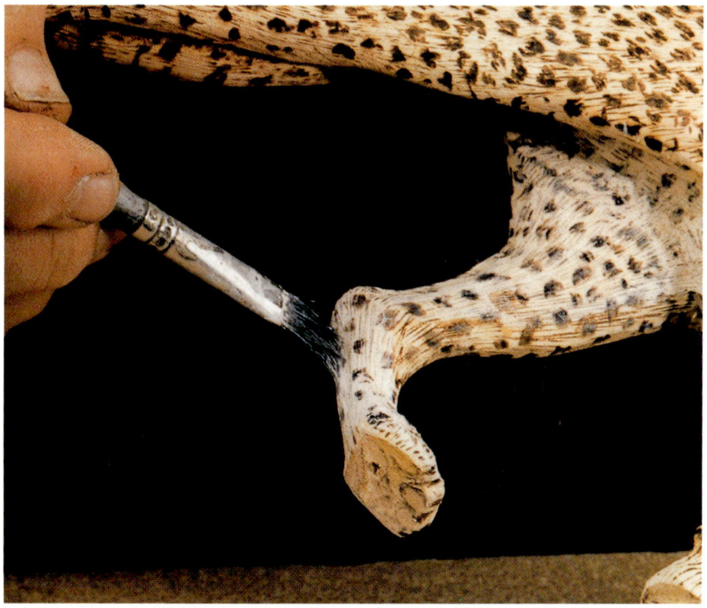

Bring the white down the back of the leg and onto the feet.

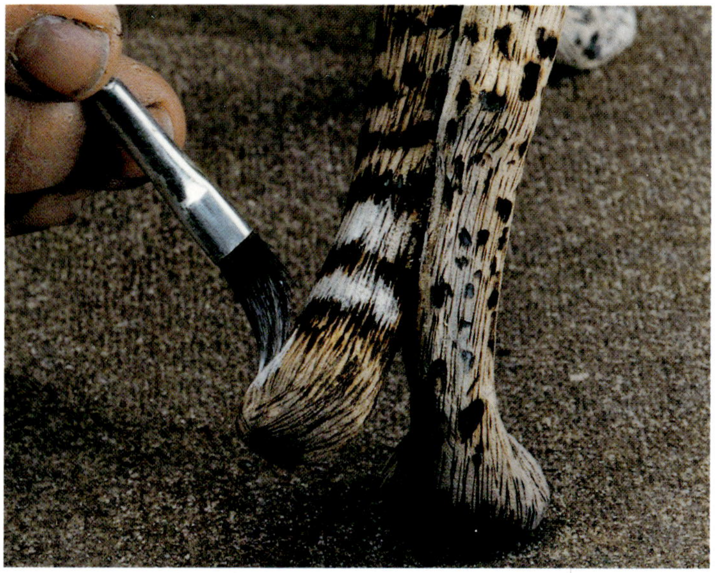

The three stripes and the tip of the tail are painted in a very strong white with very little water.

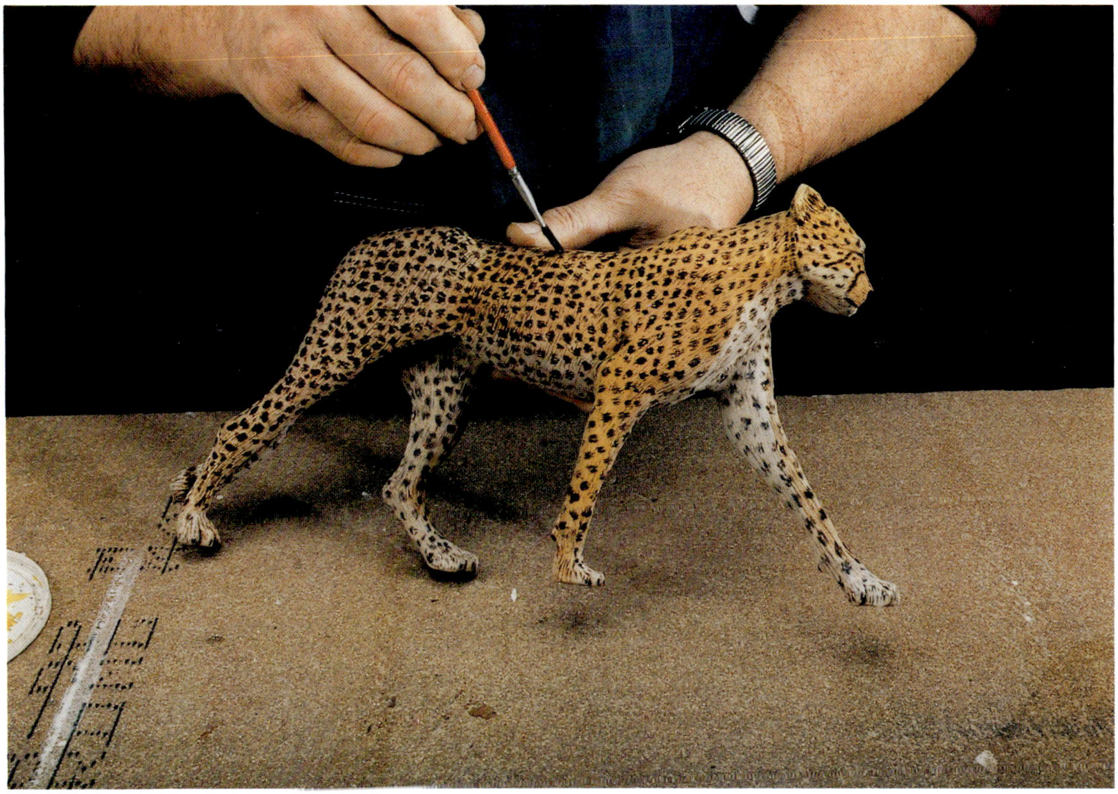

Take the yellow ochre (dipping your brush in water each time you are ready to dip your brush in the paint to create a wash of the paint) and cover the rest of the body with it as a base coat.

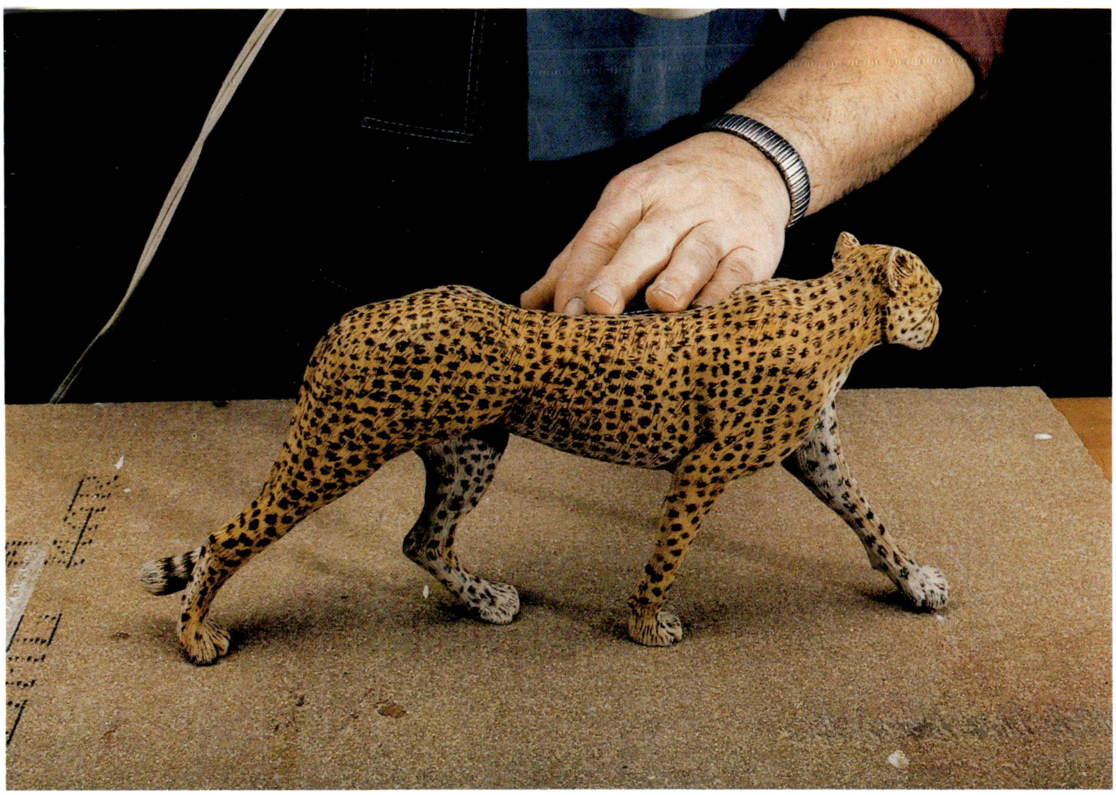

The yellow ochre base coat has been applied to half of the cheetah. Apply it to the other half.

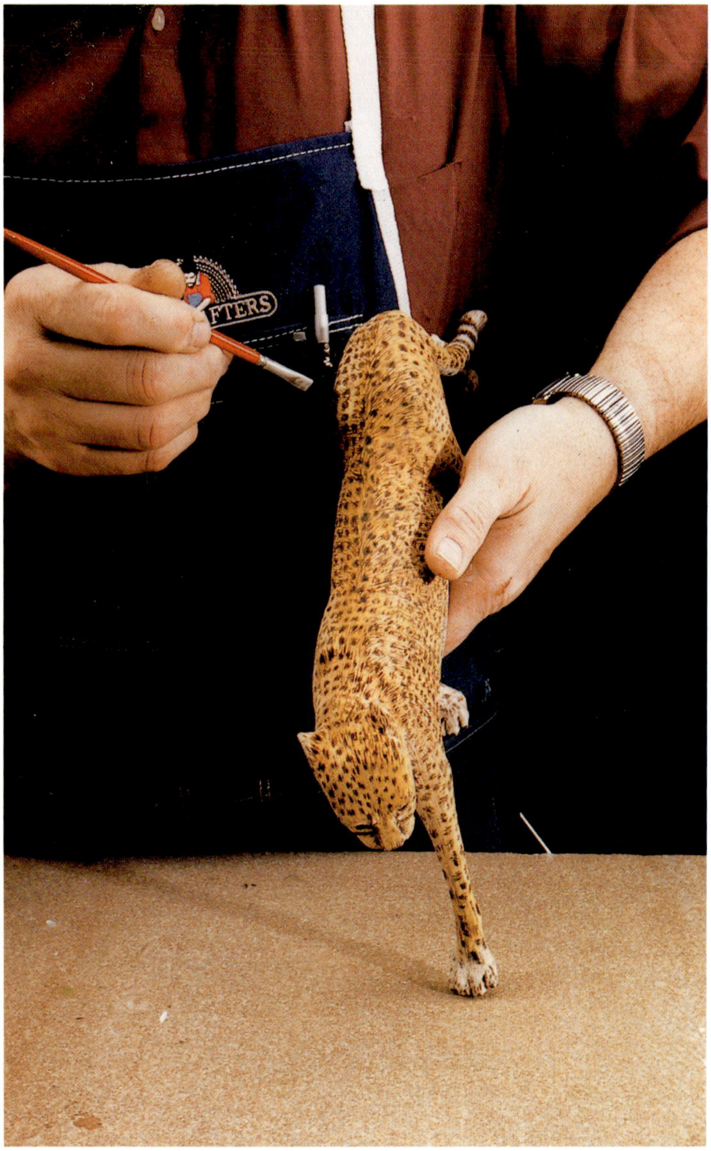

Beginning right between the ears, add a second coat of yellow ochre to the back to deepen the color right down the back, blending it onto the sides and down. Follow the spine on down the tail.

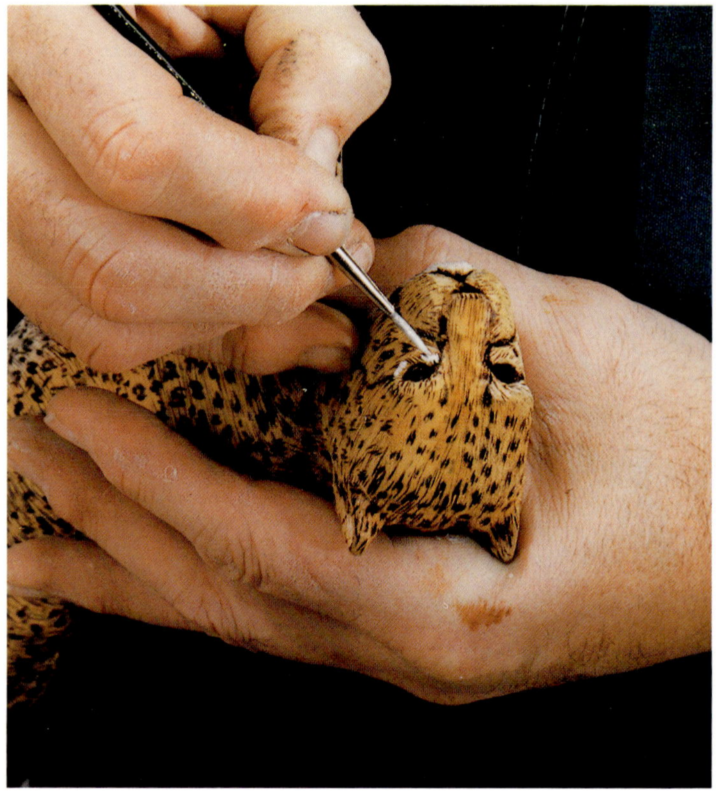

Add white to the corners of the eyes.

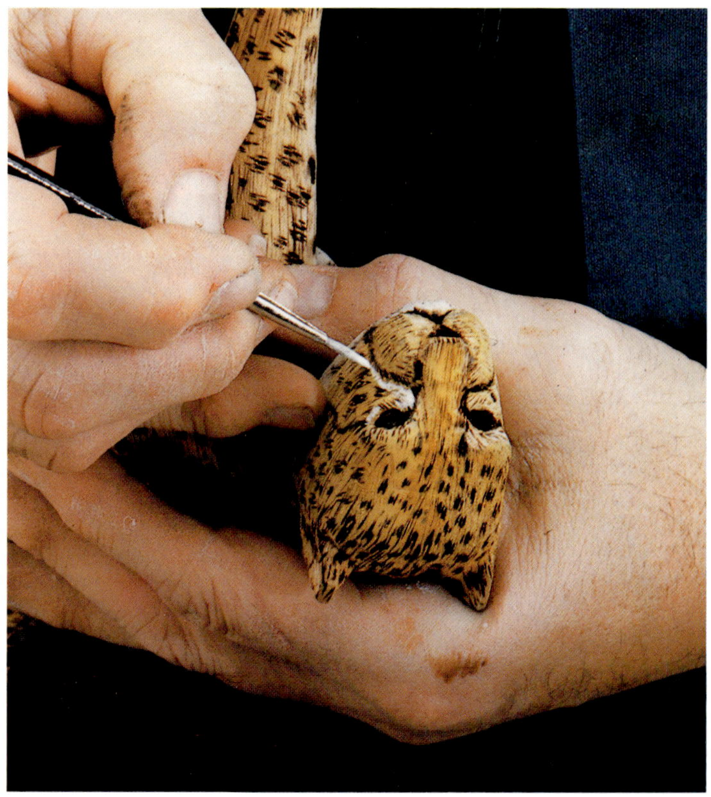

The white blends out along the distinctive black lines on the cheetah's face.

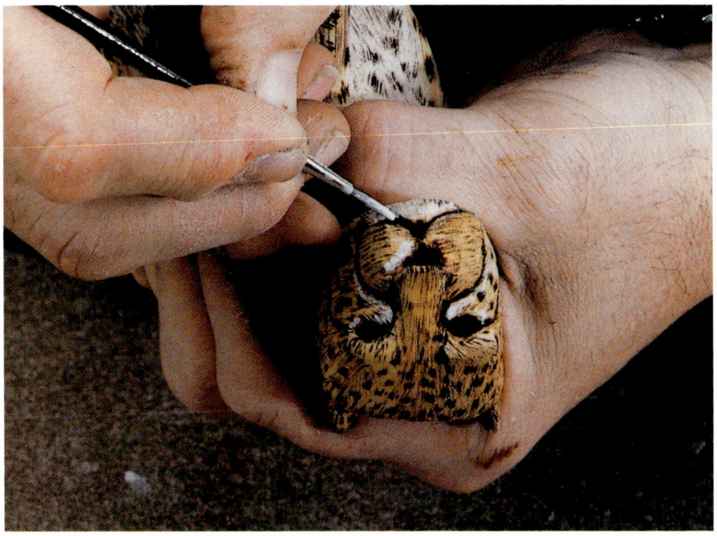

There is also white along the side of the nose.

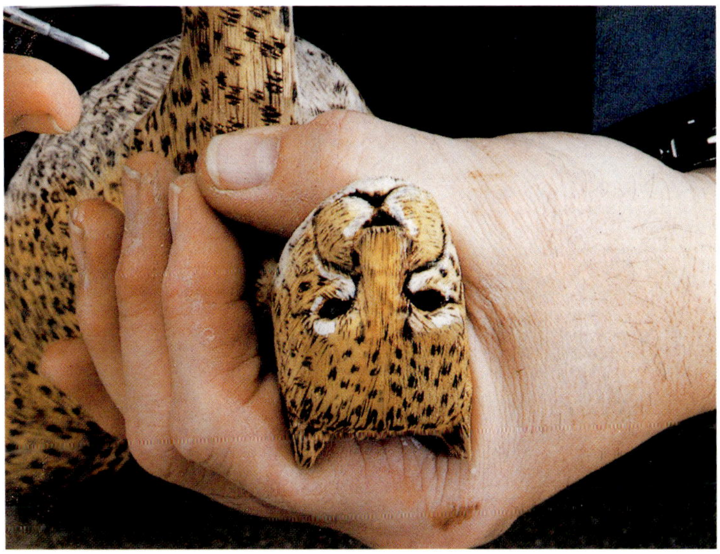

Add a little spot of white above each eye.

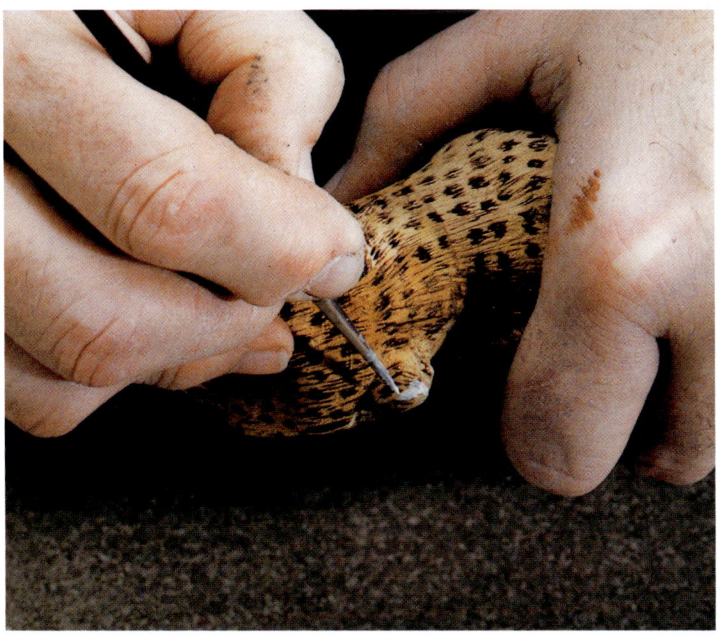

Add a small white patch to the tip of each ear as well.

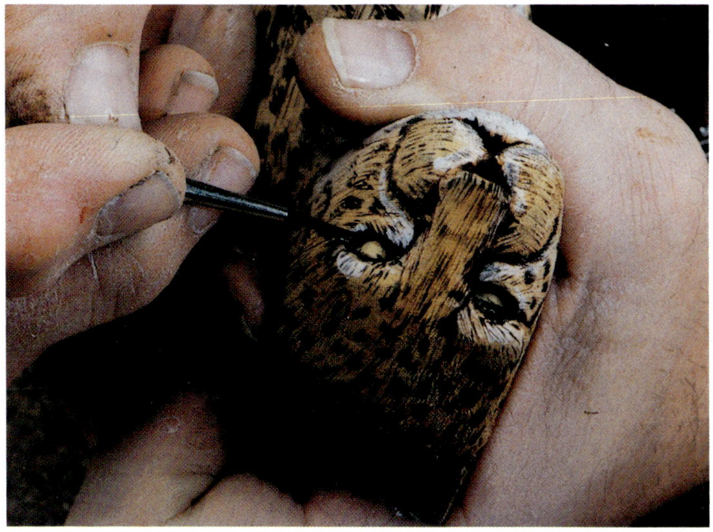

We're going to paint the cheetah's eyes. First mix yellow ochre and a small amount of white to lighten it up. Paint his eyes with that color.

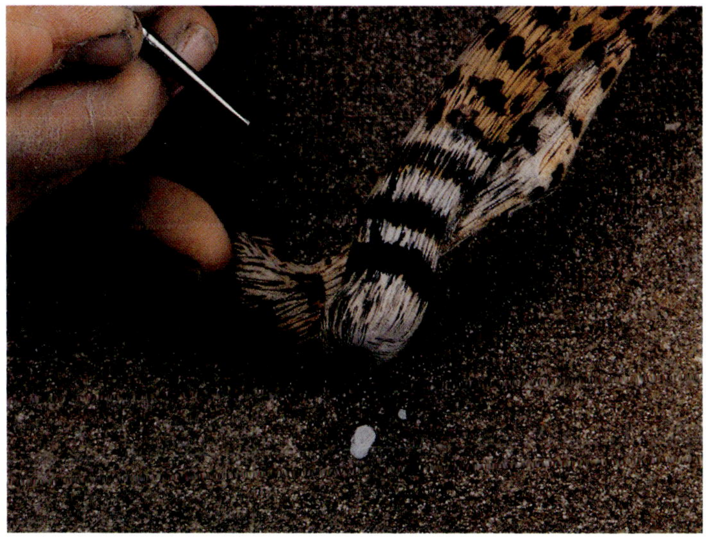

Let the eyes dry throughly and move on to the tip of the tail. Working forward and starting with the black, moisten a brush to make the black liquid and darken the three stripes at the end of the tail. Notice that the watered black will pull along the burn marks and make the hair show more clearly.

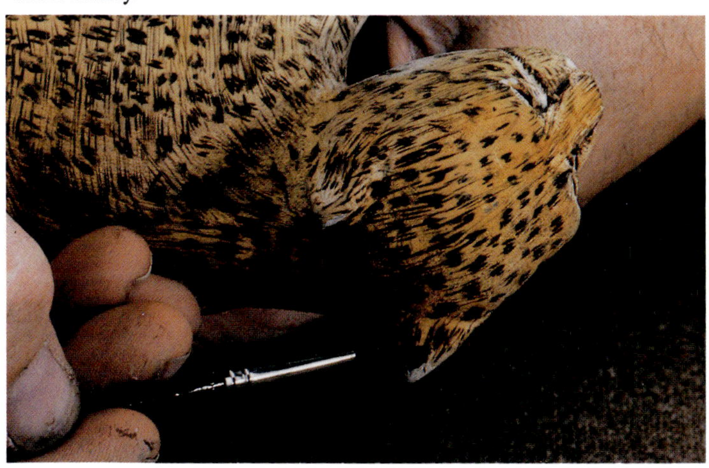

Apply black below the white patches on the ears. There is one black spot on the back of the ears. This black is almost pure, just dampen the brush before putting it on. The black should be strong enough the white does not show through it.

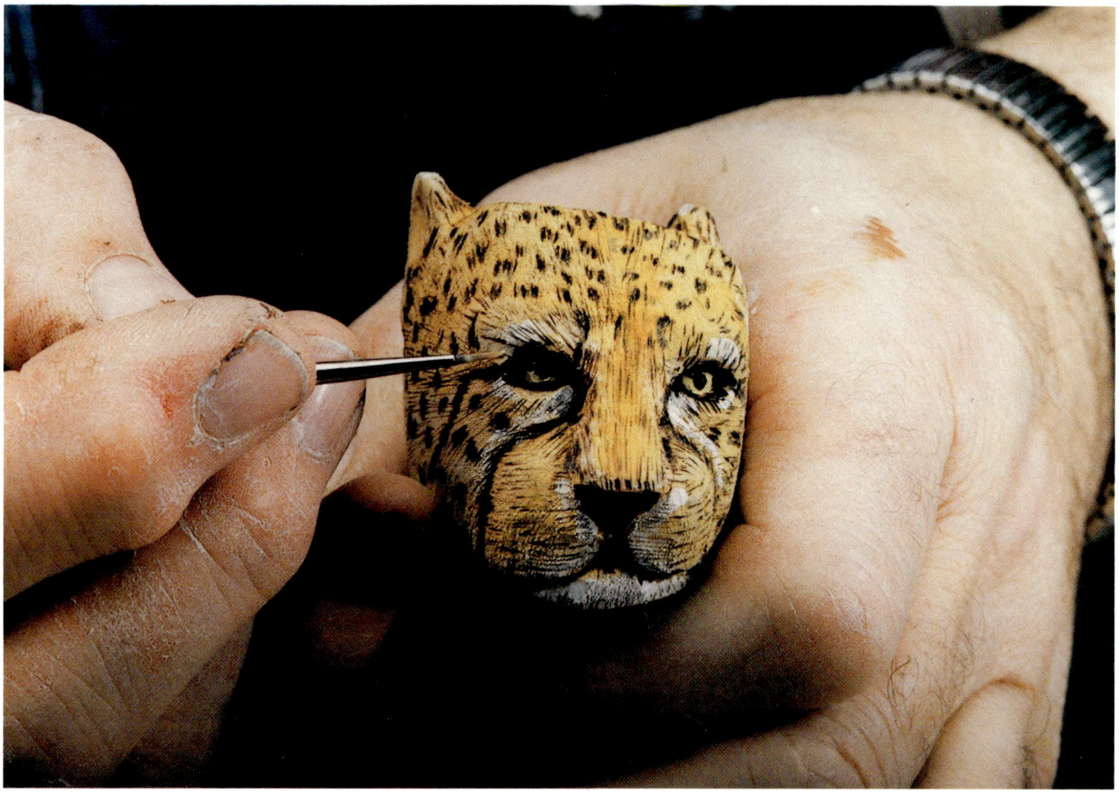

Now that the eyes are dry, apply a narrow black line above and below the eyes to indicate the eyelids. Paint the black pupils in the eyes with the finest brush you have. The cat should look almost cross-eyed.

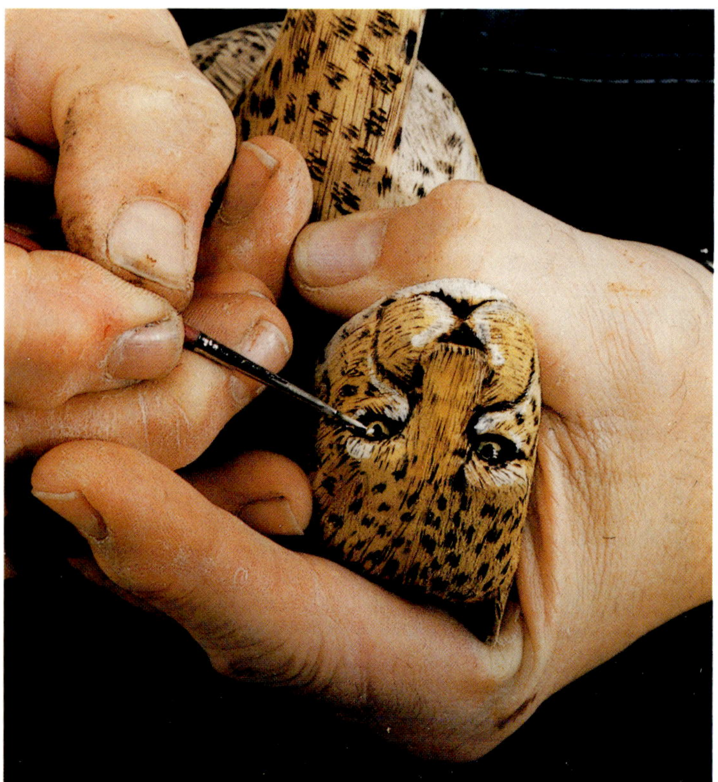

Wash your fine brush out because you are going to put a very small spot of white in each eye.

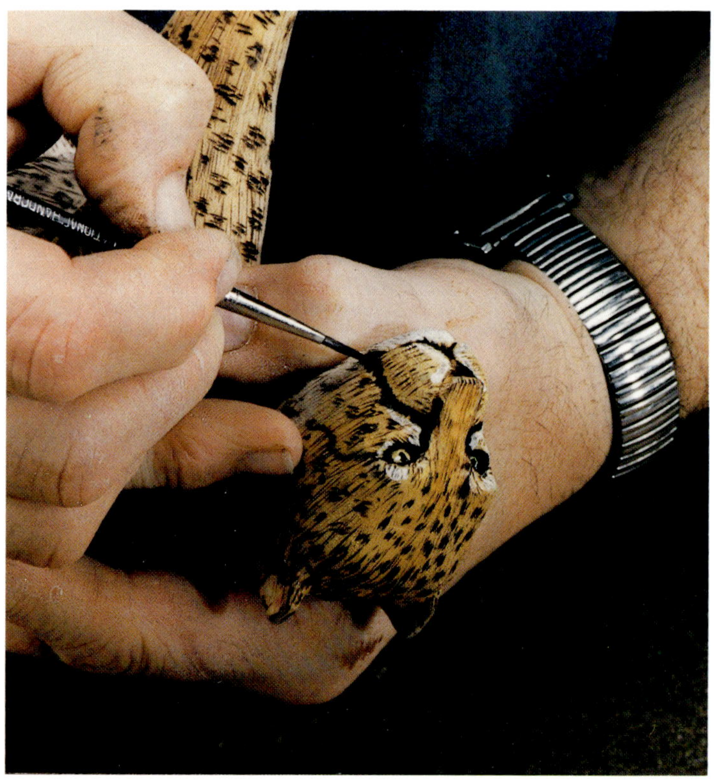

Apply black paint to the distinctive lines on the cheetah's face from the inside corners of the eyes down to the outside corners of his mouth.

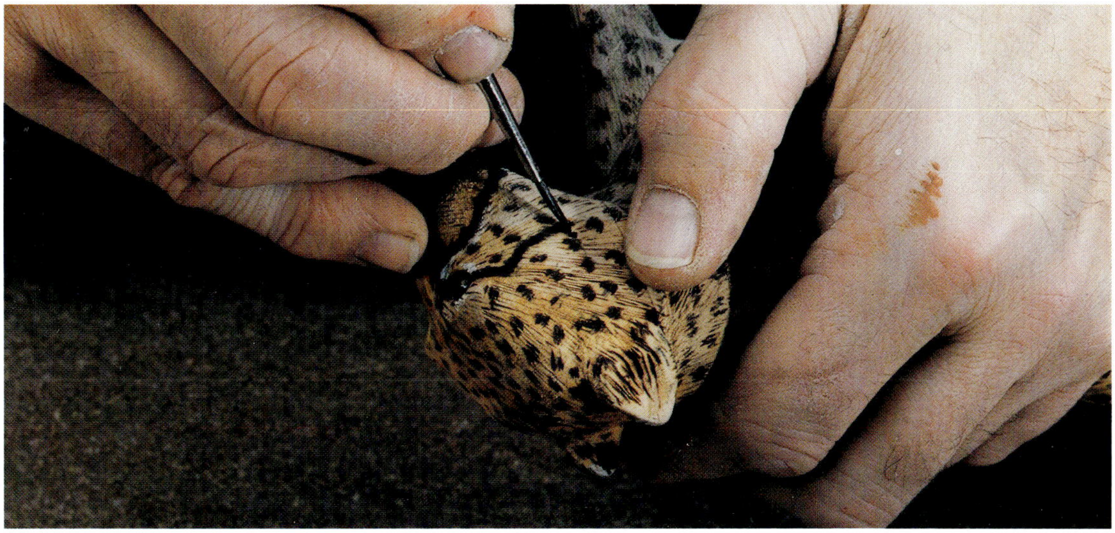

Paint in the tear lines in black.

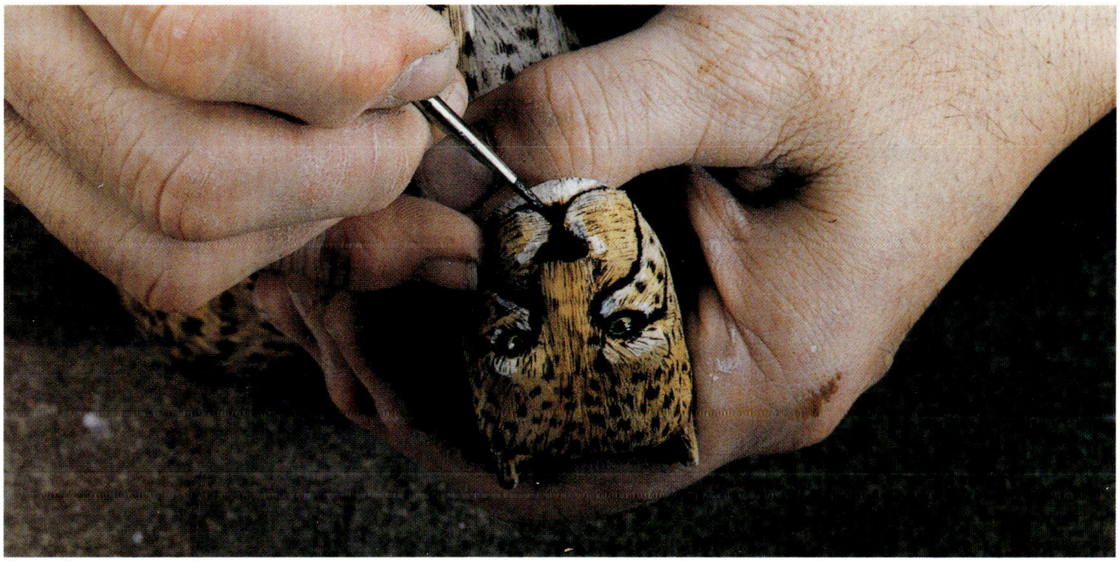

Paint the tip of the nose black.

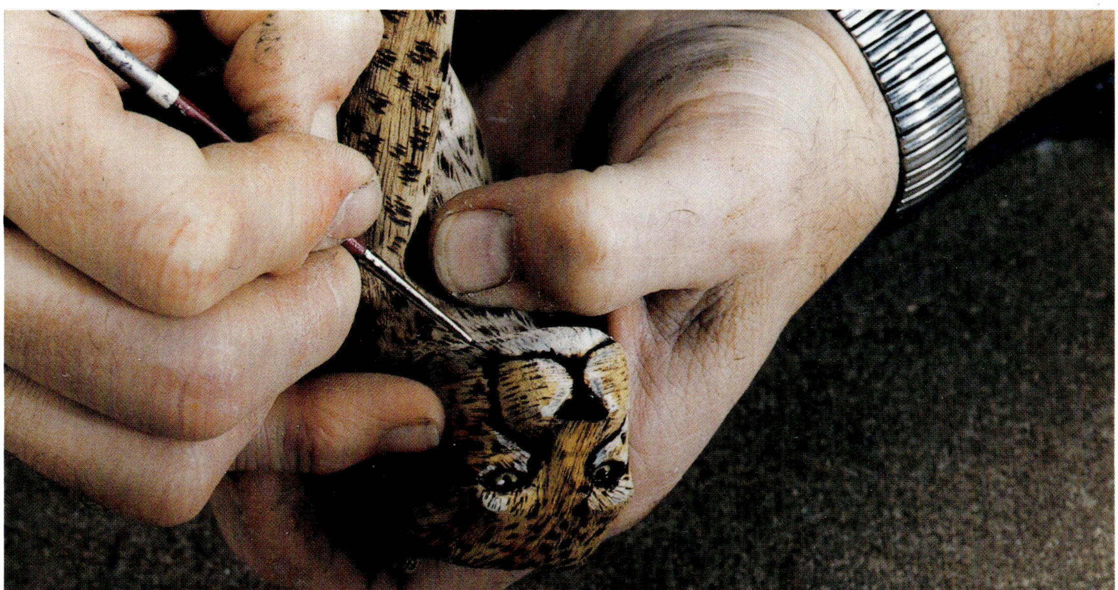

Paint the lips black. We're done!

The cheetah is finished.

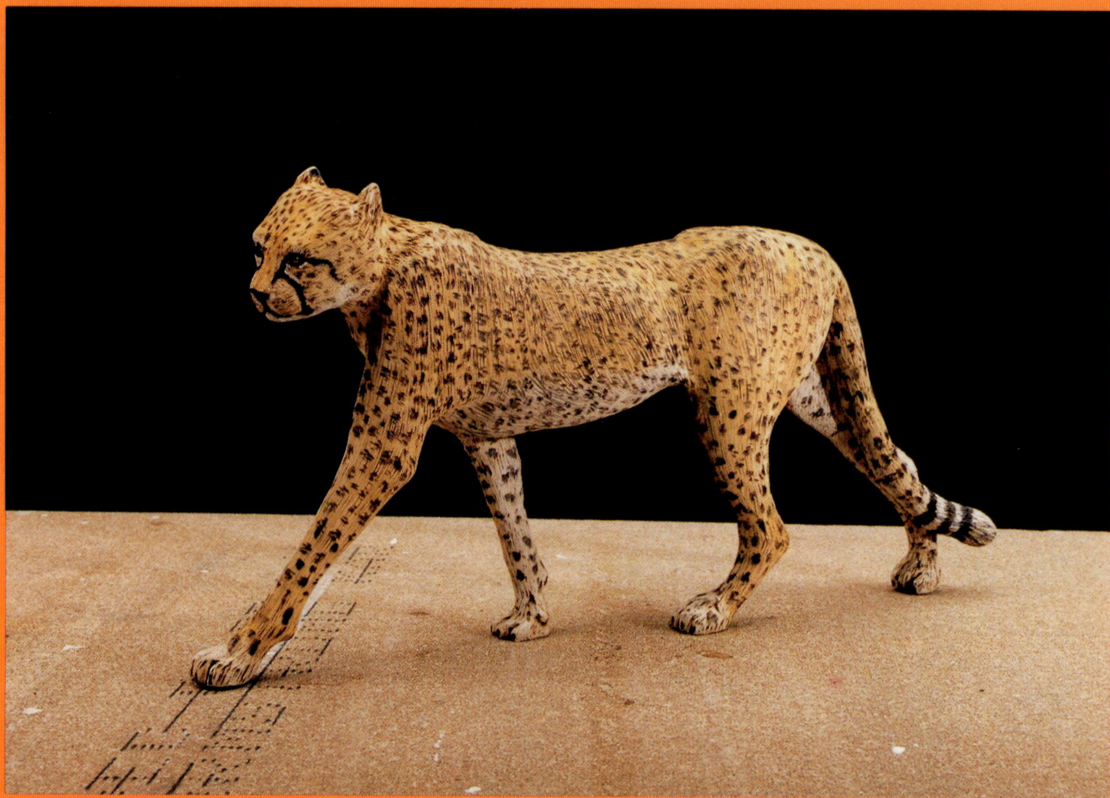

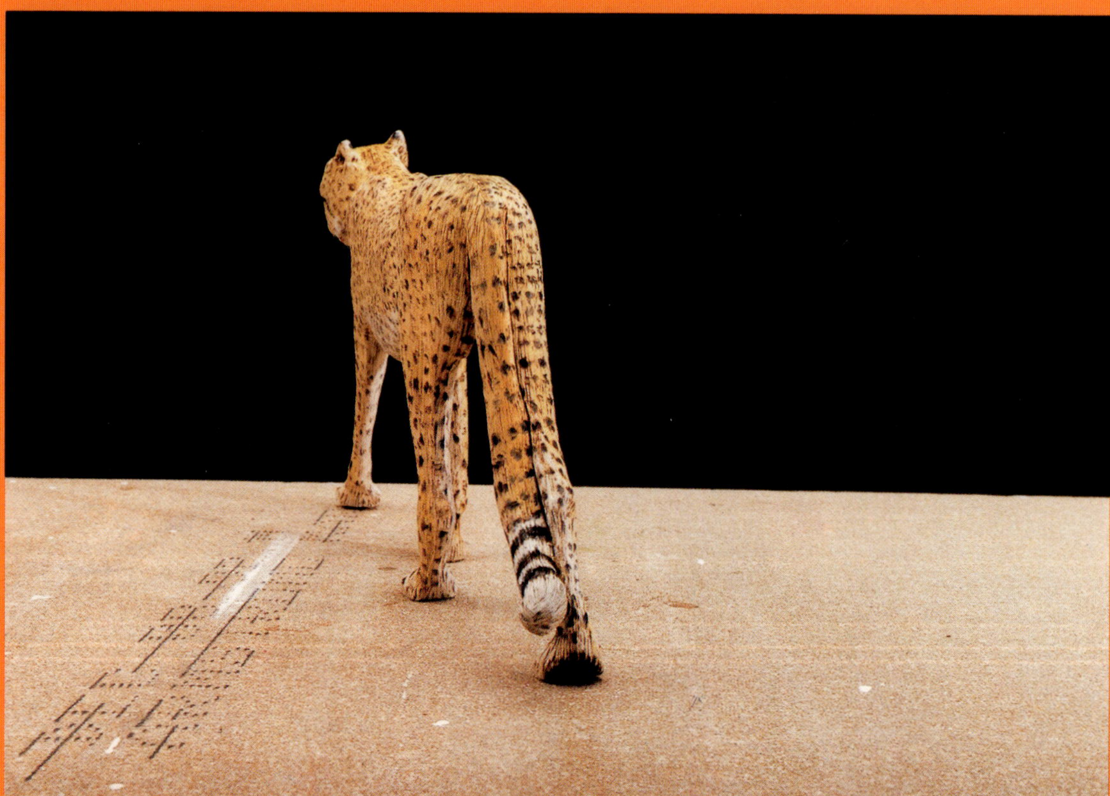

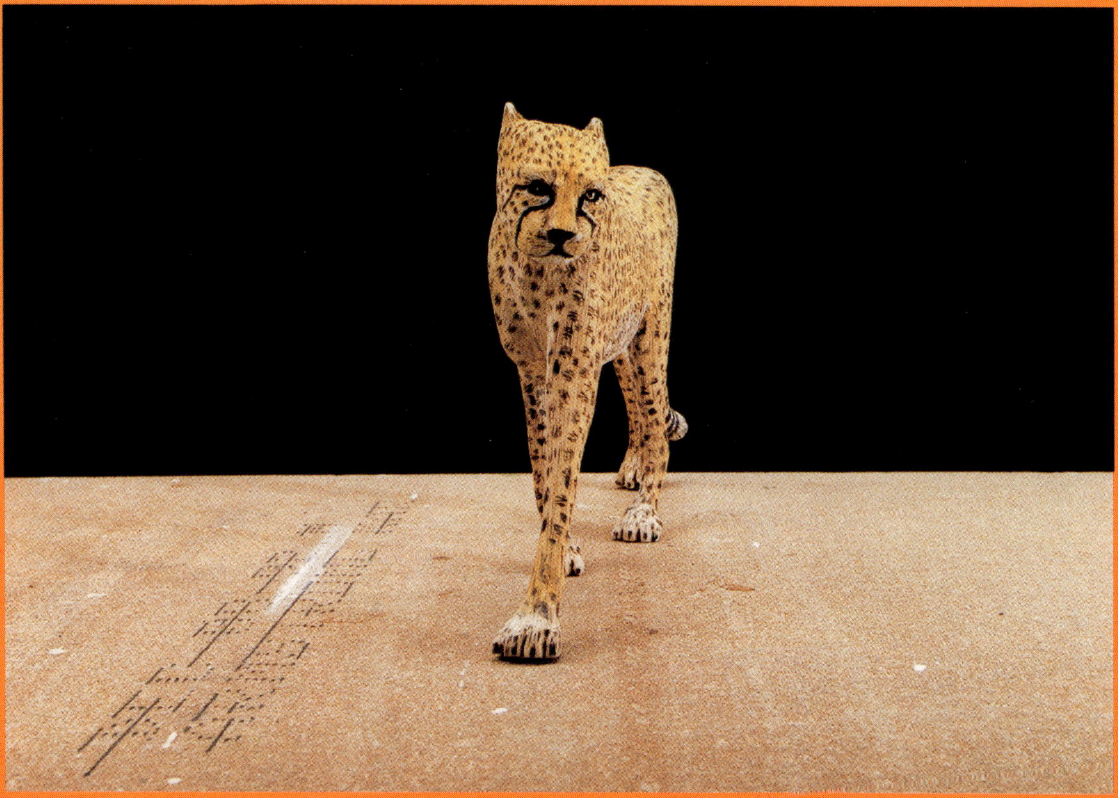

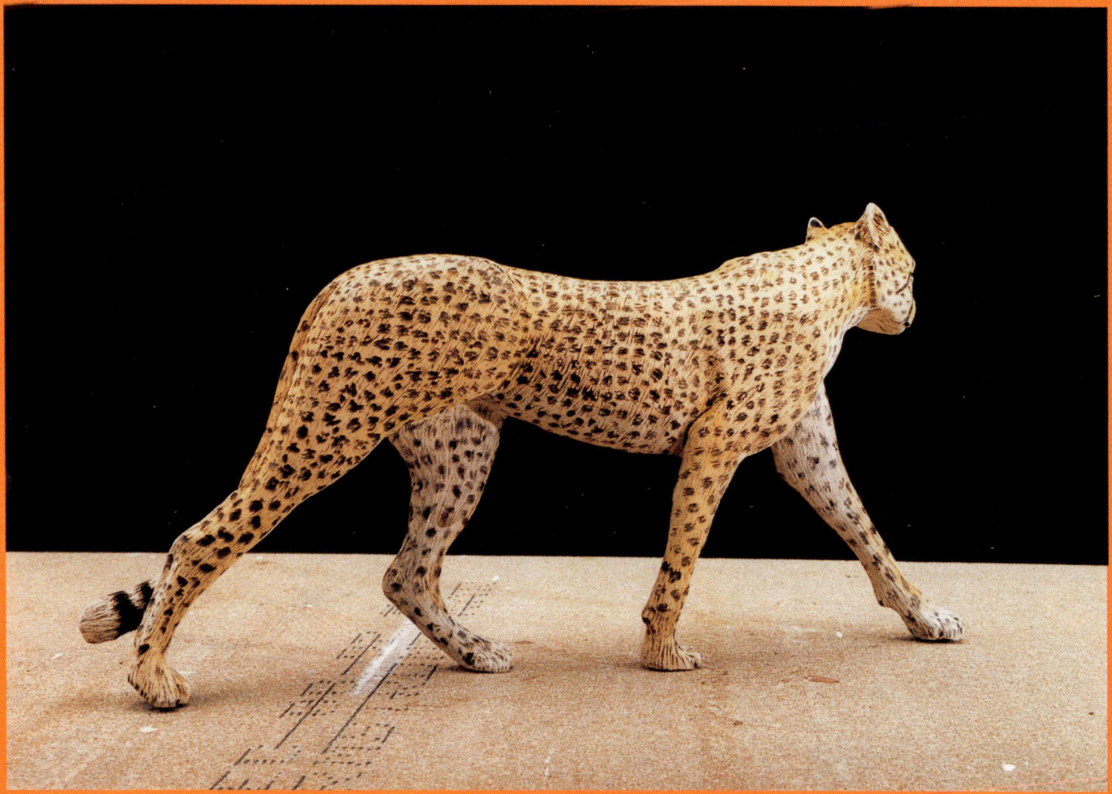

The Gallery

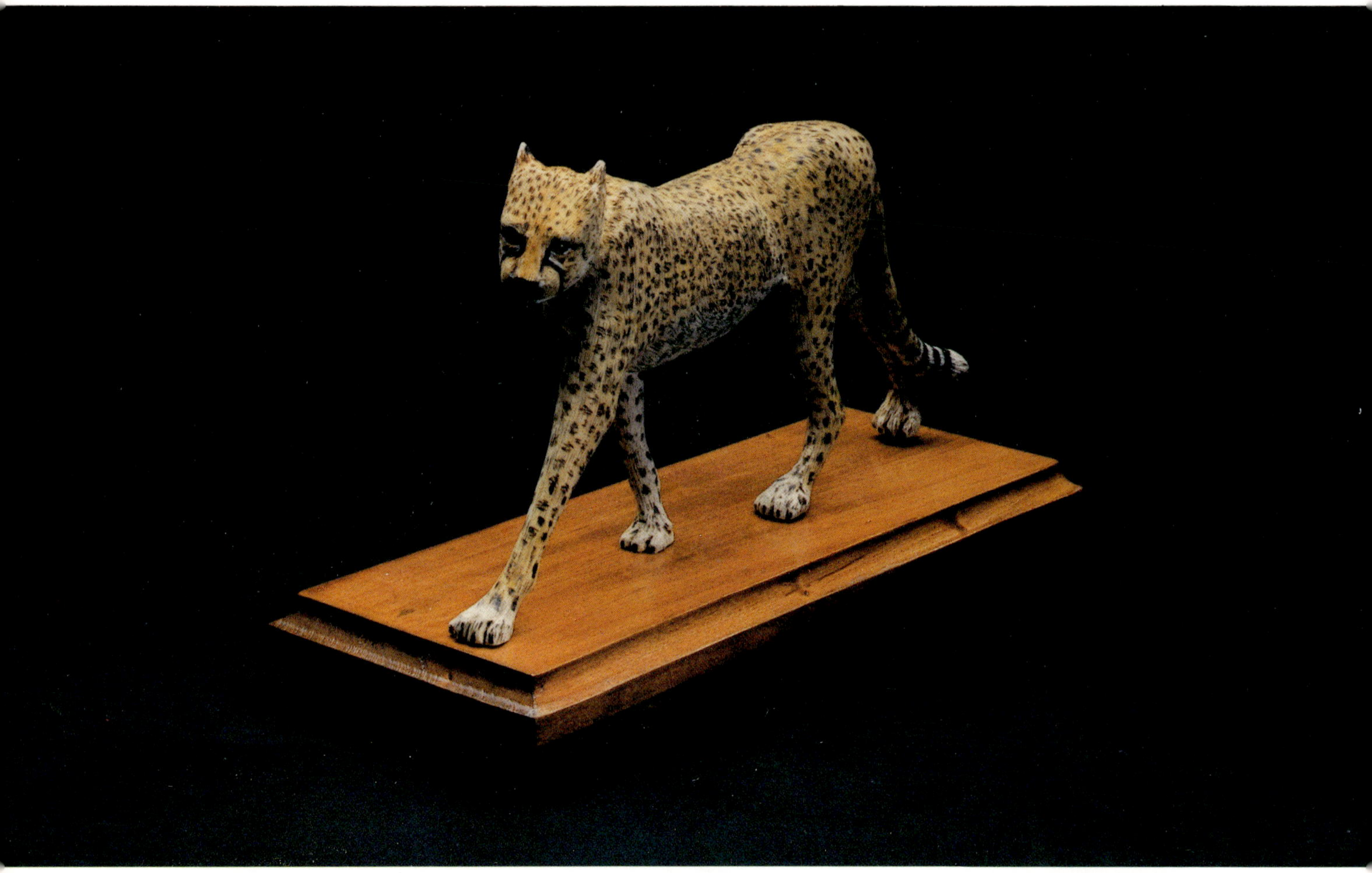

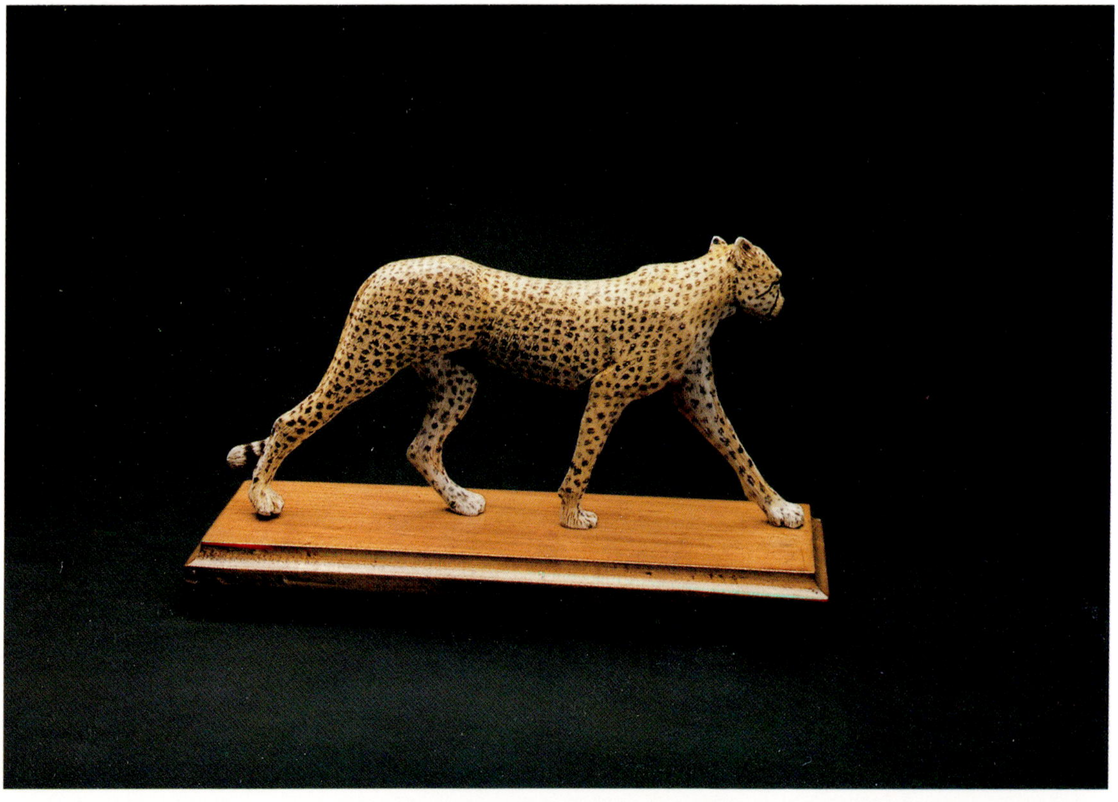

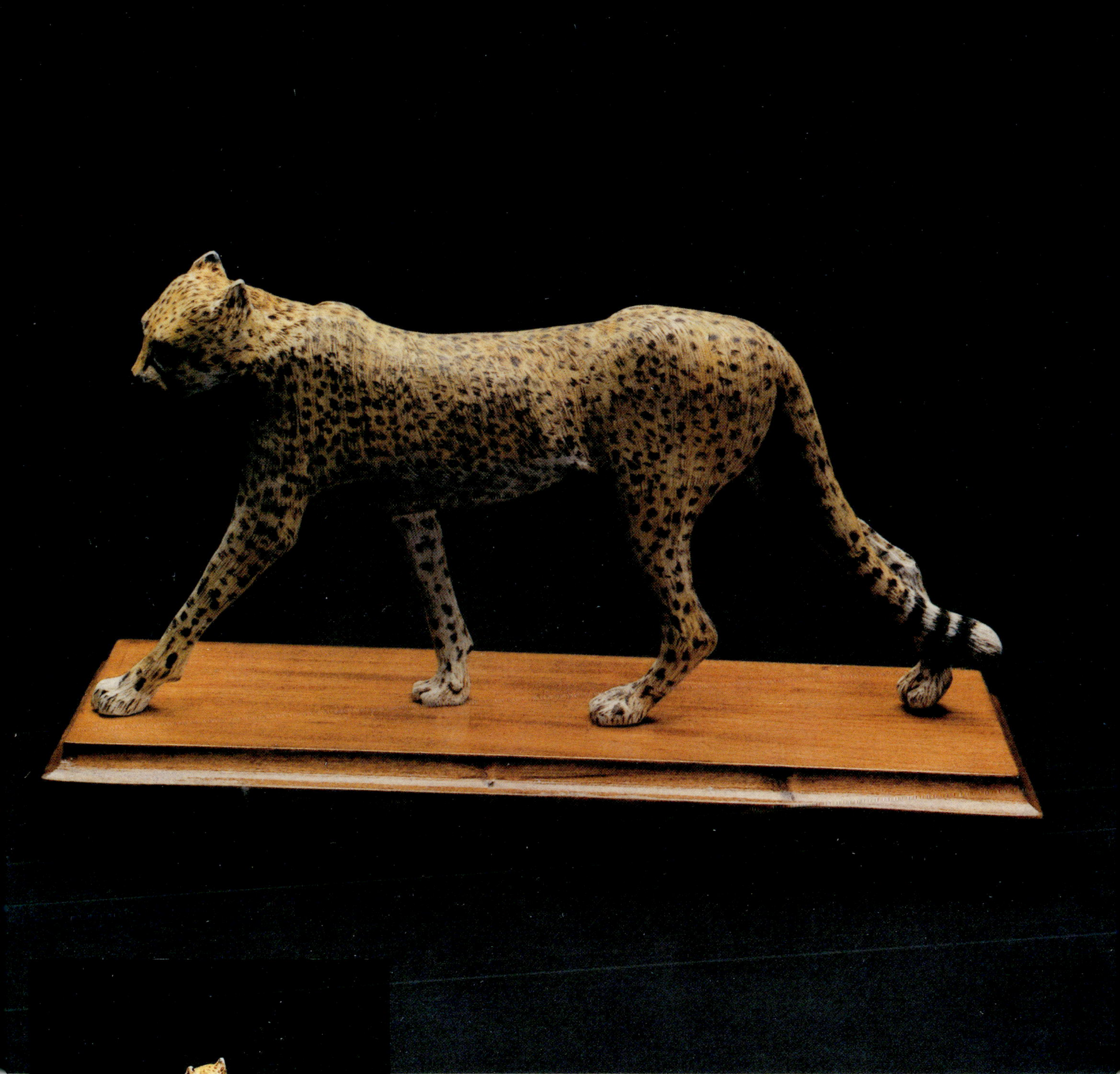

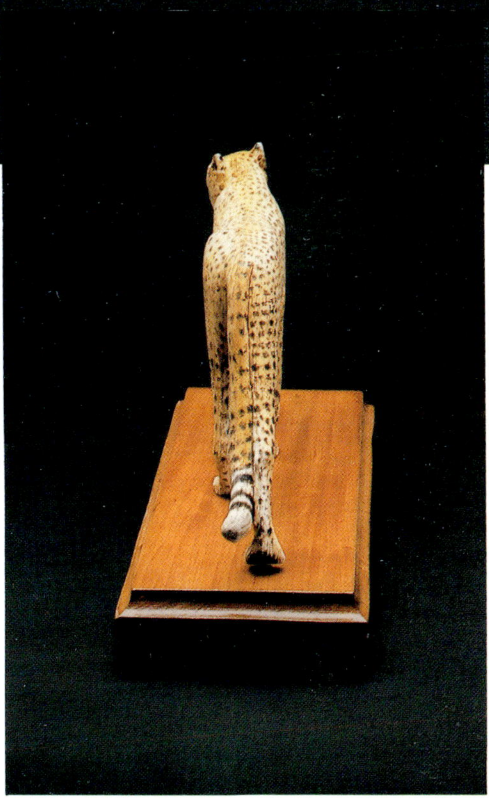

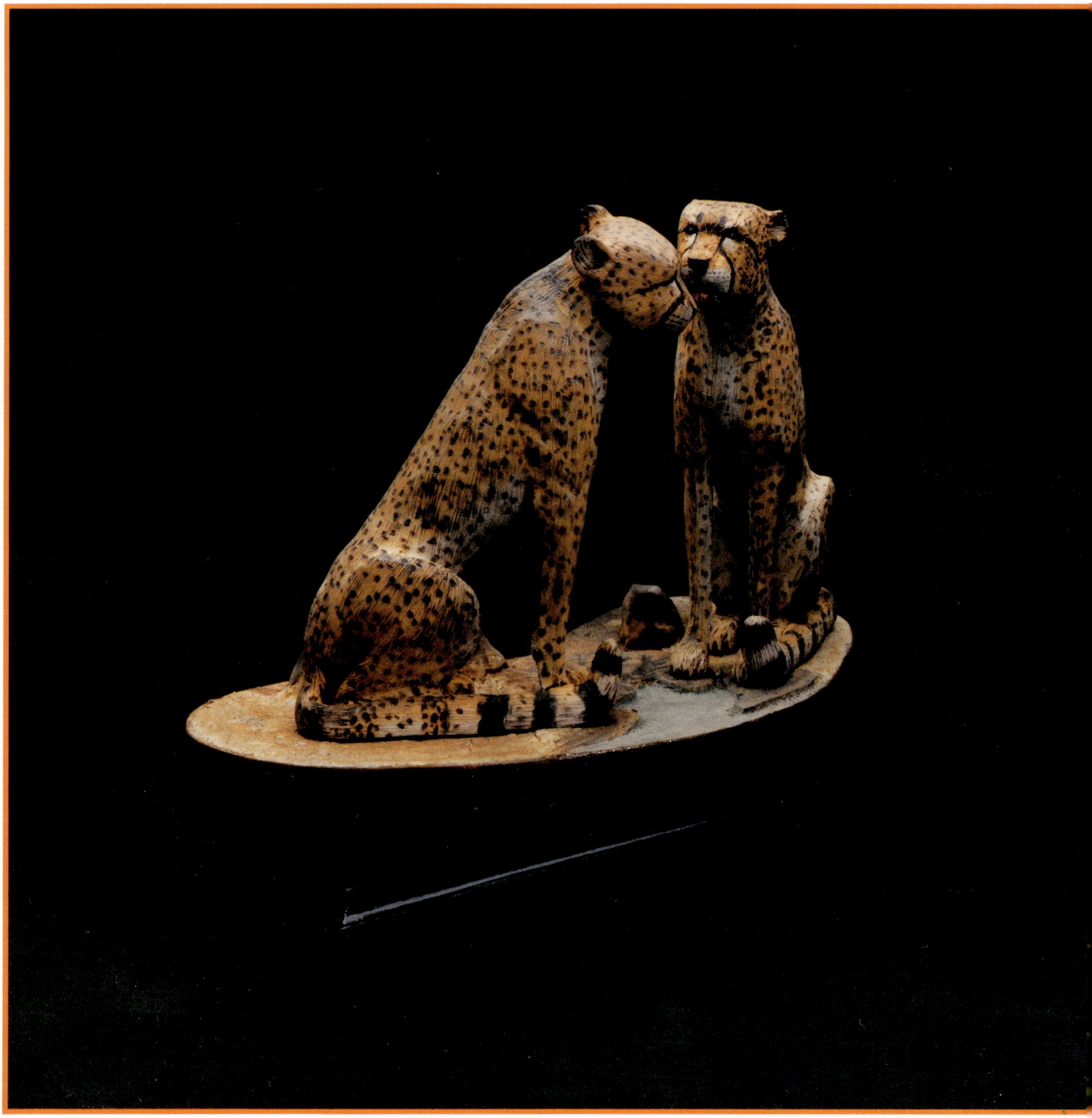

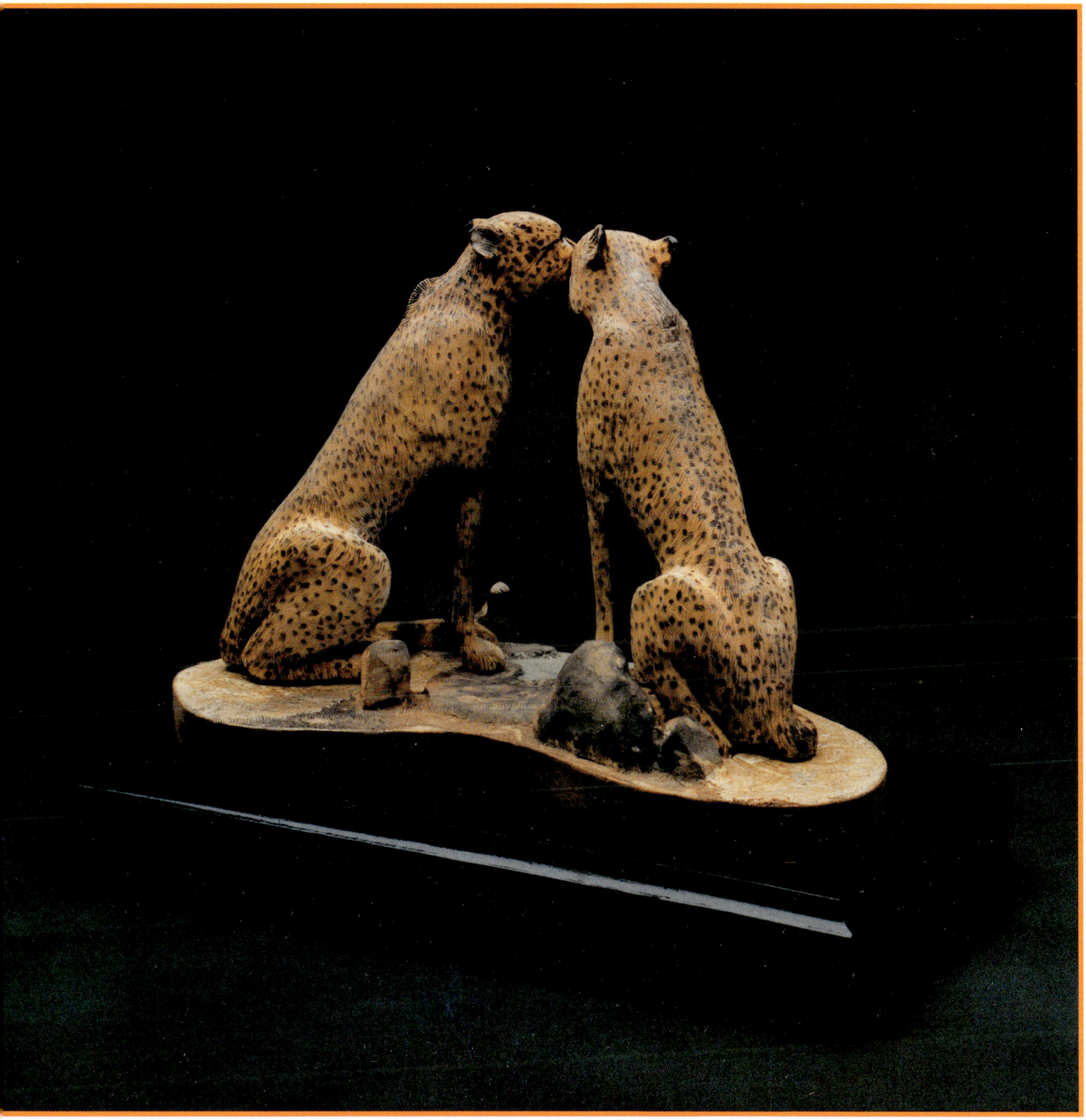

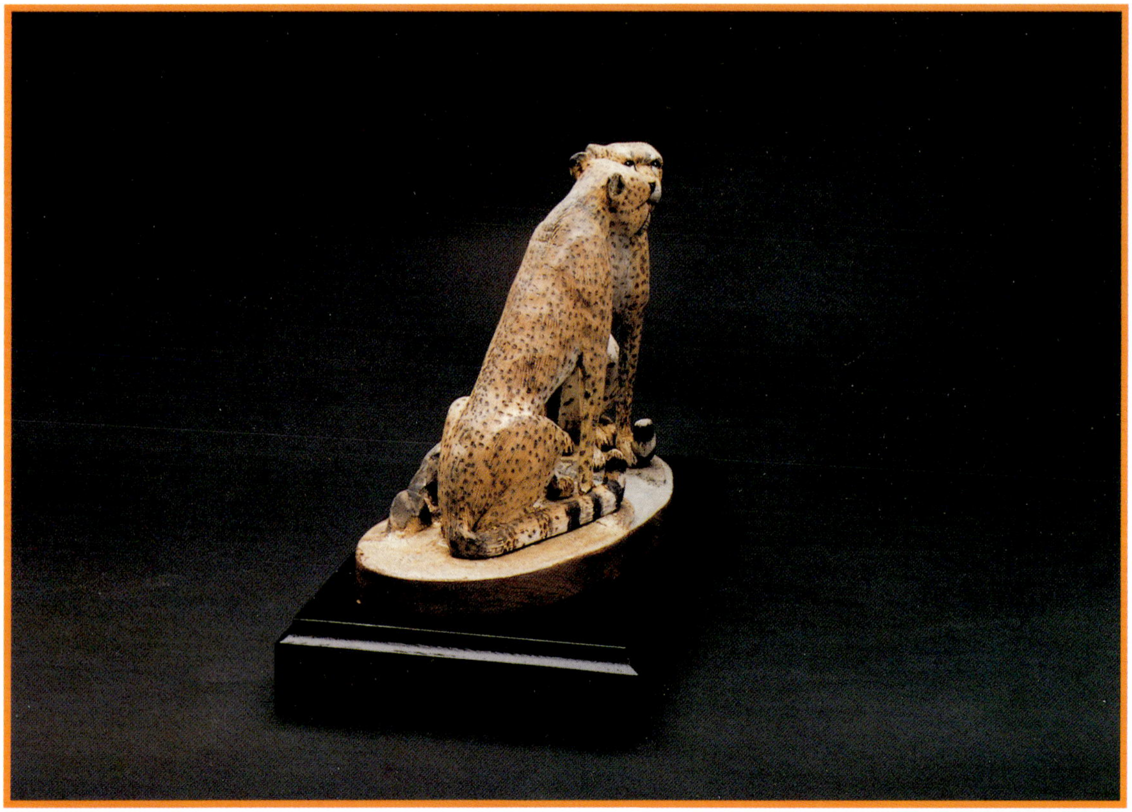

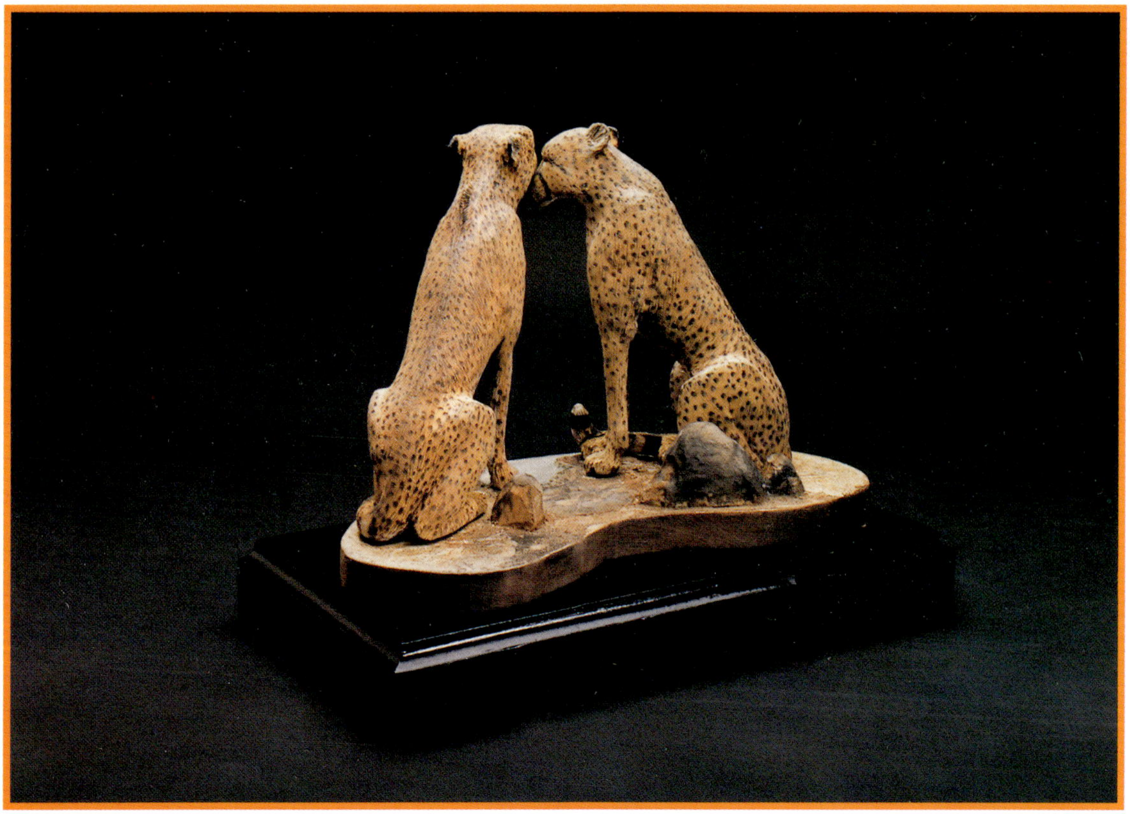

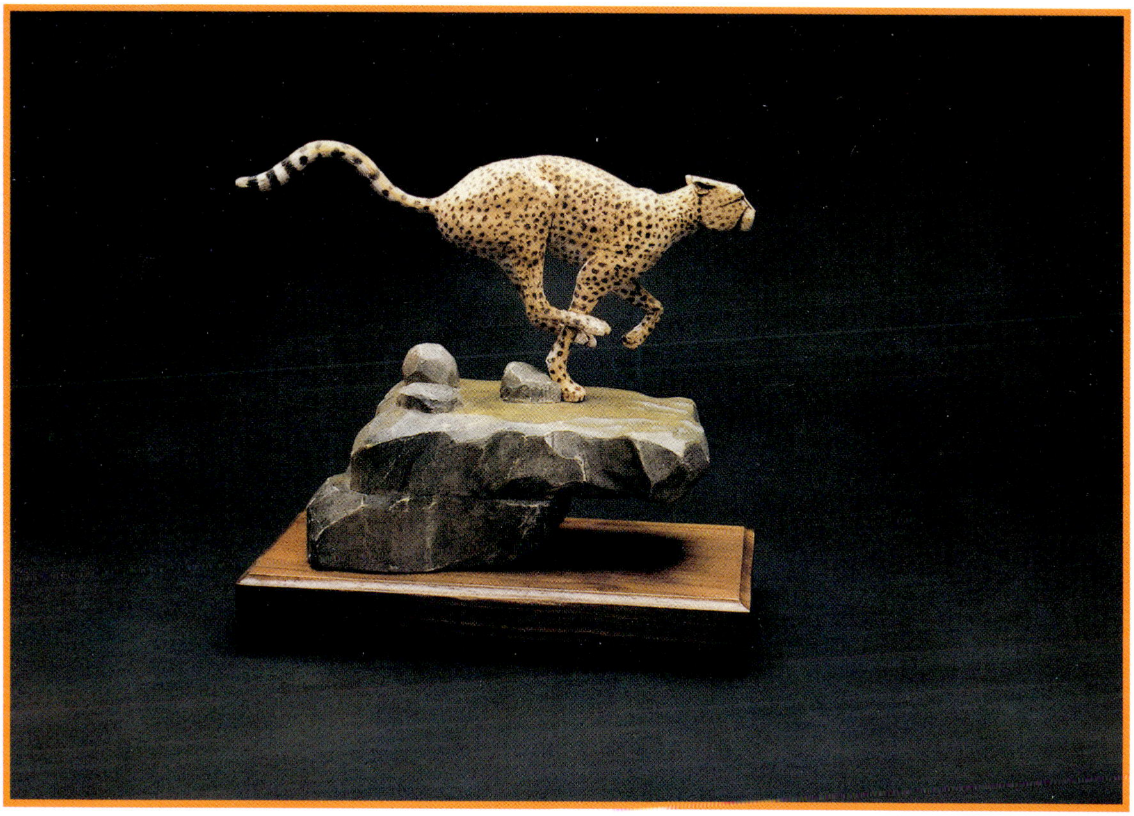

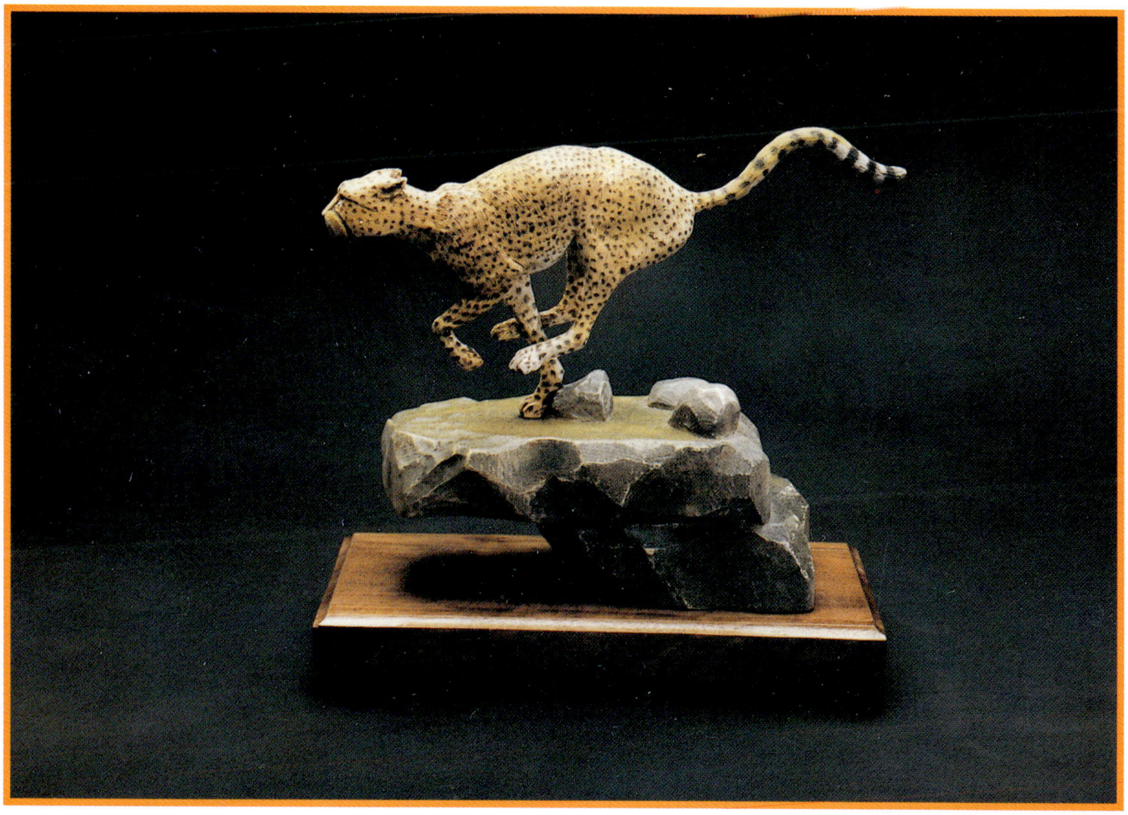

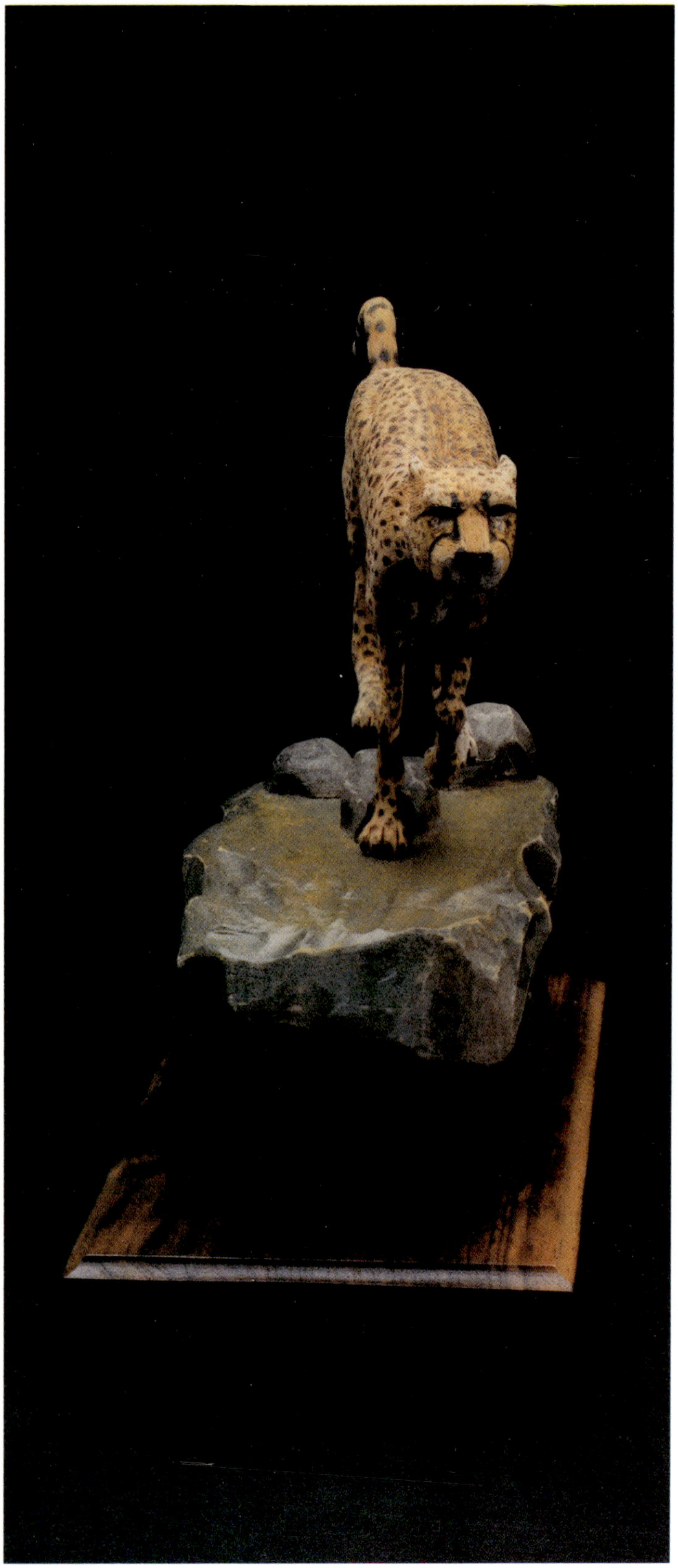

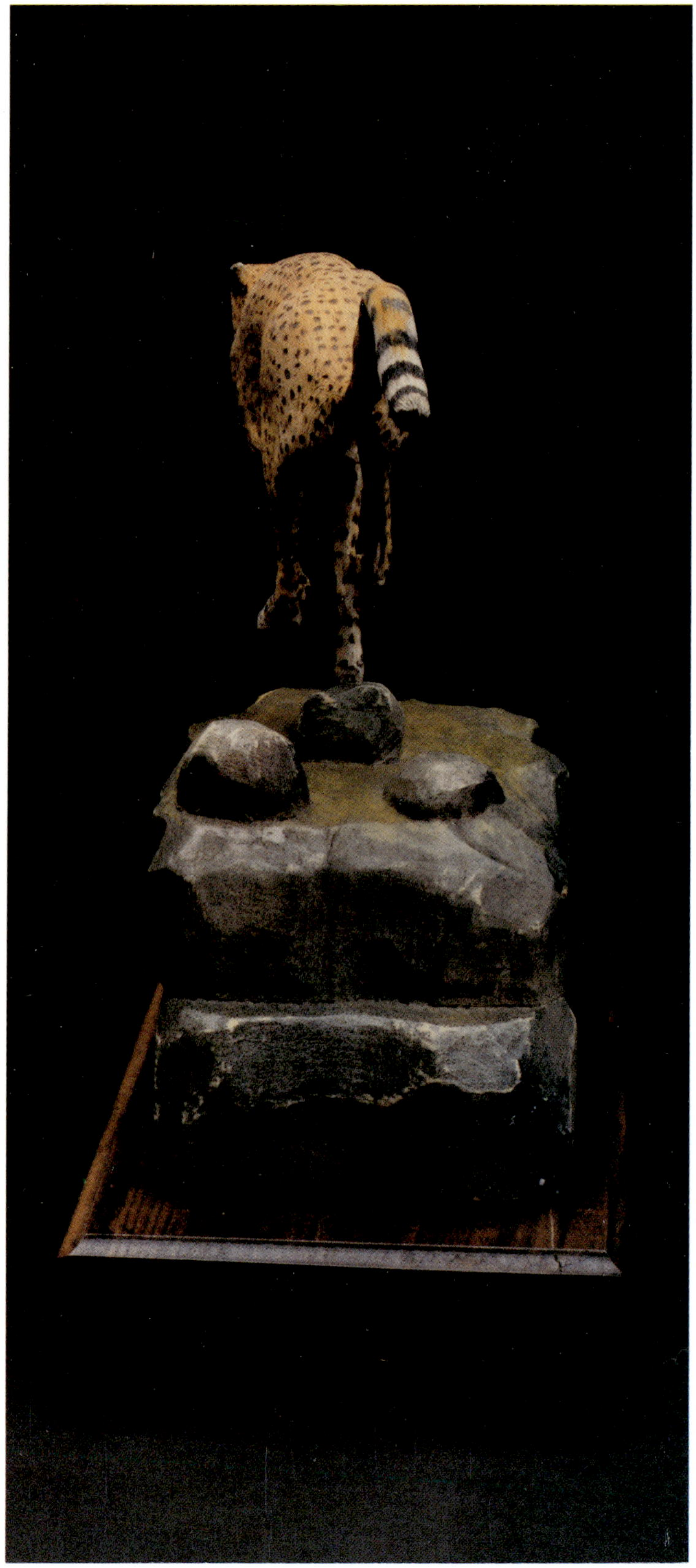